The New Role of Regional Management

By

Björn Ambos
Professor of International Management,
Vienna University of Economics and Business Institute for
International Marketing and Management

and

Bodo B. Schlegelmilch
Professor of International Marketing and Management,
Vienna University of Economics and Business Institute for
International Marketing and Management

First published 2010 by
PALGRAVE MACMILLAN

Palgrave Macmillan in the UK is an imprint of Macmillan Publishers Limited, registered in England, company number 785998, of Houndmills, Basingstoke, Hampshire RG21 6XS.

Palgrave Macmillan in the US is a division of St Martin's Press LLC, 175 Fifth Avenue, New York, NY 10010.

Palgrave Macmillan is the global academic imprint of the above companies and has companies and representatives throughout the world.

Palgrave® and Macmillan® are registered trademarks in the United States, the United Kingdom, Europe and other countries.

ISBN: 978–0–230–53875–7 hardback

This book is printed on paper suitable for recycling and made from fully managed and sustained forest sources. Logging, pulping and manufacturing processes are expected to conform to the environmental regulations of the country of origin.

A catalogue record for this book is available from the British Library.

A catalog record for this book is available from the Library of Congress.

10 9 8 7 6 5 4 3 2 1
19 18 17 16 15 14 13 12 11 10

Printed and bound in Great Britain by
CPI Antony Rowe, Chippenham and Eastbourne

Contents

Tables and Appendices

Figures

About the Authors

Professor Björn Ambos

Björn Ambos is full professor and head of the Institute for International Marketing and Management at Vienna University of Economics and Business (WU) and academic director of the Master Program in International Management/CEMS. Ambos studied business administration at the University of Hamburg in Germany, and Florida State University in the United States. He earned a Dipl.-Kfm. and a Ph.D. in international management from the University of Hamburg and a PD (Habilitation) from WU. He previously held positions at the University of Edinburgh, WU and the University of Hamburg, before rejoining WU in 2006 as one of its youngest full professors. He has taught courses, or held visiting positions, in more than ten nations in Asia, the Americas and Europe.

Professor Ambos gained several years of industry experience in international management, working in Vietnam, Italy, Paris and New York. He has conducted research with or consulted with top management teams all over the world, including Austrian Research Centers Seibersdorf (ARCS), Astellas, Die Presse, EADS, Eli Lilly, Ford, France Telecom, Hutchison 3G, Honda, Jungheinrich, JPMorgan, L'Oreal, Nike, Olympus, Pfizer, Puma, Roland Berger, Royal Dutch Shell, Royal Scottish National Orchestra, SAP, Sequenom, Siemens, Solvay, Unilever, Telekom Austria, Thyssen Krupp, Volkswagen and Villeroy & Boch. He is the recipient of several awards for excellence in teaching and research.

Professor Ambos's current research concerns global strategy, regional headquarters, knowledge management and innovation within multinational firms. He serves on the editorial board of the *Strategic Management Journal* and the board of the *European International Business Academy*. Ambos is a scientific advisor to the National Research Foundation of the United Arab Emirates and is currently serving his second term of a three-year appointment as an officer of the Global Strategy Interest Group at the Strategic Management Society.

His research has been published in *European Business Forum, European Management Journal, Journal of International Management, Journal of World Business, International Business Review, International Journal of Technology Management, Management International Review, Strategic Journal of Marketing, Strategic Management Journal and Research Policy*. The German business press recently ranked him as the most productive researcher in international management. He has presented papers and addresses at more than 70 universities and conferences in the last ten years.

Professor Bodo B. Schlegelmilch

Professor Schlegelmilch (MSc, PhD, DLitt) is dean of the Vienna University of Economics and Business (WU) Executive Academy and professor of International Marketing and Management at WU and at Leeds University Business School. He is also a fellow of the Chartered Institute of Marketing and adjunct professor of International Business Studies at the University of Minnesota, Carlson School of Management and at Kingston University, London, United Kingdom.

Prior to founding the Institute for International Marketing and Management at WU in 1997, he held tenured professorships at Thunderbird School of Global Management in Arizona, the University of Wales in Swansea and the University of Edinburgh in Scotland. At Thunderbird, he headed the Marketing group and was director of the US-government-supported CIBER Institute for International Business Ethics. At the University of Wales, he held the British Rail Chair of Marketing, and at the University of Edinburgh, he was a lecturer of marketing and international business. During his career, he also held visiting appointments at the University of California at Berkeley, the University of Cologne, the University of Miami in Florida and Thammasat University in Bangkok. He also worked for Deutsche Bank and Procter & Gamble in Germany.

Professor Schlegelmilch studied business administration at Cologne University of Applied Sciences and holds an M.Sc. degree and two doctorates (Ph.D. and D.Litt.) from the Manchester Business School. In terms of research, he has been recognized as one of the leading authors publishing in international marketing journals and has been listed in "Who's Who in International Business Education and Research." Recently, he has also been ranked among the top 25 business professors in Germany, Austria and Switzerland in terms of lifetime publishing. His work focuses on a variety of topics in global marketing management and strategy. He has published more than 200 papers in conference proceedings and academic journals, such as the *Strategic Management Journal, Journal of International Business Studies, Journal of Business Ethics* and *Journal of World Business.*

Professor Schlegelmilch has won various teaching and research awards and has taught in international marketing programs on six continents. He is a board member of the American Chamber of Commerce in Austria and has conducted executive education seminars and board-level workshops for a wide variety of major multinationals.

Professor Schlegelmilch was the first ever European editor-in-chief of the *Journal of International Marketing* and has served (or is serving) on the editorial boards of several leading academic journals, including the *Journal of Marketing, Journal of International Business Studies, International Journal of Research in Marketing, Journal of Strategic Marketing, International Marketing Review, Journal of Marketing Management, Journal of Business Research,* and *Marketing – Zeitschrift für Forschung und Praxis.*

Acknowledgements

We owe gratitude to many friends, colleagues from academia, interview partners and funding organizations that helped us realize this project. First and foremost, the authors would like to acknowledge the generous support of the Austrian National Bank (OeNB). Without funding through its research initiative, the Jubiläumsfonds, we would have been unable to conduct the extensive research study on which this book is based.

We also like to extend our appreciation and gratitude to the all the executives who shared their insights with us. In particular, we like to acknowledge the following individuals whose knowledge and experience has been most helpful in shaping our own understanding on regional strategies: Mr Aoki (Honda), Mr Alebeek (Nike), Mr Bauer (Puma), Dr Dobrocky (Boehringer Ingelheim), Dr Fibig (Pfizer), Mr Doerr (Boehringer Ingelheim), Mr Giles (Boehringer Ingelheim), Mr Grottenthaler (Boeringer Ingelheim), Mr Hoyt (Nike), Mr Hülse (Boehringer Ingelheim), Mr Hatanaka (Astellas), Mr Kaiser (Puma), Mr Köbele (Pfizer), Mr Kopp (Volkswagen), Mr Kasai (Nissan), Mr Katayanagi (Astellas), Mr Kozato (Canon), Mr Lichtinger (Pfizer), Mr Le-Brun (McDonalds), Mr Masuda (Honda), Mr Morgen (British Embassy Tokyo), Mr Nishiwaki (Asics), Mr Ohtani (Astellas), Dr Pörschmann, (Boehringer Ingelheim), Mr Ruppe (Nike), Mr Schmid (SAP), Mr Sumita (Honda), Mr Senn (Volkswagen), Mr Slater (Ford), Mr Schirmer, (Ford), Mr Suzuki (Toyota), Dr Schleef (Volkswagen), Dr Tinhof (Astellas), Mr Unbehaun (Asiscs) and Mr Vivaldi (Unicredit).

We are also greatly indebted to our research assistants, who helped us to develop the case studies. Specifically, we would like to thank Barbara Brenner, Lisa Gärber, Ursula Haas-Kotzegger, Phillip Nell, Philipp Obenaus, Nina Pröll, Ilona Szöcs and Gina Weinzierl for their contributions. A special thanks also to Ursula Zeller-Nürnberger and Hanife Ülkü, who help us formatting the manuscript, as well as Virginia Thorp and Paul Milner of Palgrave Macmillan for their support throughout the project.

Finally, we would like to thank our families for their understanding when we missed out on joint activities because we were busy with research for this book.

1
Introduction

Global ideals versus regional realities: Why regional strategy still makes sense

Globalization is dead – Long live globalization

Let us be clear from the outset. We are not committing blasphemy by denying globalization. Ever-increasing globalization is as inevitable as changing weather; we may regret it or not, but we have to live with it. We are also not bemoaning the consequences of globalization. While certainly not without its problems, on balance, globalization is doing clearly more good for the economic well being of the world than bad. Neither do we yearn for some romantic notion of cocooning countries in economic self-sufficiency. This ideology of some totalitarian states has long been empirically falsified.

However, what we do criticize is the pervasive tendency to cast the international strategy debate in extremes. Regardless of the particular perspective, strategic marketing, management strategy or the design of organization's architecture, we are usually offered extreme choices: globalization or localization,[1] integration or responsiveness,[2] standardization or adaptation,[3] centralization or decentralization.[4] In fact, there appears to be little progress since the early contributors mapped out the field. Theodore Levitt's seminal paper "The Globalization of Markets,"[5] in which he foresaw a trend towards standardized products and services on a worldwide basis, appears to drive the discussion still. The underlying message: the more uniform, that is, global, integrated, standardized or centralized the firm operates, the better it is able to take advantage of economies of scale and scope.

Although the black-and-white contrast of global versus local is appealing for its simplicity, the real world looks more complex. Internationally operating companies are constantly striving to find the right middle ground between local and global. And this holds regardless of whether companies are selling predominantly products or services, durables or fast-moving consumer goods, or whether they are in the business-to-business or business-to-consumer domain. Consequently, the key question is not whether companies should be globally integrated, that is, coordinate *all* their activities worldwide, but *which* activities and *which* components of the product and services they offer should be centralized or decentralized, standardized or adapted.

This question is relevant for all corporate activities, be it R&D, procurement, manufacturing, human resource management, finance or marketing. To this end, the success of an internationally operating company does not merely hinge on whether it is a global company or remaining a local player, but on getting the balance right between local responsiveness and global synergies.

The regional imperative

Although most management scholars and practitioners alike would subscribe to these arguments, it is precisely here where we see a need to sharpen the debate. Specifically, the right balance between local responsiveness and global synergies is not just a question of a headquarters deciding on the appropriate mandates of subsidiaries. It involves the design of a much more intricate mesh of organizational structures and processes in which *regional structures* and *regional coordination and control processes* play an important role. For the time being, we use a fairly coarse-grained definition of region, namely, something bigger than one country and smaller than the entire world. Well-designed regional structures and processes have the ability to bridge and gel together national subsidiaries and central headquarters and efficiently and effectively coordinate functional and divisional activities across corporate networks. However, as we will discuss later in this book, one of the unresolved questions remains the size and dominant logic behind forming regions.

Notwithstanding the importance of regional strategies and structures in practice, relatively few scholars emphasize the regional dimension of international business. One such scholar is Pankaj Ghemawat, who coined the term "semiglobalization" in his work on corporate strategy. In his view, differences between countries are far larger than generally acknowledged, and companies that presume complete integration are emphasizing standardization and scale expansion too strongly.[6]

Other eminent scholars who stress the importance of regions are Alan Rugman and Alain Verbeke,[7] In his analysis of Fortune 500 companies, Rugman points out that even among these large multinational corporations (MNCs), more than 80 per cent generate more than 50 per cent of their sales in their home region. In fact, only 6.6 per cent of these MNCs have at least 20 per cent of their sales in two regions, and only 2.4 per cent of these MNCs are global, that is, derive at least 20 per cent of sales from each of the three triad regions.

Although Rugman's analysis, in particular, has been criticized[8] and, in addition to global market presence, other dimensions of globalization should also be considered (notably the globalization of the capital base, the globalization of the supply chain and the globalization of the corporate mind-set[9]), the inevitable conclusion has to be that regional strategy matters. As Rugman and Verbeke put it:

> Regional strategy, meaning differentiating the MNC's approach to doing business in the various regions considered relevant, may paradoxically be the most effective approach towards achieving a global market position, in the sense of a more balanced distribution of sales across borders.[10]

The majority of companies still has a very pronounced regional focus and has built regional organizational structures. Because we can safely assume that not all of these companies simply failed to recognize the merits of globalization, this raises at least five important questions:

- Why do regions continue to play such an important role in the age of globalization?
- What best defines a region: geography, language, stage of economic development or some other characteristic?
- Which value-chain activities should be located at country, regional and headquarters level?
- How can companies best organize their regional structures, coordination and control processes?
- What impact do regional structures have on interregional coordination, and especially on knowledge transfers within and between regions?

In the following, we are initially focusing on the rationale behind the enduring importance of regional structures. Specifically, we are discussing five drivers that contribute to the regional imperative.

Regional homogeneity

Ask anybody from Europe what distinguishes Europeans from, say Americans, and a plethora of specifically European and specifically American characteristics will emerge. Invite a British citizen to compare himself with a Frenchman or an Italian and again, lots of differences will surface. The same will happen when a Scot compares himself with someone from England or Wales. And of course, more differences will appear when someone from Glasgow compares himself with a person from Edinburgh. At the end of the day, we all are – and love to be – different. However, differences and similarities are all a matter of degree.

We have learned from generations of sociologists that variations in interests, values, ethnic and linguistic background and kinship ties define group memberships, and how one group uses more or less subtle techniques and signals to differentiate itself from others. Widening our perspective, we can easily recognize that differences *within* any given region usually tend to be smaller than differences *between* regions. This applies when we define a region merely as two countries that share a common language, say Austria and Germany, and compare it with any other formation of countries. But it also holds if we focus on a much broader political and economic region, for example, the European Union and compare it with Asia or the United States. In both examples, intraregional communalities tend to be larger than interregional communalities.

Usunier and Sissmann[11] introduce the concept of cultural affinity zones. These zones are said to display similar characteristics in terms of language, religion, family life patterns, work relationships and consumption patterns. From a business perspective, not only the consumer characteristics are important, but also factors like the regulatory system, the industry structure and competition and the marketing infrastructure. Moreover, companies tend to have an organizational heritage that connects them to a region. This may be evident in close connections to local partners, existing licensing agreements or dealer networks. In addition, it may simply be borne out by their better understanding of the motivational structure of managers and employees from the region in question. To this end, it is very likely that differences in the external environments and factors connected to the organizational heritage become more acute when companies cross regional boundaries.

Limits to economies of scale and scope

In many industries, factory automation has lowered scale economies, enabling companies to supply regional and even local markets efficiently.[12] This is evident, for example, in the car industry, where the idea of a standardized world car has long been given way to an ever-increasing array of models that are tailored to specific regional demand conditions. An example for this is the Tata Group's introduction of a low-cost car, the Nano, for India. But even where production costs are of relatively minor importance, marketing costs, transport costs and administrative and overhead costs may increase rapidly when operations cross regional boundaries.[13] Compare, for example, the marketing costs for adding a new product to an already existing product line sold under an established brand franchise with a situation where a company has to establish its brand in a new region in order to introduce the same product.

Finally, economies of scale and scope may also be optimized at regional level, because the transfer of ideas, experience and knowledge is limited by increasing differences between regions (stickiness of knowledge).[14] Insights into the idiosyncrasies of Islamic banking, the principles of open-air markets in India, the business impact of the Chinese New Year or the significance of the wedding industry in Japan vividly illustrate that business knowledge loses its value when transferred out of its regional context.

Regional liability of foreignness

From the management literature, the concept of liability of foreignness is well known.[15] The key argument posits that there are a series of costs that place foreign companies at a competitive disadvantage. These include costs directly associated with spatial distance, for example, the cost of travel, transportation and coordinating, as well as firm-specific costs such as unfamiliarity with and lack of roots in a local environment. Moreover, there are also costs resulting from the host country environment and the home country environment. The former stem from a lack of legitimacy of foreign firms or economic nationalism; the later may result from restrictions on high-tech sales to certain countries, for example.

The troubles of Austria's leading oil and gas concern OMV illustrate the impact of both economic nationalism and the threat of restrictions. When OMV attempted to acquire Hungary's oil and gas company MOL, economic nationalism in Hungary was stirred up. MOL strenuously opposed the deal and, to this end, was partly relying upon the protectionist support of Hungary's socialist-led government. Hungary even contemplated passing a law that would restrict the ability of a foreign government-controlled entity to invest in the country's energy sector. However, this would have been clearly against the principle of a liberalized European Union (EU) energy market.[16] In another deal, OMV was considering investment in Iran with the objective of developing the South Pars gas field. This led to heavy cross fire from the US government, which threatened that the Iran Sanctions Act could lead to sanctions against any company that invested more than 20 million US dollars in one year in Iran's oil and gas sector.[17] Thus, here the threat of sanctions did not come from OMV's home country, but from the US government attempting to extend its authority beyond the boundaries of the United States.

The liability of foreignness is clearly present each time a company crosses national boundaries, and the Hungarian – Austrian example shows that it may even be quite severe when neighbouring countries are involved that belong to the same economic and political union, namely, the EU. However, we would argue that liability of foreignness becomes more acute when companies cross *regional* boundaries. Of course, this holds particularly true for travel and transportation and coordination costs. Within Europe, of example, it is easily possible to arrange a face-to-face meeting in one of the capital cities where participants fly in and out on the same day. In contrast, the same would not be possible if participants from Asia or the United States were involved. And even phoning colleagues is getting more complicated when different time zones are involved. Assuming a workday lasts from 9 o'clock in the morning to 5 o'clock in the afternoon, it is virtually impossible for a company located in continental Europe to reach a US company located on the west coast during its business hours.

And while there tends to be plenty of bickering between countries within a given region, the existence of various more or less loosely knit regional trade blocs, such as NAFTA, ASEAN, CACM and MERCOSUR, demonstrates that more common ground between countries can usually be found at the regional level, regardless of whether the regional blocs are mere customs unions or organizations with a far-reaching political agenda like the EU.

Prevailing regiocentric management orientation

The form and substance of a company's international operation greatly depends on management's assumptions and beliefs about the nature of the world. As early as 1969, Howard Perlmutter developed the EPRG framework to capture the worldview of corporate management.[18] EPRG stands for ethnocentric, polycentric, regiocentric and geocentric. In a company with a regiocentric orientation, management views regions as unique and seeks to develop an integrated regional strategy. Thus, a European company that focuses its attention on the EU follows a regiocentric orientation.

However, a regiocentric orientation does not necessarily imply that corporate activities are exclusively focusing on one region only. Where more than one region is involved, the strategic and organizational logic of the company will mainly centre on regions. Wind et al.[19] discuss this issue with reference to the development of international marketing strategies. Similarly, Malhotra et al.[20] argue for a regional perspective on the grounds that cultural factors still inhibit the development of homogeneous markets.

Given the cognitive and emotional embeddedness of managers within a particular region, such as Western Europe or Latin America, it is likely that managers will not only find it easier to conduct business in their home region, but will mostly also be more efficient and effective in the way they carry out their work.

Organizational complexity

A final argument supporting a stronger emphasis on regional strategies lies in the enormous organizational complexity of global structures. Even very large companies, such as Procter & Gamble (P&G), struggle with this issue. In 2005, P&G started an organizational restructuring program that attempted to shift primary profit responsibilities from four regional organizations to seven global business units (GBUs). In addition, the company created seven market development organizations (MDOs) responsible for implementing global strategies. However, to complicate issues further, in developing markets, MDOs and not GBOs were primarily responsible for profit.

Yet another dimension was added in the form of the global business service unit (GBS) that coordinated transactional activities such as accounting, human resources or information technology (IT). And to obscure the organizational structure further, specific teams and task forces are woven into the structure. In his case study on P&G Japan, Christopher Bartlett[21] describes the impact of this reorganization and the struggle of the Beauty Care Global Leadership Team (GLT), a group that was comprised of managers from key MDOs, the GBU and some decision makers from GBS. He concludes that P&G's reorganization was causing a good deal of organizational disruption and management distraction. This sentiment was shared with Mike Thompson, then head of P&G's beauty business in Europe, who explained in the case:

> We swung the pendulum 180 degrees, from a local to a global focus. Marketing plans and budgets had previously been developed locally, strongly debated with European managers, then rolled up. Now they are developed globally – or at least regionally – by new people who often did not understand the competitive and trade differences across markets. We began to standardize and centralize our policies and practices out of Geneva. Not surprisingly, a lot of our best managers left the company.[22]

The P&G example shows that even very large MNCs struggle with a globally integrated organizational structure. For the majority of small and medium-sized corporations, the P&G example raises the question whether the potential gains of a tightly integrated global organizational structure are not offset by the inevitable organizational complexity. Expressed differently, for most firms there appears to be an argument supporting the development of strong pan-regional structures, while keeping interregional structural links at a minimum. Thus, for the majority of companies, efforts to reduce organizational complexity are likely to result in an organizational architecture that centres on regions.

The case for a regional strategy

In the preceding paragraphs, we criticized the extant strategy literature for its tendency to focus either on single countries or on the development of global strategies. What appears to be lacking is an appreciation of the middle ground. To this end, we presented a number of arguments that support strategy development cantering on regional markets (two countries or more) rather than focusing on a country-by-country approach or a completely integrated global approach. Specifically, we emphasized that national idiosyncrasies are always present, but their extent increases when crossing regional boundaries. Moreover, we pointed out that modern production techniques increasingly permit scale and scope optimization at the regional level without requiring a detailed global coordination of all processes. Next, we underlined that the so-called liability of foreignness also increases substantially when crossing regional boundaries. Taking these perspectives together with the organizational complexities MNCs need to handle when attempting to achieve a global integration and the prevailing regiocentric focus of most managers, there appear to be strong arguments for accentuating the regional

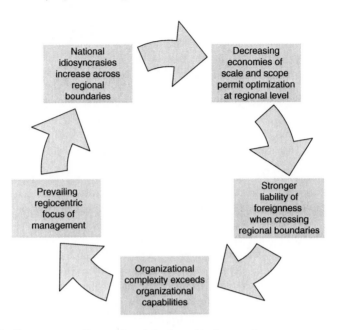

Figure 1.1 Forces supporting regional strategy development

dimension of strategy. Figure 1.1 depicts the key forces supporting regional strategy development.

Underlying research and structure of the book

This book is based on extensive research conducted during the past four years. Our research consists of three broad phases (see Figure 1.2). The purpose of this three-phased research design is to seek triangulation by covering the spectrum from relatively "fine-grained" to relatively "coarse-grained" methodologies within the same project to assess the same set of issues.

In the first phase, we use a case method and develop case studies based on nine MNC's. The goal of case study research is to generate theory that subsequently permits rigorous empirical testing. In selecting industries and cases we followed a 3-x-3 matched-case study design that enabled us to compare and contrast different companies from different industries (automotive, pharmaceuticals and sport shoes) and different triad regions (United States, Europe and Japan). Based on these criteria, we selected the following nine firms for our study: Asics, Astellas, Boehringer Ingelheim, Ford, Honda, Nike, Pfizer, Puma and Volkswagen (see Figure 1.3).

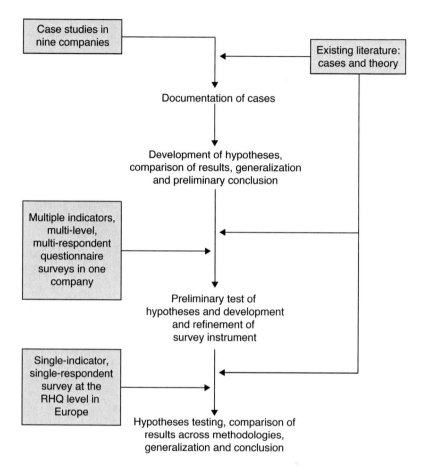

Figure 1.2 Research design

With the exception of Astellas Pharma, all nine companies belonged to the leading companies (Top 20) in their respective industries. In order to filter out perception differences regarding the role and function of regional firm units in the network of multinational corporations, we conducted interviews at three different firm levels: headquarters level, regional headquarters level and subsidiary level. For the latter, we always interviewed managers from subsidiaries in a small market and a large market, because we expected perceptions to be shaped by differences in the importance of the market. In total, we conducted more than 60 interviews with senior- or executive-level managers at all levels of the organization.

Based on our qualitative interviews, we first attempted to draw out some of the key challenges faced by US and Japanese companies operating in

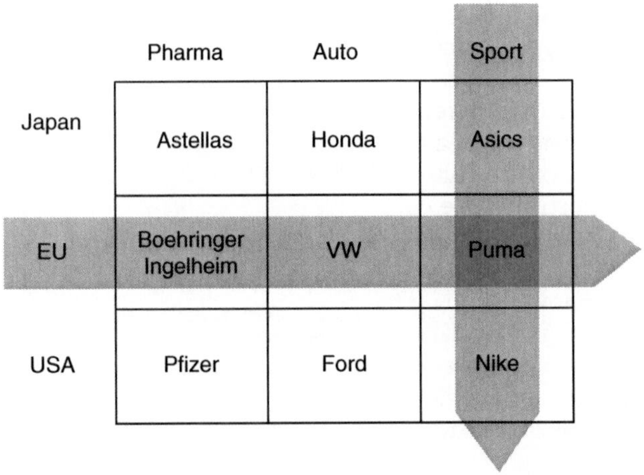

Figure 1.3   Research design for the conducted qualitative interviews

Europe and looked at commonalities and differences in how they managed these challenges. Next, we developed six case studies:[23] two for each industry. Within each industry, one case study is always cast in a teaching case format, while the other is a description of the regional structure of the company in question. Although all cases are based on our research, at times companies requested that we disguise the actors in the case. Taken collectively, the case studies offer extensive insights into the regional strategy and structure of the analysed companies.

The second phase of our research involved an in-depth empirical analysis using multiple indicators at one of the nine case study firms (Boehringer Ingelheim). The objective was to formalize the hypotheses that were generated in the first phase, to carry out preliminary tests of some of those hypotheses and to develop suitable instruments for conducting a large sample survey that permitted us to test the hypotheses more rigorously in the third phase of the study.

In the third phase of the study, we conducted two surveys that were carried out at the regional headquarters and subsidiary level on a large sample of MNCs. The first survey was targeted to European subsidiaries, irrespective of whether they were reporting directly to global headquarters, divisional headquarters or regional headquarters. This survey allowed us to compare and contrast the value added of different parent structures and architectures. The second study surveyed regional headquarters in particular, enabling us to probe deeper into idiosyncratic challenges of managing a regional headquarters. Overall, our data is based on more than 250 detailed corporate responses.

This book reflects the logic of our research program. Part I sets the foundation of this book. In Chapter 2, we will get a closer look at the European market. The objective is to highlight commonalities as well as differences between markets in different countries. Although our findings indicate that we are far away from a homogeneous Europe – and some might celebrate this as part of the cultural diversity and richness of Europe – we will argue that, collectively, the commonalities are sufficient to justify a focus on regional and, where appropriate, subregional strategies. In Chapter 3, we return to the dilemma of global integration and national responsiveness and show how regional strategy and regional structures can help in managing the global-local tensions. In the next two chapters, we take a closer look at the structural (Chapter 4) and managerial (Chapter 5) challenges in building up a regional presence. Building on these insights, Part II takes a closer look at the challenges and responses of US and Japanese firms competing in Europe. Looking at Ford, Nike, Pfizer and Asics, Astellas and Honda, we examine how national heritage, distance to the market and firm strategy influence the structure, value-chain configuration and management of their European operations. In the final part of the book, Part III, we take an industry focus. For each of the three industries examined, we present two cases that illustrate specific best practices for different aspects of regional management. We end the book with a brief summary of our key findings.

Part I

Succeeding in Europe

2
The European Market

Is there common ground between Spain and Slovakia or Italy and Ireland?

Companies aiming to succeed in Europe must develop a thorough understanding of Europe as a region. How are European countries interlinked? Are European states completely different, or does the continent show signs of homogeneity? And what about European consumers? Are consumption patterns similar across national borders, or do country differences and peculiarities result in a fragmented consumer market? Ultimately, this leads to the question of how much common ground there is among the country markets that make up the European region.

In this chapter, we will showcase the significance of the European region, analyse its position in international trade, illustrate how its countries are commercially interlinked and, finally, highlight how homogeneous or heterogeneous Europe really is.

Europe as the number one "hot spot" for trade

According to the World Bank, international trade increased, on average, almost twice as fast as the gross domestic product (GDP) between 1990 and 2006. Moreover, stocks of foreign direct investment rose about five times as fast as world GDP.[1] Generally, the EU-27 has been increasingly integrated with the rest of the world in recent years. Flows of goods corresponded to 10.8 per cent of the GDP in 2006, which was significantly higher than the rate of 8.6 per cent achieved in 2003.[2] Over the last ten years, exports of both goods and services grew on average by about 6.2 per cent annually. During that period, services remained stable with an average 22 per cent share of international trade. Moreover, in 2006, the export of goods could generate a significantly higher growth rate than did the export of services (9.3 per cent against 6.9 per cent).[3]

Trade in goods

Over the last few decades, the European Union has positioned itself as one of the strongest players in international trade, accounting for around one-fifth of world trade in goods. As shown in Figure 2.1, the European Union is the world's largest exporter and second biggest importer after the United States. Its trade balance has been consistently unfavourable over recent years, growing from €45 billion in 2002 to €192 billion in 2006.[4] However, the United States, being the biggest net importer, recorded a much higher deficit of around €700 billion in 2006, whereas China, Japan and Canada showed a surplus.

Europe's most important exports were in "machinery and vehicles" (43.5 per cent), followed by "other manufactured articles"[i] and "chemicals". The EU showed a clear comparative advantage, with a €102 billion surplus in the trade of machinery and vehicles, and chemicals reporting a surplus of €75 billion. By contrast, the EU-27 countries were net importers of fossil fuels and had a deficit of €282 billion in the trade of energy products.[5]

Concerning the EU's main trading partners, the United States remains number one. However, China has caught up, taking the number one spot as main provider of imported goods in 2006. China is now the main source of "manufactured products" and "machinery and vehicles", with the latter being the most important import category (30 per cent of extra-EU imports). Russia is Europe's most important supplier of "energy products", while the United States remains the leading seller of "chemical products".[6] As far as exports are concerned, the United States is the European Union's most important market, accounting for 23.2 per cent of all extra-EU exports. US sales of "machinery and vehicles" – the most important group of export items – made up 22.4 per cent of exports in 2006. Furthermore, large shares of energy and chemical products went to the United States in 2006, making up 31 per cent and 30 per cent of total exports, respectively. However, exports in these product groups to Russia and China increased significantly over the last few years, showing growth rates of 26 per cent and 20 per cent, respectively, between 1999 and 2006.[7]

Data on the individual European countries indicate that Germany is Europe's main participant in extra-EU trade (27.7 per cent of exports and 19.4 per cent of imports in 2006). Other big exporters are Italy, France and the United Kingdom, with shares above 10 per cent. Major importers after Germany are the United Kingdom, the Netherlands, Italy and France, with shares between 10 per cent and 15 per cent. However, one has to be aware of the so-called Rotterdam effect, which exaggerates Dutch imports because goods bound for other EU countries are recorded as extra-EU imports by the Netherlands.[8]

---

[i] "Other manufactured articles" include iron and steel, professional, scientific and controlling instruments and apparatus and nonmetallic mineral manufactures.

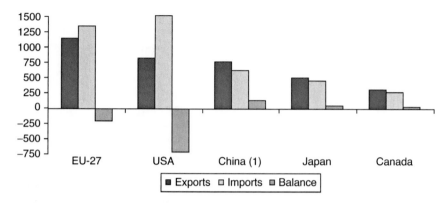

Figure 2.1   Main world traders: Exports, imports and trade balance, 2006 (per billion euros)

Source: European Commission (2008) *European Economic Statistics*, Luxembourg, copyright © European Communities, p. 88.

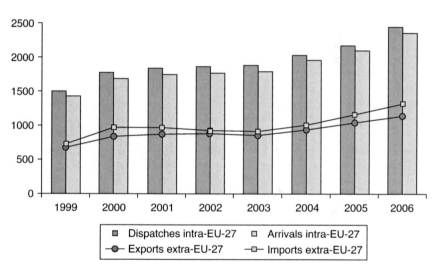

Figure 2.2   Intra-EU dispatches and arrivals, extra-EU exports and imports, 1999–2006 (per billion euros)

Source: European Commission (2008) *Panorama of European Union Trade – Date 1999–2006*, Luxembourg, copyright © European Communities, p. 36.

Notwithstanding the strong position of the EU in international trade, extra-EU trade represents only a minor share of the whole volume traded by the European Union (see Figure 2.2). *In each of the European countries, the majority of trade in goods is conducted with other European nations.* Therefore, intra-EU trade is far more important to European countries than extra-EU trade, with the former making up two-thirds of total trade in 2006. In the period between 1999 and 2006, intra-EU dispatches made up between 67.8 per cent and 69.1 per cent of total exports, whereas arrivals accounted for between 63.5 per cent and 66.2 per cent of total imports. Both arrivals and dispatches increased at an annual rate of around 7.3 per cent.[ii] Total EU dispatches (intra-EU exports) increased up to €2.5 trillion in 2006, whereas total EU arrivals (intra-EU imports) amounted to €2.4 trillion.[9]

The magnitude of internal trade in goods is best shown with the ratios demonstrating the weight of intra-EU trade compared to total trade in the individual European countries. These varied between 83.1 per cent in the Czech Republic and 58.6 per cent in Italy in 2006. Of course, geography plays a major role, as countries like the Czech Republic (83.1 per cent), Slovakia (81.0 per cent) or Luxembourg (79.3 per cent) show major percentages due to the fact that they are landlocked and therefore bound to trade more with neighbouring states than countries like Italy (58.6 per cent) or Greece (58.8 per cent), which are more sea-faring nations.[10] The most important European dispatchers are Germany, the Netherlands and France. Regarding product arrivals, Germany also heads the intra-EU list, followed by France and the United Kingdom.[11]

In general, smaller countries export larger quantities to their main trading partners within the EU, especially when they are neighbours. For example, 42 per cent of Austria's dispatches went to Germany in 2006, Poland directed 34 per cent of its intra-EU exports to Germany and the Netherlands directed 32 per cent to Germany. This, of course, also holds true the other way around. Germany was the main supplier of intra-EU arrivals to all of the trading partners shown in Figure 2.3, excluding Belgium, which sourced more goods from the Netherlands. Again, smaller countries purchased larger quantities from Europe's main suppliers. For instance, Austria sourced 71.6 per cent from the five main intra-EU traders.[12]

Trade in services

Services are becoming more and more important and play an ever-increasing role, especially in the European economy. However, this does not hold true for international trade. Here services account for only around 22 per cent of overall international trade.[13] This relatively low number has its roots in the nature of services, which are subject to more constraints than trade in goods. Nevertheless, with the evolution of tradability of services in recent years, service transactions have been recording similar growth rates as trade in goods, hence outshining growth of services in general.

In 2006, the European Union held a 26.9 per cent share of global exports and 23.4 per cent of imports of services, making it the world's largest trader

---

[ii] Intra-EU trade registered marginally lower growth rates than extra-EU imports (8.9 per cent) and exports (7.8 per cent).

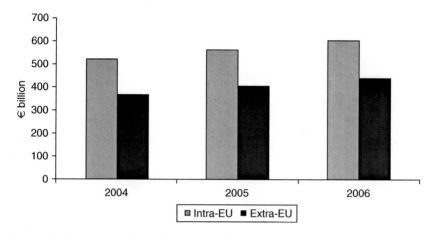

Figure 2.3 Intra-EU and extra-EU exports of services (per billion euros)

Source: European Commission (2008) *European Union International Trade in Services – Analytical Aspects*, Luxembourg, copyright © European Communities, p. 13.

in services. US service exports ranked second (18.8 per cent), followed by that of Japan (6.2 per cent) and China (4.7 per cent). The EU recorded a surplus of €68.5 billion in 2006, which meant an increase of 9.6 per cent in exports and 6.6 per cent in imports, compared to 2005.[14]

The United States remains the European Union's most important trading partner when it comes to services. In 2006, 30.5 per cent of total exports went to the United States and 32.7 per cent of total imports came from the United States. The United Kingdom remained Europe's most important exporter of services, with a share of almost one-quarter, followed by Germany and France. Germany led the European countries in terms of service imports with more than 19 per cent of total EU imports.[15]

However, just as is the case for trade in goods, *extra-EU trade in services is far less important than the total service transactions within the European Union*. In 2006, the intra-EU share of European trade in services amounted to nearly 60 per cent, meaning that European countries traded more with other European nations than with the rest of the world.[16] The value of intra-EU exports made up €599.9 billion (see Figure 2.3). Total intra-EU imports amounted to €566.6 billion.[17]

Among the individual European countries, Germany accounts for 15 per cent of all intra-EU service transactions, followed by the United Kingdom (12 per cent), Spain (9 per cent) and Italy (9 per cent). Germany has by far the largest intra-EU service deficit (€−26.6 billion), whereas Spain has the biggest surplus (€20.7 billion). The country that showed the highest share of intra-EU exports in total exports of services is Slovakia with almost 80 per cent. Romania, Malta, Portugal, Austria and Poland all had a share of over 75 per cent. Bigger countries like Germany, France or the United Kingdom showed shares below average.[18]

Foreign Direct Investments

In recent decades, foreign direct investments (FDI) have been playing an ever-increasing role in economic globalization. The ability of a region to participate in global FDI activities reflects its competitiveness and goes well beyond the traditional trading activities involving goods and services. FDI complements and spurs the evolution of trade flows, as both investing firms and host countries feed on a wide range of benefits that come along. According to the United Nations,[19] world FDI flows have risen substantially since 1970. Remaining below 1 per cent of the global GDP until 1989, FDI flows surged and reached a peak in 2000 (3.9 per cent of the GDP) before dropping again until 2003 when positive growth returned. In 2006, FDI flows amounted to 2.5 per cent of the GDP.

The EU plays an important role in world FDI flows. With the exception of 2004, it has consistently been the largest investor over the last few years. In 2006, when world FDI flows increased by 85 per cent, the EU held a 34 per cent share of total world FDI flows.[20] In fact, in 2006, out of the ten largest developed investor nations, six were European. With outflows of $115 billion,[iii] France remained the second largest investor worldwide, after the United States. Spain, Switzerland and especially Germany (plus 43 per cent) could continue their outward expansion.[21]

In 2006, FDI flows into the EU increased by 9 per cent, amounting to a total of $531 billion. A lower volume of inflows into the United Kingdom, the Netherlands and Spain was compensated for by the surge inflows to Belgium, Germany, Italy and Luxembourg. Nevertheless, the United Kingdom remained the largest recipient of FDI flows in Europe, and the second largest worldwide.[22]

It is interesting to note that, in 2006, eight of the world's ten largest cross-border mergers and acquisitions (M&As) were carried out within the European Union.[23] *Again, it can be seen that intra-EU transactions were respon-sible for the higher amount of inflows into the EU.* In fact, the percentage of intra-EU FDI inflows out of total FDI inflows has increased over the past few years, reaching 76 per cent for the period 2004 to 2006 (see Figure 2.4).[24]

In the light of the above, we can conclude that, in the course of the past few decades, Europe has been ever more integrated with the rest of the world and has positioned itself as one of the world's major trading partners. For European countries, the home market, namely, the European market itself, is far more important than turning towards trade with the rest of the world.

[iii] The authors would like to draw the reader's attention to the fact that UNCTAD uses the US dollar as its currency of denomination, whereas EUROSTAT uses the euro.

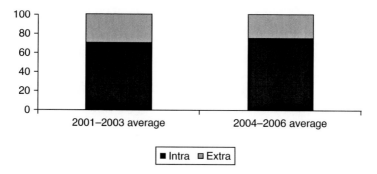

Figure 2.4   Weight of extra- and intra-EU FDI in total EU FDI flows (per cent)
Source: European Commission (2008e), *European Foreign Direct Investment Yearbook 2008 – Data 2001–2006*, Luxembourg, copyright © European Communities, p. 12.

Intra-EU transactions far outnumber extra-EU trade in goods, external trade in services and FDI flows with the rest of the world. This section has highlighted the significance of Europe as a region and has shown that this region is a major hot spot for trade. In a nutshell, there is a lot more trade going on within the boundaries of the European Union than there is with the outside world.

Homogeneity in Europe – dream or reality?

The analysis of trade figures in the previous section has shown that Europe, as a region, is truly a hot spot for trade. Nevertheless, questions regarding homogeneity in Europe have yet to be answered. Companies need to know to what extent Europe can be targeted as a homogeneous market, or whether they have to address each and every individual country market separately. Hence our chapter heading: Is there common ground between Slovakia and Spain or Ireland and Italy?

To establish whether European countries have some common ground, we have analysed a sample of 15 countries[iv] according to different macroeconomic indicators and studied several consumer goods categories to better understand consumer behaviour in these selected nations. In a first step, European countries are analysed regarding macro-oriented, environmental

---

[iv] These countries, representatives of the respective European regions (Scandinavia, Central Europe, Southern Europe, Eastern Europe, the Mediterranean and the United Kingdom and Ireland), were Austria, Bulgaria, Denmark, France, Germany, Ireland, Italy, Norway, Poland, Portugal, Romania, Slovakia, Spain, Sweden and the United Kingdom. Norway, the only non-EU member country in the sample, was included in the study in order to analyze if European policies, regulations and restrictions also have an impact in Europe outside the EU's boundaries.

variables. This provides insights into the degree of homogeneity *among countries*. In a second step, consumption patterns in different product categories are scrutinized to obtain an understanding of the homogeneity *among European consumers*.

Homogeneity among countries: Macroeconomic indicators?

The EU has a number of programs aimed at increasing integration; some key programs are presented here in more detail. On a macroeconomic level, issues such as the economic divide between Western and Eastern Europe, declining population, aging population and labour market difficulties affect all countries in Europe, yet at differing degrees.

The European Union and the euro

Europe consists of numerous nations of various sizes with rich histories and traditions, different people and cultures. The idea of a more integrated Europe had already been debated in 1850,[25] but for that idea to gain real momentum and be put into practice, the continent had to go through two World Wars and the resulting political and economic crises. In the early 1950s, there finally was real political willpower for a unified Europe and six countries, among them Germany and France, lay the foundation stone for the European Union (EU) by establishing the European Coal and Steel Community (ECSC).[26]

A push for integration: As a trading bloc, the EU's aim is "to abolish all customs barriers within the Community and establish a common customs tariff to be applied to goods from non-EEC countries."[27] However, the EU is much more than a trading bloc. Internally, the EU aims to increase integration among its member states on an economic, political and social level, and this makes it unique in the world. Furthermore, the EU member states also share common political institutions and 15 of them share a common currency, the euro. Even though the EU has accomplished many goals, it will never be the United States of Europe[28] because the member states remain sovereign countries with their own political and social systems.

From a purely economic point of view, the EU is highly successful because it combines the consumer spending power of 500 million people into one single market.[29] This makes it "the world's leading trading power"[30] and therefore an important partner in international negotiations.[31] Given the globalization pressures that every country faces today, it is essential to have a unified Europe because "no individual EU country is strong enough to go ... alone in world trade".[32]

The free movement of capital, services and labour has many implications for businesses in Europe – now they can easily source funding from anywhere within the EU, have access to all consumers in Europe and hire any European citizen as easily as hiring a local. In addition, the establishment of the single market has spurred the overall quality of goods and has led to "an increase in the variety of products available to both businesses and consumers".[33] Consumers can now buy products in foreign markets without having to pay additional import duties; this has increased the need for companies to have more or less similar price levels in all European countries.[34] Easier access to new markets has also led to an increase in competition as both European and international companies can now establish themselves much more easily within the EU.[35]

For most products, the EU member states have agreed to the "principle of recognition of national rules".[36] This simply means that if a product can be legally sold and/or manufactured in one member state, it must be allowed to enter the markets of all other member states.[37] This "recognition of national rules"[38] has led to an increase in the variety of goods in the member states, and it is now common that EU supermarkets carry French cheese, Spanish ham and German sausages in their standard product ranges. In theory, this also applies to the service sector, but in practice "a service company is still mainly bound to local culture and language".[39]

To facilitate the free movement of goods, the European Union has spent much time and money to ensure that consumers are confident to buy products from all member states. Throughout the European Union, all consumers benefit from the same high standards for quality assurance, product guarantees and protection of fraud. In a nutshell, the European Union protects consumers against rogue traders, misleading advertisements and faulty products.[40]

The European Union has brought about many changes for its member states, yet the road ahead to entirely free movement of goods, capital and labour is still long with many obstacles along the way. The European Union has fundamentally changed the way business is done in Europe and, together with the euro, has increased competition and price transparency. What is good for consumers, on the other hand, is not good for non-competitive companies, because they face difficult economic times due to increased competition from more competitive companies in other EU member states and non-EU countries.

The euro: In 1992, the ratification of the Maastricht Treaty resulted in the foundation of the Economic and Monetary Union (EMU). The EMU has three pillars: the euro as the single currency; a common, independent central bank and aligned monetary policies.[41] From a political point of view, the euro is also a deterrent of conflict in Europe because now the major European nations are financially interlinked and must align their governmental policies as well.[42] An additional political aspect of the euro is that the dominance of the US dollar is being challenged. The US dollar is unparalleled as "an investment vehicle",[43] and to date, oil prices are quoted only in dollars. Yet European hopes for the euro's strength remain high. According to a survey, "Europe's business leaders believe that the Euro will overshadow the American dollar within 20 years".[44]

For companies in the euro zone,[v,45] "the headaches of juggling 14 or so different currencies"[46] is finally over. The costly exchange of national currencies and exchange rate uncertainties are now relics of the past, and ultimately consumers benefit from increased competition as prices have fallen in many areas.[47] In general, consumers have received more bargaining power because it has become a lot easier for them to compare prices across different markets. Therefore, in addition to the elimination of internal tariffs, companies can no longer hold on to "country-to-country price differences" of up to 40 to 50 per cent.[48]

It may still be too early to say whether the economic benefits of the euro outweigh its costs. But what can be stated is that the euro zone has so far enjoyed low inflation and low interest rates, which have led to a strong common currency.[49] By and large, the euro has helped create a more unified Europe with ever-increasing economic ties.

EU programs for increased integration

To facilitate further integration among EU member states and to create a single market with similar levels of development across all countries, the EU has designed many reform programs. Three of these will briefly be discussed below.

Education: European countries spend significant parts of their budgets on education (on average 5 per cent of GDP in the EU-27) because education is crucial to ensure economic growth and future innovations. Each member state remains responsible for its own education system. The EU does, however, promote cooperation in this field through a number of processes and programs (Bologna process, Socrates, Erasmus, and so on).[50]

The Bologna Process was initiated in 1999 and is a European reform process that aims to form a European Higher Education Area by 2010.[51] This process introduced reforms to make European higher education more "compatible and comparable, more competitive and more attractive for Europeans and for students and scholars from other continents".[52] The main objectives, among others, were to introduce a system of comparable degrees, a two-cycle system of university qualifications (undergraduate/graduate), and a European credit transfer system (ECTS) to make it easier for students to move from one country to another for the purpose of education or employment.[53] It is important to note that the Bologna Process aims at "translating" degrees and credits across all European countries and not at unifying the national curricula.

---

[v] The euro zone includes the following countries: Austria, Belgium, Cyprus, Finland, France, Germany, Greece, Ireland, Italy, Luxembourg, Malta, the Netherlands, Portugal, Slovenia and Spain.

Information and communication technologies: Information and communication technologies (ICTs) are considered essential for improving the competitiveness of European industries and thus hold great potential for Europe as a whole. Regarding Internet access, figures across Europe are diverse. Interestingly, several regional country groups emerge. Scandinavian countries lead, with penetration rates of slightly below 80 per cent of total households in 2007. Mediterranean countries like Italy, Portugal and Spain show rates between 40 per cent and 50 per cent. Eastern European countries such as Bulgaria and Romania lag behind, with 19 per cent and 22 per cent, respectively.[54]

In order to tackle the European Internet divide, the European Commission has designed the i2010 initiative, a strategic policy framework introducing broad guidelines for the information society by 2010. Its core objectives are to spur efficiency, ensure that Europe's citizens, governments and businesses make the best use of ICT and help social and geographical differences to be overcome, thus building an inclusive digital society.[55] The EU wants to create a "Single European Information Space", which "promotes an open and competitive market for information society and media services".[56]

Transportation: Transportation plays an essential role in modern economies, whether it is delivering goods from manufacturers to customers, or bringing people from one place to another for work or pleasure.

The data regarding national road networks show a significant difference between the Eastern European countries and the rest of Europe. Poland and Romania only have 1 kilometre of motorways per 100,000 inhabitants. Spain has the most in Europe, amounting to a total of 27 kilometres per 100,000 inhabitants, followed by Portugal and Austria with 22 and 20 kilometres, respectively.[57] The reason for this significant difference between Eastern European countries and the rest of Europe is the level of economic development. Transport performance is closely related to the development of an economy. This is particularly true for the transport of goods, but also holds true for passenger transport demand.[58]

To secure the free movement of goods and services within the European Union, the European Union has initiated the Trans-European Transport Network (TEN-T) policy, with which major transnational transport routes will be unblocked and sustainable transport ensured.[59] By 2020, transport within EU member states is likely to have doubled, and TEN-T will include 89,500 kilometres of roads and 94,000 kilometres of railways. The inland waterway system will grow to 11,250 kilometres, including 210 inland ports and 294 seaports. Furthermore, 366 airports will finalize the ambitious initiative of implementing a common European transport network.[60]

These programs are all aimed at bringing European countries closer together and eradicating the vast differences that still prevail in many industries. Because many of these programs involve structural changes and high infrastructure investments, they all have long implementation and adoption time frames. Once completed, these programs will reduce differences among European countries regarding education systems, access to ICTs and transportation networks.

Key issues affecting Europe

In Europe, a number of important issues can be identified that affect all nations, even though at differing degrees and with different outcomes. These issues not only bring Europe closer together but also form subregions that can help companies in developing their strategies.

Economic divide between Western and Eastern Europe: The economic divide between Western and Eastern Europe can best be seen in the GDP per capita rates (see Figure 2.5). The data for the 15 countries analysed show very

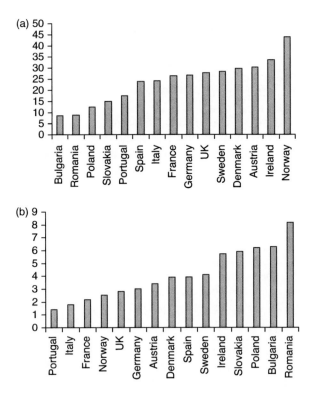

Figure 2.5   Development of GDP in Europe (a) GDP per capita, 2006 (in €1,000 per year), (b) GDP growth rate, 2006 (percentage change from previous year)

Source: Eurostat Database 2008.

clearly that the Western European countries are more developed than the Eastern European ones (Bulgaria, Poland, Romania, Slovakia) because their GDP per capita rates are about twice as high. Yet GDP growth rates show that the developed Western European economies are growing at a very low rate compared with the high growth rates of the Eastern European economies. As a result, the Eastern European countries will be catching up with Western standards in the near future. Out of the 15 countries, Romania has the highest annual growth rate (8.2 per cent), followed by Bulgaria (6.3 per cent), Poland (6.2 per cent) and Slovakia (5.9 per cent). Interestingly, Ireland also has a very strong growth rate (5.9 per cent), which can be largely attributed to the establishment of foreign businesses, as corporate taxation and legislation on holding companies are very favourable.[61]

The reasons for this economic divide are rooted in history. Eastern European countries were trapped behind the iron curtain in command economies until 1989, and growth after the opening of the economies did not start immediately.[62] To this day, Eastern European countries like Bulgaria, Poland, Romania and Slovakia still lag behind the EU-27 average in terms of GDP per capita, expenditure on infrastructure, innovation and education. However, with the accession to the European Union in 2004 and the resulting strong growth rates, it can be expected that they will catch up in the near future. To further accelerate growth in Eastern Europe, the European Union is funding many infrastructure programs.

Declining and ageing population: In 2007, there were 495.1 million inhabitants in the European Union (EU-27).[63] The 15 markets analysed had 425.3 million inhabitants, with Germany, France, the United Kingdom, Italy and Spain being the most populous countries (see Figure 2.6). These 5 countries together had a combined population of 310.1 million people. The combined size of Europe's population makes it one of the biggest consumer markets in the world and thus an attractive and lucrative market for businesses.

However, the size and structure of the European market are likely to change in the future because the European population is declining and aging. Even though the overall EU-27 population still grew by 2 million in 2005, this "population increase ... is ... mostly due to migration"[64] as net migration was 1.7 million and the natural population change amounted to only 0.3 million. The future outlook indicates that migration will not be able to offset the overall population decline, as "many believe the main wave of emigration from Eastern to Western Europe is over".[65] Recent migration patterns and projections indicate that many of the former emigrants have actually been moving back home as some developed economies hit recessions or the opportunities in their home countries have improved. From 2001 to 2005, many of the countries we analysed were already stagnating, that is, showing population growth rates of around zero, and some countries, notably Romania, Bulgaria and Poland, were experiencing a decline in population.

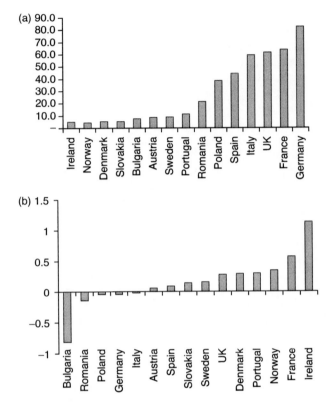

Figure 2.6 Demographic developments in Europe (a) Population size, January 2007, (b) Population growth rate, 2001–2005 (percentage difference from previous year)

Source: Eurostat Database 2008 and United Nations (2007), *World Population Prospects – the 2006 Revision*, New York, Department of Economic and Social Affairs, pp. 54–9.

In Western European countries, the population decline is primarily attributed to low fertility rates. In the Eastern European nations, the population decline is attributed to the migration of their citizens to seek employment elsewhere, because either their economies cannot provide enough jobs (push factor) or the attractiveness of foreign labour market conditions incentivize them to move abroad (pull factor).

The current population decline is paired with changes in the population structure. "It is now well understood that the population structure of nearly all developed economies will undergo dramatic changes over the next 30–40 years",[66] yet these changes are taking place fastest in Europe. For Europe, this means that "the population is projected to become older in all member states, Norway and Switzerland".[67] In 2006, the average percentage of the population aged 80 or more in the 15 countries we analysed was 3.9 per cent, and in some nations (Sweden, Germany and France), it was almost 5 per cent. Since the second half of the eighteenth century, living conditions have changed profoundly, and as a result, life expectancy has "increased significantly within just a few generations".[68] As the population is expected to get increasingly older, it will be necessary for the European governments to restructure the current health care and pension schemes.

The age group of 65 to 79 year olds is increasing steadily; in 2006, many of the countries we analysed had more than 10 per cent of their population in this age bracket and expected this proportion to increase to 30 per cent over the next 20 years (see Figure 2.7).[69] Thus, a much smaller working-age population will have to support a much larger senior population. This situation will force not only governments to restructure and rethink current processes, but also businesses as they need to retain older staff and incentivize them accordingly. Unfortunately, "many organizations fail to adequately prepare for an upcoming wave of departing workers".[70]

The low fertility rates in Europe call for a more detailed analysis as they symbolize many decisions young women and families are making nowadays. In the 15 countries analysed, not a single country reaches the 2.1 children-born-per-woman threshold known as the *natural replacement rate*. This rate shows "the average number of children per woman required to keep the natural population stable in the long-run, under the ... assumption of no migration".[71] A main driver for the low birth rates is that women are choosing to have children at a later stage in life and fertility rates drop significantly after the age of 30. Comparing the mean age of women of childbearing age in 1995 and 2005, in every country we analysed the mean age had increased significantly[vi] and now is somewhere between 25 and 31.

The indicators analysed show a diversified continent with four different regions. The Scandinavian countries boast high fertility rates despite having the highest average age of women at childbirth. Mediterranean countries have slightly higher than average age of women at childbirth and slightly higher-than-average birth rates. Eastern European countries also have low fertility rates and are, in addition, dwindling due to emigration. However, in the future, it can be expected that migrants will return home as their economies develop. The Central European countries like Germany and Austria face a rapidly aging population, and Germany is being faced with a real decline in population from 2005 to 2010.[72] Unless far-reaching policies are introduced to stimulate the fertility rates, the European populations will see a drastic change in their size and structure.

[vi] Except in Germany, where the mean age in 1995 was already at a very high level. The following year, 2006, the mean age increased again.

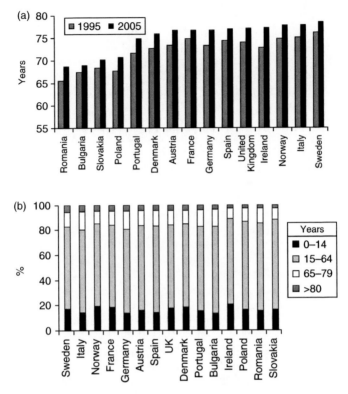

Figure 2.7   Ageing population in Europe (a) Life expectancy at birth, 1995 and 2005, (b) Population by age class, 2006 (percentage of total population)
Source: Eurostat Database 2008.

Labour market difficulties: Overall, the European labour market is less flexible and more regulated than the American one.[73] Over the last few decades, employment rates have continued to increase and are now at rates of 60 to 70 per cent of the total population (see Figure 2.8). Yet rates are much lower for females in all countries analysed, with the lowest female employment rates registered in Italy (46.6 per cent), Romania (52.8 per cent) and Slovakia (53.0 per cent). In the future, it will be crucial to increase female labour participation and at the same time increase birth rates. Countries with the highest GDP per capita are also the ones with the highest female employment rates, like Norway (74.0 per cent), Denmark (73.2 per cent) and Sweden (71.8 per cent).

European unemployment rates have been quite high, and many blame excessive labour market protection and generous unemployment benefits of

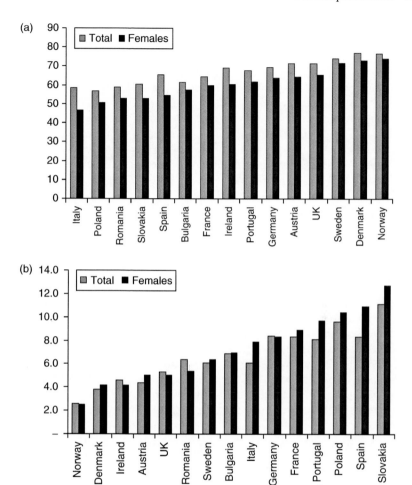

Figure 2.8 Employment rates and unemployment in Europe (a) Employment rate, 2007 (percentage of total population), (b) Unemployment rate, 2007 (percentage of total population)

Source: Eurostat Database 2008.

some countries.[74] Unemployment rates are high in two groups of countries, the first being the Eastern European countries of Slovakia, Poland, Bulgaria and Romania, where the economies still cannot provide for enough jobs, and unskilled labour is widespread. The second group consists of countries that have very generous unemployment benefits and structural difficulties[75] like Germany (8.4 per cent), France (8.3 per cent) and Spain (8.3 per cent).

Concerning the labour market, Europe can be divided into three distinctly different regions. Scandinavian countries such as Norway, Sweden and Denmark boast low unemployment rates and high employment rates, both for men and women, which makes them powerful economies with high per capita GDP rates. Western European countries like Germany, France and Spain also have high employment rates, yet their female employment rates lag behind, and the unemployment rates are significantly higher due to excessive labour market protections. Finally, Eastern European countries such as Bulgaria, Slovakia and Romania have lower total employment rates and also lower female employment rates. Their unemployment rates are also significantly higher than in the rest of Europe because their economies are still not strong enough to provide a sufficient number of jobs for their working-age population.

Is there homogeneity among European countries?

Europe as a whole is a diverse continent with different people and backgrounds, yet common ground does exist. The most important common ground factor is the membership of the European Union. Countries joining the European Union pledge to work more closely together, to integrate their economies, and to abolish all borders between one another. The implications of these decisions go further than the member states' borders, as many non-EU countries adopt European principles, standards and practices in order to sell their goods and services to the European Union member states.

Overall, countries in Europe face the same challenges of economic development, declining and aging populations and labour market problems. Yet, there are different reasons and characteristics for these challenges. The measures taken by individual European countries to counter these issues are often very different and usually highly country specific. Yet in the future, all countries will need to further align their policies to address these issues effectively and to ensure a common European direction.

So, yes, there is certain homogeneity among European countries regarding the trends and problems they are facing today. Yet many differences still prevail. The most significant differences lie in the degree of development of GDP, infrastructure, living conditions and access to technology and educational spending. In the future, assuming that growth rates in Eastern Europe remain high, Eastern European countries will catch up with the Western European economies and the differences will be minimized. To this day, it is difficult to forecast when exactly the Eastern European countries will catch up, but there is no doubt that they will.

Homogeneity among European consumers – dream or reality?

Do the British like the same ice cream as the Spanish? Do Bulgarians drink as much coffee as Italians? Are there any differences between France and Romania when it comes to alcoholic beverages – and what about toilet paper?

To answer whether there is common ground between European countries, we went beyond trade figures and macro-analyses and looked at the consumers themselves. Their consumption patterns, their preferences and their tastes tell us whether companies face a halfway homogeneous European consumer market or a fragmented, diverse market for each and every single country. Below, we have taken a closer look at consumption patterns in a few selected product categories to help us understand whether convergence outweighs fragmentation in Europe. The product categories we analysed are tobacco, alcoholic drinks, ice cream, hot drinks, cosmetics and toiletries, and toilet paper.[76, vii]

Tobacco: Not even a decade ago, consumption patterns across Europe were still quite diverse. However, in recent years, the European Union has developed a very comprehensive tobacco control policy in order to cut down smoking in Europe, with the effect that national tobacco industries are becoming more and more alike. The policy includes legislative measures that comprise tobacco advertising bans, tobacco sponsorship bans, severe tax raises and smoking regulations at work and in public places such as football stadiums, restaurants, bars and nightclubs. These regulations are minimum standards that have to be met by each EU member state. Austria and Germany, for example, have a tradition of rather liberal government views when it comes to smoking. After long resistance, the German government finally implemented the advertising ban in 2006, but debates concerning smoking being banned from restaurants and pubs are still taking place. On the other hand, there are countries like Ireland, the United Kingdom and Italy that are known for quite restrictive attitudes towards smoking legislation. These countries have imposed regulations that go even further than the EU legislation. Eastern European countries such as Poland and Romania have also adopted strict anti-smoking policies and moved away from their less stringent pre-EU regulations. All EU directives also apply in Norway, the only non-EU member in our analysis.

When it comes to health awareness, again it can be seen that European consumers are moving closer together. EU anti-smoking campaigns, combined with national anti-smoking promotions, have led smokers to cut down on their consumption. In some countries, especially Bulgaria and Poland, people are not yet taking on the trend towards healthier lifestyles; however, it is very likely that rising living standards will lead to increased health awareness in these countries. Smokers in these Eastern European nations, but also French smokers, have been known for their love of very strong cigarettes. However, in 2004, the EU set a maximum tar yield at 10 milligrams and forbade the production of high-tar cigarettes. Hence, the common standards across Europe are making cigarette consumption patterns similar.

[vii] The Euromonitor International Database is the source of all data in this section.

Nowadays, mid-tar cigarettes are the leading market segment in every single European market, with the trend going towards lighter, low-tar cigarettes. This illustrates that government regulations are very much able to shape and change consumption patterns.

The goal of cutting down cigarette consumption across Europe is bold, but the policies mentioned above work. Across Europe, volume sales are stagnating or decreasing (with the exception of Denmark).[viii] Cigarette tax increases, anti-smoking campaigns and smoking bans have indeed brought Europe closer together and decreased and consolidated cigarette consumption.

Nevertheless, and this is important, consumers have reacted differently to these policies. Romanians and Germans, for example, have started to replace cigarettes with RYO (roll your own) tobacco. In these countries, consumers think that by trading their cigarette for rolling tobacco, papers and filters, they can cut down on smoking and smoke "more healthily" since they can control the volume of tobacco in each cigarette. On the other hand, there are countries like Sweden and Norway where many cigarette smokers are turning more and more to snus. Snus is a non-smoking tobacco that is normally put between gum and upper lip. It is a traditional tobacco product in those two countries and has experienced substantial growth rates in the last few years due to the tobacco policies and constantly increasing cigarette prices mentioned above. Smokers believe that the snus is healthier than cigarettes, because it does not contain any tar. Moreover, after the smoking ban, many smokers turned to snus because they could still use smokeless tobacco in restaurants, bars and other public places. Since 2000, the total volume sales of snus in Norway have increased by about 18 per cent annually. If the same increase continues, the forecast shows that by 2010, there will be more people using snus than smokers.

Even though the European tobacco market is consolidating, it is important to note that different consumer habits still exist and that these differences will even grow. Cigarette consumption will very likely continue to decrease; however, companies will face different consumer reactions across Europe and will have to react carefully when targeting their customers with the right product.

Ice cream: The European ice cream industry is experiencing several trends, which all go in the same direction. However, at the time of writing, consumers across countries still show quite different ice cream consumption patterns. Moreover, in this industry, we can easily group certain countries together in regions with similar ice cream preferences.

---

viii CAGR (Volume Growth 2002–2006 in per cent): Austria (–2.9), Bulgaria (–0.5), Denmark (4.1), France (–7.7), Germany (–8.0), Ireland (–3.6), Italy (–1.3), Norway (–2.1), Poland (–1.6), Portugal (–0.6), Romania (–7.3), Slovakia (–6.3), Spain (0.1), Sweden (–0.8), and the United Kingdom (–1.5).

Looking first at per capita consumption, we can see a great divide between regions. On top of the list are the Scandinavian countries, with Norwegians and Swedes both eating more than ten litres of ice cream per year. At the bottom end of the spectrum are Eastern European countries like Romania and Bulgaria, where per capita consumption does not even reach two litres per year (see Figure 2.9).

One of the key trends in the European ice cream industry at the moment is the polarization of consumers opting for either health and wellness or

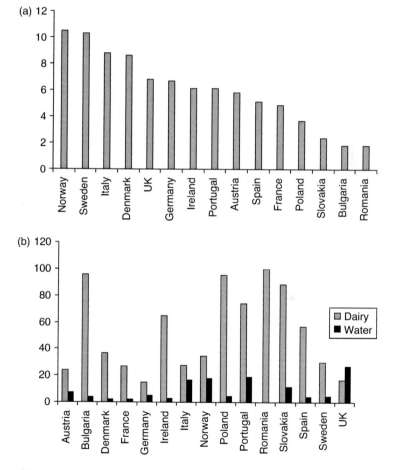

Figure 2.9 European consumption of ice cream (a) Per capita consumption of ice cream 2007 (kilograms), (b) Market shares of ice cream by subsector (percentage of volume sales)

Source: Euromonitor International Database 2008.

indulgence. On the one hand, European consumers are increasingly demanding low-fat and low-calorie ice creams, but many are not willing to sacrifice taste. This demand is being met by manufacturers with probiotic ice creams and products called "Skinny Cow" or "Milk Time".[77] On the other hand, there is a move towards indulgence and luxury ice cream that disregards the popular calorie count. Consumers increasingly want to award themselves with rich and satisfying ice creams, and manufacturers are meeting this demand by introducing value-added ingredients and high-quality premium products that include fudge swirls, caramel chunks and sophisticated new flavours. The trend towards healthier ice cream alternatives is almost universal throughout Europe – almost, because Italy and France do not fit into the picture. In the Eastern European countries, this polarization is only just beginning. But with growing disposable income, it can be expected that they will catch up with the rest of Europe quite soon.

Another trend in the ice cream industry is a move towards enjoying ice cream all year long. In the past, ice cream was always consumed in warm, summer months and was thus a seasonal summer product. However, with the rise of take-home, bulk ice cream, consumers across Europe are more and more indulging in their ice cream around the year. It should not come as a surprise that take-home ice cream has by far the largest share in Scandinavian countries, where climates are relatively colder compared with the rest of Europe (Norway – 67.5 per cent, Sweden – 65.6 per cent). Growth rates in the take-home sector can also be seen in warmer climates. Consumers in Spain and Portugal, however, are still very impulse driven and therefore still prefer purchasing ice cream on impulse (65.8 per cent and 71.1 per cent, respectively) over take-home products. Even though there is a trend towards a consolidated "take-home ice cream market", the divide between European countries is still quite big. Warmer climates prefer impulse ice cream; colder climates opt for take-home products.

The majority of Europe prefers dairy ice cream. Vanilla, strawberry and chocolate are the three most popular flavours in the respective markets. However, again, there are a few countries that do not fit in. Consumers in the United Kingdom prefer water-based ice cream over dairy products, and in Romania, water-based ice cream is not even being sold. And when it comes to vanilla ice cream, the French prefer theirs yellow and beanie in taste, whereas the Germans like theirs much whiter and buttery.

There could not be an analysis of the European ice cream sector without mentioning ice cream's country of origin. Italy is world-famous for its traditional ice cream production. As a result, artisanal ice cream[ix] has a market share of almost 70 per cent in Italy, whereas artisanal ice cream has only marginal shares all across the other countries in comparison. Only the

---

[ix] Artisanal ice cream is hand-made ice cream sold at traditional ice cream parlours and bakeries for immediate consumption.

Eastern European countries and France have artisanal ice cream shares larger than 20 per cent.

Taken collectively, the European ice cream sector is experiencing similar trends across countries. However, at the time of writing, consumer patterns in individual countries were still far apart. Hence, even though there might be consolidation in some areas of the industry, it will most likely still take a long time for individual country traditions and personal tastes to change.

Alcoholic drinks: The European alcoholic drinks industry is characterized by two trends that substantially differentiate the Eastern European countries from the rest of Europe but ultimately will bring these two regions closer together. On the one hand, we have a mature, saturated market in the West, where volume sales are stagnating or even decreasing, whereas on the other hand, there is a block of markets in the East with a lot of growth potential.[x] (see Figure 2.10) The downward trend of volume sales in the Western countries in recent years has several reasons: changes in demographics, new lifestyle choices, a rise in the health and wellness consciousness and political pressure on manufacturers to curb certain advertising practices. The older people get, the less alcohol they tend to consume, and when they do enjoy a drink, they opt for quality instead of quantity. The rise in health consciousness and an enlarged media focus on alcohol consumption among minors have contributed to an increased awareness of the perils of excessive alcohol consumption. Furthermore, legislative measures across Europe such as the introduction of harsh drunk-driving regulations or advertising bans have led to a slowdown in volume sales. Romania, Poland, Bulgaria and Slovakia, on the other hand, face a different situation, which leads us to the second trend. The rise in disposable income increases consumption of nonessential products. Hence, Eastern European markets have experienced high sales growth rates for alcoholic beverages in recent years. Integration into the European Union, increase in foreign direct investment and the lowering of import duties on foreign imports have led to higher purchasing power and, therefore, to higher volume sales of alcoholic drinks. As these two trends unfold, Western and Eastern Europe are likely to level consumption rates somewhere in the middle.

It is interesting to note that in 12 out of the 15 countries in our analysis, consumers buy the majority of their alcohol in the off-trade channel.[xi] Ireland, the United Kingdom and Spain, on the other hand, prefer to

---

[x] CAGR (Volume Growth 2002–2007 in per cent): Austria (0.5), Bulgaria (5.5), Denmark (–1.8), France (–1.2), Germany (–0.6), Ireland (0.0), Italy (–0.2), Norway (2.6), Poland (5.8), Portugal (2.6), Romania (10.0), Slovakia (2.1), Spain (1.5), Sweden (–1.0), United Kingdom (0.4).

[xi] Off-trade channels refer to all retail formats/channels such as supermarkets, kiosks and so on, whereas the on-trade channel combines restaurants, pubs, bars and nightclubs.

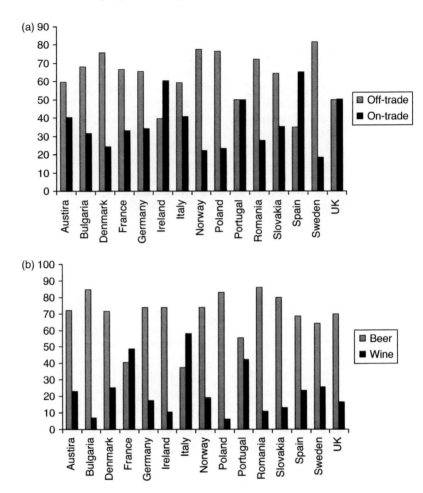

Figure 2.10 Consumption of alcoholic drinks in Europe (a) Market share by distribution channel 2007 (per cent), (b) Market share by alcoholic drinks subsector (per cent of volume sales)

Source: Euromonitor International Database 2008.

enjoy their drinks in pubs, restaurants and clubs – the on-trade channel. Of course, Ireland and the United Kingdom are well known for their love of pubs, where they spend their business lunches as well as their leisure time get-togethers with friends. However, this is not the whole story, and times are changing. In nearly all European countries, including Ireland and the United Kingdom, alcohol prices in pubs and restaurants are increasing. This, together with higher living costs, stricter drunk-driving regulations and smoking bans, is causing European consumers to shift their consumption patterns away from their favourite pubs and towards their homes.

There are a few countries that do not fit the trend. In Scandinavia, it has become quite trendy to go out and share a drink with friends in a local bar. Norwegian and Swedish consumers have increasingly adopted these continental European alcohol consumption patterns in recent years. According to the Euromonitor, this can be attributed to the fact that Scandinavians are travelling more. Furthermore, Austrians, for example, would rather enjoy their wine in bars and restaurants than go for the cheaper versions in the off-trade channel. However, even though there are a few countries that show different consumption patterns, it can be concluded, for now, that the majority of alcoholic drinks in Europe is sold off-trade.

Another interesting trend is that there are signs of market polarization. The alcoholic drinks market is facing increasing demand for premium and high-end alcoholic drinks on the one hand, and cheap, value-for-money products on the other. More and more consumers are opting for quality instead of quantity. This can be attributed to the aging population, as well as the increased health trend and the rise of purchasing power in the East. On the other hand, for example, in Germany, consumers are increasingly opting for economy beer, owing to the strong position of discounters and the high level of minimum quality standards of the Deutsches Reinheitsgebot. In the Eastern European countries, this market polarization can be seen quite clearly. With economic concentration in major cities, people who work there have started to buy premium beers and wines. On the other hand, in rural areas, where economic growth still lags behind, people often brew their own alcohol. In 2007, 25 per cent of total alcohol consumption in Romania was either homemade or un-branded.

Of course, the most interesting part of the analysis is to see whether all European countries have the same likes and dislikes when it comes to the different alcoholic drinks on the market. The volume share of beer is very high in every country analysed. As regards the different types of beer, lager is the most popular choice in Europe, with market shares of over 80 per cent in almost all European markets. However, there are some peculiarities when it comes to European beer tastes. Germans are known for their wheat beer (market share of 16.9 per cent), British consumers love their dark ale (market share of 24.0 per cent) and the Irish are keen on stout (market share of 31.3 per cent), with the world-famous Guinness brand (see Figure 2.11a). Furthermore, Irish and British consumers also like their cider. Whereas cider shares across Europe are only marginal, cider reaches 8.5 per cent and 11 per cent of alcoholic drink purchases in the United Kingdom and Ireland, respectively.

Wine sales are not as high as those of beer in most countries. However, in Italy (57.9 per cent) and France (48.8 per cent), wine sales outnumber beer purchases. Moreover, the majority of countries in the sample are experiencing a

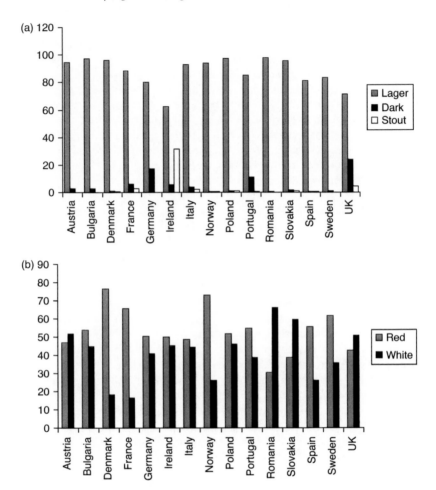

Figure 2.11   Beer and wine consumption in Europe (a) Market share by type of beer 2007 (per cent of volume sales), (b) Market share by type of wine 2007 (per cent of volume sales)

Source: Euromonitor International Database 2008.

rise in wine sales. This can be attributed to the fact that wine is considered healthier than beer or spirits and is seen as a more sophisticated drink. With changing demographics, increased health awareness and the trend towards high-quality products, wine has experienced healthy growth rates in the recent past. Nevertheless, there are three countries in the sample experiencing declining demand for wine. These countries are France, Italy and Spain – the most important European countries when it comes to wine production and consumption. Declining volume sales can be attributed to the fact that companies are faced with highly saturated wine markets and traditional wine drinkers belong to a generation that is getting older and thus drinks less – and they are not being replaced, because younger age groups prefer other beverages, mostly soft drinks and beer. When it comes to the question whether Europeans like their wine red or white, the answer is quite clear: they prefer red wine. Only Austrian, Irish and British consumers prefer white wine to red wine (see Figure 2.11b).

Wine does not play a major role in Eastern European volume figures. For example, in Poland and Bulgaria, even the share of spirits sales is higher than the wine market share. This can be attributed to the fact that, for instance, in Poland, the price for a bottle of Vodka is almost the same as the price for a bottle of wine. Therefore, Polish consumers prefer to stick to their traditional drink, vodka, rather than opt for the relatively higher priced, imported wines.

In conclusion, factors such as economic growth, demographic changes, busy lifestyles and health trends are changing the European alcoholic drinks sector. Even though there are a few trends that go in different directions across the European countries (declining demand in the West; growing volume sales in the East), we predict that European alcohol sales will become more and more alike in the long run. Differences in tastes, however, do exist. Some like their wines red, few like it white; the Irish like their stout, and the Germans like their wheat beer. These country idiosyncrasies are likely to persist in the foreseeable future, and companies will have to deal with them when operating across Europe.

Hot drinks: Coffee is the preferred hot drink in the majority of the 15 countries analysed (see Figure 2.12). Interestingly, it is the Scandinavian countries of Denmark, Norway and Sweden that consume the most coffee, ranging from 5 to 6.6 kilograms per capita in 2007. There, filtered coffee is the preferred type of coffee, which needs more ground coffee than, for example, a cup of espresso. Therefore, per capita data, which is expressed in kilograms, might slightly distort reality. The only two countries that drink more tea than coffee are the United Kingdom and Ireland. Although the 13 coffee-drinking countries are not strong tea drinkers, a trend towards more tea is evolving due to the associated health and wellness benefits. This health trend is affecting the hot drinks industry as people look for relaxing attributes in their hot beverages and want to combine indulgence with added effects of well-being. Inspired by this move towards healthy lives, consumers are motivated to turn to hot drinks like green tea and teas with added antioxidants.

Concerning the location of hot drink consumption, Spain and Portugal are the only two countries that buy almost as much coffee in food-service outlets as in retail stores (40.4 per cent and 41.7 per cent, respectively). As the lives of people are getting more and more stressful and long working hours are the norm, more and more consumers are looking for time-saving

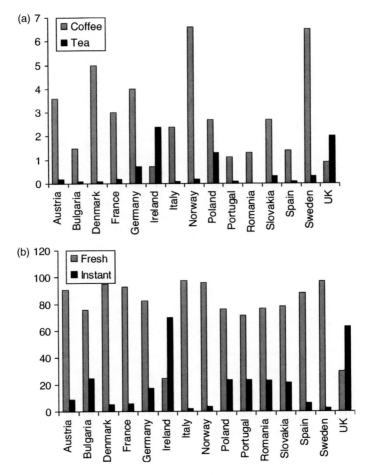

Figure 2.12   Consumption of hot drinks in Europe (a) Per capita consumption of hot drinks 2007 (kilograms), (b) Market shares of coffee by subsector (per cent of volume sales)

Source: Euromonitor International Database 2008.

options and consume hot drinks on-the-go. This demand is being met by sprawling coffee chains all over Europe. North American and British chains are also increasingly focusing their operations in Eastern Europe in the hopes of generating high growth rates in the future.

Another time-saving product is instant coffee. Generally, in almost all European countries, instant coffee sells much less than fresh coffee. Nevertheless, people in Ireland and the United Kingdom consume more instant coffee than fresh coffee.

Overall, European consumers prefer tea and coffee to other kinds of hot drinks, and chocolate and milk-based hot drinks are experiencing diminishing market shares. Everywhere in Europe, lifestyles, consumption patterns and household sizes are changing, and as a result, more and more consumers are looking for convenient, on-the-go consumption of hot drinks. The times when coffee and tea were consumed only at the breakfast table are over. We expect the hot drinks segment will see some changes in the future, with the key trends being health, wellness and convenience. In an otherwise relatively homogeneous segment, the 15 nations we analysed show some differences regarding the preference of coffee over tea and fresh coffee over instant coffee.

Cosmetics and toiletries: The cosmetics and toiletries industry has been registering strong sales volumes in all European countries and is set for growth in the near future as income levels across Europe are rising and consumers are trading up to premium products and brands. This trend is multiplied with an aging population and the desire to look and feel young, which is leading to unprecedented demand for cosmetics and toiletries.

Europe's favourite places to shop for cosmetics are supermarkets, grocers and perfumeries. For example, store-based purchases in Germany, Ireland and Portugal amount to 95.6 per cent, 96.1 per cent and 94.9 per cent, respectively. It is interesting to note that in all Eastern European countries analysed, a high percentage of all purchased cosmetics is bought via direct selling, a retail format pioneered in the United States in the late 1960s. Direct selling is especially successful in Bulgaria and Romania, where it accounts for 27.3 per cent and 31.2 per cent of all purchased cosmetics and toiletries, respectively. Another interesting, if slightly outdated distribution format, is the home shopping channel on TV, which in general is not very popular across Europe. However, consumers in France buy more cosmetics via home shopping channels[xii] than over the Internet.[xiii]

When digging deeper into the cosmetics and toiletries data of the 15 countries we analysed, it becomes clear that a large part of total cosmetics expenditure is spent on perfume (see Figure 2.13). Unsurprisingly, France, the country that created perfumes centuries ago, is one of the heaviest users with a yearly per capita consumption of about 74 millilitres. Only consumers in Spain sprayed more perfume on themselves, with a per capita usage of 116 millilitres in 2007. In all remaining European countries, per capita consumption was between 40 to 50 millilitres but Norwegian and Bulgarian consumption fell much lower than the average (23.6 and 35.7 millilitres, respectively). Norway and Bulgaria represent both extremes on the GDP

[xii] 63.3 per cent of non-store based purchases, which make up 7.9 per cent of the French cosmetics market.

[xiii] 19 per cent of non-store based purchase.

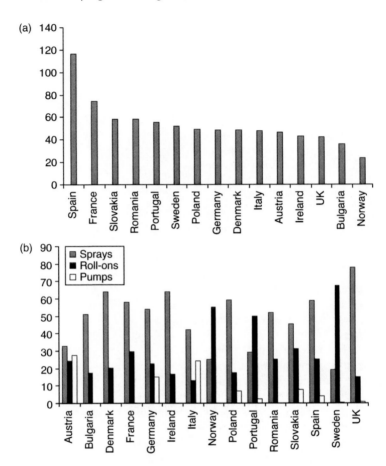

Figure 2.13 Consumption of fragrances and deodorants in Europe (a) Per capita retail volume of fragrance (millilitres), (b) Market share of deodorants by subtype (per cent of volume sales)

Source: Euromonitor International Database 2008.

income level and also on consumer expenditure charts, as Norway is the richest in the sample and Bulgaria the poorest. The conclusion must be that perfume consumption is not determined by disposable income but by personal preference.

Another interesting product within the industry is deodorant, which comes in various shapes and sizes, such as deodorant sprays, pumps, roll-ons, creams and wipes. In most countries, deodorant sprays are the most popular deodorant product, with the only exceptions being Norway, Portugal and Sweden, where sales of roll-ons are more than twice as high as those of sprays. Deodorant pumps have failed to achieve significant market shares outside of Austria and Italy, where they have reached 27.7 per cent and 24.2 per cent, respectively.

The cosmetics and toiletries industry is an important industry because consumers spend significant parts of their income on these products, and consumption is expected to increase in all markets studied. Within the industry, two large consumer regions in Europe emerge: the Eastern European and the Western European consumers. In the Eastern European markets, the manufacturers enjoy high growth rates, but from a lower starting point. In Western Europe, manufacturers deal with mature markets in which consumers are replacing standard products with more luxurious ones. Country peculiarities emerge when it comes to different product types and retail channels.

Toilet paper: Across the 15 European markets, per capita consumption of toilet paper can be split into two large groups: one group of heavy consumers with an annual consumption of about four kilograms or more, and a group of light consumers with about three kilograms or less per year (see Figure 2.14). The light consumers are Bulgaria (2.7 kilograms), Poland (2.9 kilograms), Romania (2.0 kilograms), and Slovakia (3.2 kilograms). The other extremes are the United Kingdom with a per capita consumption of 6.9 kilograms per year, followed by Ireland and Germany, both with 6.5 kilograms. The data seem to indicate that toilet paper use is closely linked to disposable income and that consumers with lower disposable incomes are more parsimonious in their consumption.

Germany is a good example of a trend towards market polarization in the toilet paper industry. In general, economy products enjoy a high popularity in Germany, due to the fact that discount chains are on the rise, amounting to a 30 per cent market share. Hence, economy toilet paper has a staggering market share of 45 per cent. On the other hand, luxury products make up 31.5 per cent of the market. This move towards the two opposite ends of the spectrum leaves standard products facing declining demand. In this context, it is interesting to note that in Spain and the United Kingdom, economy toilet paper only reaches 2.0 per cent and 4.6 per cent of consumers.

The neighbouring countries France and Germany are quite different regarding their preference for toilet paper type. In Germany, the economy toilet paper has the biggest market share (45.3 per cent) and in France, it is the luxury toilet paper that has the highest percentage of the market (56 per cent). Spain, Italy and the United Kingdom, in contrast, all favour standard toilet paper, with market shares of 61 per cent, 48.6 per cent and 73.6 per cent, respectively. In all markets, luxury products are gaining market shares as opposed to economy products, which are losing market shares, except in Germany.

The toilet paper industry has seen some new brands and innovations being introduced in the last few years; however, in general, it can be considered a

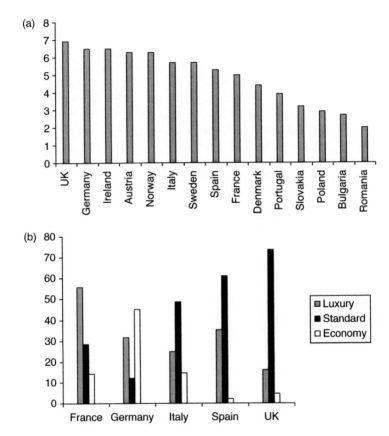

Figure 2.14   Toilet paper consumption in Europe (a) Per capita consumption of toilet paper 2007 (kilograms), (b) Market shares by types of toilet paper 2006 (per cent of volume sales)

Source: Euromonitor International Database 2008.

rather mature market with limited growth potential except for the Eastern European countries. For the next few years, it is very likely that the Eastern European countries will increase their toilet paper consumption as their disposable income increases, and therefore, they will blend in with the rest of Europe. Even though the 15 countries in our comparison seem quite similar, a few differences can be found regarding quality preferences.

Is there homogeneity among European consumers?

Based on our analysis, several trends appear to emerge. These trends drive consolidation among European consumers; they diminish country differences and push consumption patterns closer together. In particular, these trends include market polarization, the health and wellness trend, faster lifestyles, demographic change, and EU policies and governmental regulations.

Market polarization: This trend describes a market situation where a split between low-end and high-end products is taking place, causing the middle segment to lose market share.[78] Examples in the alcoholic drinks and toilet paper industry have shown that consumers across Europe are increasingly opting for either value-for-money products or high-end premium goods. Similarly, the ice cream industry shows market polarization between healthy, low-calorie products and premium indulgence ice creams.

Health and wellness: The health and wellness trend is quite widespread in Europe. According to data taken from the Euromonitor International Database, consumers are increasingly changing consumption patterns towards healthier product choices all across Europe. As we demonstrated in our analyses, European consumers are opting for reduced calorie products, are choosing healthier foods and drinks, have started to drink less alcohol and are smoking less.

Faster lifestyles: In recent decades, lives in Europe have become more stressful than ever before. Economic growth and technological development have made lives faster. Consumption patterns indicate that people are more and more looking for time-saving options when it comes, for instance, to the consumption of foods and beverages. Hence, food-service chains that offer fast service and specialize in on-the-go concepts experience increasing popularity and are spreading rapidly all over Europe.

Demographic change: Demographics are changing significantly in Europe: people are getting older. With an aging population comes a change in consumption patterns. For instance, the older people get, the more concerned they are about their health. As a result, they opt for healthier product choices. Thus, older people tend to drink less alcohol, and when they do enjoy a drink, they opt for wine instead of beer, and choose quality over quantity.

EU policies and governmental regulations: The analyses of the tobacco and alcoholic drinks industries in particular have shown quite clearly that political pressure can shape consumer behaviour. Advertising regulations, smoking bans, political campaigns and strict drunk-driving regulations are all examples of how politics influences and consolidates European consumption patterns.

With these trends in mind, it can be concluded that the European consumer market shows signs of consolidation. But is it really one single market yet? The trends are omnipresent and are clearly pushing towards one homogeneous consumer market. However, it cannot be ignored that these trends do lead to different reactions in a few countries and that, in general, country differences and consumer peculiarities are still quite prominent. As we have shown, Italians love their traditional artisanal ice cream and Irish consumers prefer water ice cream, whereas in Romania, water ice cream is not even on the market. Germans prefer beer, yet Spaniards opt for wine, and Polish consumers still choose vodka over wine. Austrians like their wine white, Italians like it red. Germans love their wheat beer, the Irish like their stout. And while the majority of Europeans prefer coffee to tea, consumers in the United Kingdom and Ireland drink much more tea than coffee. Moreover, consumers in these two countries are the only two that prefer instant coffee to fresh coffee.

These country peculiarities exist and are deeply rooted in their culture and traditions. Hence, it can be concluded, for now, that homogeneity among consumers is not a reality, yet. Nevertheless, the trends mentioned above indicate that there will be more homogeneity in the years to come. There is some common ground between Spanish, Slovak, Italian and Irish consumers, but for now, Europe cannot yet be considered a truly single consumer market.

Conclusion

Is there common ground between Spain and Slovakia, or Italy and Ireland? This question, posed at the very beginning of this chapter, illustrates the core of the analysis presented here. The purpose of this chapter was to showcase the significance of the European market as a region, analyse how it stands in relation to the rest of the world, illustrate how European countries are commercially interlinked between one another and, finally, highlight how homogeneous or heterogeneous the European market really is. Possible answers to this question were given along the way, a clear and definite answer, however, has yet to be formulated. In order to do that, we shall briefly summarize the key insights from our analysis.

Europe is a hot spot for trade. Over the last few decades, the European Union has positioned itself as one of the strongest players in international trade. Even though the European Union has excellent commercial ties with its international trading partners, for European countries, the home market, namely, the European market itself, is far more important than trade with the rest of the world. *Thus, there is common ground.*

Europe is a diverse continent. However, countries are faced with the same challenges, such as economic development, declining and aging populations and labour market problems. These similarities, together with the unifying force of the European Union, are pushing countries closer together. Nations work together closely, integrate their economies and abolish borders between one another. So, yes, there is a certain degree of homogeneity among European countries regarding the trends and problems they are facing today. Yet many differences still prevail. The most significant differences lie in the degree of development of GDP, infrastructure, living conditions and access to technology and educational spending. *Thus, there is some common ground, but homogeneity is not a reality yet.*

The European consumer market shows signs of consolidation. Certain trends are pushing consumer behaviour closer towards a more homogeneous European consumer market. However, country differences and consumer peculiarities are still quite prominent. These differences are deeply rooted in the individual countries' cultures and traditions and are not likely to change rapidly in the near future. *Thus, there is some common ground, but country differences slow down the convergence of consumer behaviour across Europe.*

Taken collectively, we conclude that European countries share a lot of common ground. However, country differences are still very prominent and, to this end, homogeneity in Europe is not quite a reality yet. Nevertheless, the above-mentioned trends, together with the unifying force of the European Union, lead Europe on a path towards increased homogeneity. With this in mind, chances are high that there will be a lot more common ground in the years to come.

3
Managing the Integration Responsiveness Dilemma

Navigating in the global integration – national responsiveness space

As outlined in the introduction to this book, one of the most persistent challenges for any firm doing business at an international scale is to manage the latent trade-off between global integration and local adaptation.[1] On the one hand, there are pressures to respond to the unique needs of the individual country markets. On the other hand, there are efficiency pressures that encourage companies to de-emphasize local differences and conduct business in a similar way throughout the world. The global integration – local responsiveness trade-off engages the firm at multiple levels, involving its overall strategy, the architectural configuration of the firm as well as the operational aspects of the firm, for example, the adaptation of individual prices or advertising campaigns to a given market. In this section, we will first summarize the key drivers of local adaptation and global integration. Based on this understanding, we will discuss common approaches to deal with this global – local trade-off. Building on our own data and recent evidence by an increasing number of scholars,[2] we conclude that, for most firms, the integration – responsiveness dilemma is probably best solved on a regional basis.

The advantages of local adaptation

Firms that follow a local responsiveness strategy tend to customize their operations and products to accommodate individual market differences. A set of strong factors that favours local adaptation represents variations in consumer needs. Consumers' preferences can differ on the basis of culture, religion, geographic and climate differences among countries, or their relative purchasing power. Kentucky Fried Chicken and other fast-food chains, for example, have adapted their product portfolio in Muslim countries to cater to the needs of Islamic consumers by offering food that is "Halal". As Chapter 2 indicated, even in Europe, large differences in consumer habits persist, for example, when it comes to beer vs. wine or the consumption of ice cream that may warrant a localized market approach. In addition, political pressures or industrial standards may require the firm to adapt its product offerings and operating processes to local market needs. To obtain an operating permit for a car in Germany, for example, the brake system has to go through much tougher testing than would be required for the US market. Governments may also require a certain level of production to take place locally (local content requirements). As a consequence, firms sometimes come up with quite creative localization strategies. General Motors, for example, de-assembles its ready-to-drive cars in Poland and ships them as bundles of components to the Ukraine where it reassembles them, just to avoid import taxes. On a larger scale, the formation of regional trade blocks has led many MNCs to build up local production facilities in each region of the Triad to circumvent the cost associated with importing goods from other Triad markets. Toyota, for example, set up its first plants in the United States and the United Kingdom to respond to trade restrictions and import duties. The advantage of such a responsive strategy is mostly a higher market fit or, if localization is the pre-condition to sell, market access. Irrespective of the reason, a local adaptation strategy should ultimately lead to higher profits for the firm by achieving higher sales in the respective markets.

The advantages of global integration

Although the benefits of local adaptation help to achieve a better market fit, the key advantage of global integration lies in the potential to drive down costs through market integration. One key strategy to reduce costs is to standardize processes and products across all markets and achieve economies of scale. This, in turn, avoids the inherent costs of local adaptation. Over the last few decades, development costs in many industries have surged. Development costs for Hollywood movies or video games, for example, easily climb up to $50 million; blockbuster drugs seldom come for less than twenty times that amount, with current patent protection lasting about five to seven years in the market before the competition enters the game.[3] To recoup these high development costs, firms are pressured to look for ways to scale their business beyond the local markets. Operating at a global or regional scale not only helps to refinance R&D expenditures, it also gives firms with standardized marketing huge cost advantages over their competitors. Coca Cola's marketing budget, for example, averages only 0.02 cents per case, whereas its much smaller competitors need to invest about 0.15 cents per case.[4] This puts smaller firms at an absolute and relative cost disadvantage when it comes to marketing. For similar reasons, most car manufacturers centralize technology development and research to a few key sites, rather than letting each individual market come up with a separate solution of how to reduce carbon dioxide emissions in a new combustion engine.

The reduction of costs within the global firm also often has implications for the global configuration of the value chain. Countries possess different labour cost structures, making it feasible for globally operating firms to move production to countries with the lowest possible cost structure, while concentrating other functions in different locations to maximize the overall benefit for the firm. Firms achieve the highest benefit of global integration by allocating each value-added activity in the best possible location and then coordinating and integrating the activities to achieve overall superior performance. Asics, for example, centralizes its research and design in Kobe, Japan. Manufacturing and prototyping of key components such as the cushioning gel take place in South Korea, while the bulk of shoe manufacturing is located in China.[5]

Dealing with both pressures simultaneously

In reality, neither a strategy focusing exclusively on local adaptation nor global integration will ultimately lead to success. In an increasing number of industries, firms need to manage both demands at the same time. However, bridging these two conflicting demands puts the organization under a lot of stress. For illustration, take the global – local dilemma of a multinational restaurant chain like McDonald's. It is known for serving a standardized selection of food, like the Big Mac, in a consistent quality. However, differences in taste, religion and consumer preferences force McDonald's to adapt its products locally. McDonald's reacts by introducing a non-beef version of the Big Mac in India for the Hindu population or adding beer to the menu in Germany. However, its localization efforts can only go to a certain level without losing too much of its original image and selling proposition. If the balance tips towards localization, McDonald's would run the risk of alienating its international consumers who would find it hard to recognize the products by their look and taste.

Although the McDonald's case may be quite obvious, global integration may also be exhibited in more subtle forms of local adaptiveness as, for example, "the speed to react". Take the decision to locate production in a low-cost country. On the one hand, the firm may gain by such a move, through lowering its absolute production costs. On the other hand, the resulting global configurations may cause inefficiencies due to higher coordination costs, the inability to control intellectual property and disadvantages with respect to speed to the market. The latter case is one of the key reasons why Inditex, the owner of the Spanish fashion label ZARA, decided to produce the large majority of its garments in Europe and not in the Far East. With factories centrally located in the European home region, Inditex is able to respond very quickly to changing consumer preferences and styles. In fact, ZARA's inventory turnaround is just two weeks, compared to the six to nine month of other fashion houses.[6] For ZARA and Inditex, these coordination advantages far outweigh the drawbacks of a high-cost production base.

Bridging the dual demands often also causes power and competence conflicts that prove hard to overcome. An often-cited example is Philips,[7] a company that internationalized in times of high trade barriers. The prevalent environment led Philips to rely on a very decentralized organizational structure, where the national organizations controlled almost the complete value chain in their respective countries. Although this structure initially helped Philips to succeed with locally adapted products, Philips faced troubles when trying to coordinate and integrate activities across markets. One prime example of Philips difficulties was the US subsidiary's independent decision not to use the Philips own Video 2000 standard but instead to license its competitor's VHS standard for the US production of videocassette recorders.

As the discussion above reveals, increasing pressures on both sides of the spectrum prohibit headquarters from following a one-sided strategy geared either for global integration, global standardized marketing or pure local adaptation. The quest to reduce costs on a global level is more frequently a constant trade-off among multiple pressures stemming from the opportunities to minimize the cost structure of the global firm by means of arbitrage, aggregation or both, while at the same time being locally responsive to consumers.

Common organizational solutions

Scholars have suggested various organizational responses to deal with the dual pressures. Stopford and Wells suggested that organizations internationalize along different trajectories depending on whether their internationalization is triggered by an increasing number of products sold abroad or an increasing number of countries served.[8] In the former case, internationalization will centre on product divisions leading to what the authors call a worldwide product structure. In the latter case, firms internationalize around a small set of products in an increasing number of markets and create a worldwide geographic structure. These two evolutionary development patterns have been linked and empirically supported by Bartlett and Ghoshal,[9] who found that firms who put a strong emphasis on global integration tend to organize around worldwide product divisions, whereas firms that put a strong emphasis on local adaptation tend to implement worldwide geographic structures (Figure 3.1).

A common suggestion made in the literature is that, as pressures of global integration and local responsiveness increase, firms will ultimately move towards global matrix structures or transnational networks.

The global matrix structure

Compared to product divisions or geographic structures, matrix structures are said to have a clear set of advantages. The matrix structure explicitly recognizes the multidimensional nature of global strategic decision-making.

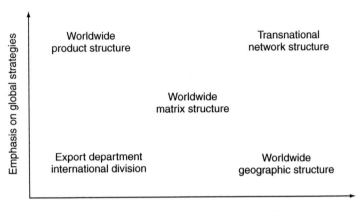

Figure 3.1   Multinational strategies and structures
Source: Based on Cullen and Parboteeah.[10]

It emphasizes dual (sometimes triple) responsibilities and a dual chain of command. For example, a matrix might consist of geographic areas and business divisions. The design helps to internalize the pressures for global efficiency, leverage and local responsiveness, as well as achieving synergies among businesses. In case of conflict, managers will consult both reporting lines to reconcile the conflict and achieve a coordinated set of actions. Thus, in principle, the global matrix should foster a team spirit and cooperation among business area managers, country managers and/or functional managers on a global basis. However, reality has shown that the various dimensions do not always carry equal weight, often leading to one dimension overruling the other. Although organizations show a matrix structure in their chart they are, in fact, often driven by geographic structures or product divisions. Thus, the matrix has often failed to produce a culture of "thinking globally, acting locally."

The transnational network

To address some of the latent shortcoming of the global matrix, Bartlett and Ghoshal popularized an organization form that they call the transnational network.[11] Like the global matrix, the transnational network aims to internalize all the advantages of various structural options. However, unlike the symmetric matrix structure, the transnational network has no basic form. Instead, the transnational network tries to link different types of subsidiaries across the globe. Responsibilities are divided according to the individual competence profile of the subsidiaries. This could result in the marketing "headquarters" sitting in Boston, component manufacturing in Hanoi and market responsibility in Miami. Within the network resources, goods and knowledge are supposed to flow in all directions without structural hierarchies. Coordination within these networks is achieved through a mix of various control instruments. It assigns social integration and a shared culture a prominent role. Thus, in essence, the transnational network is a centreless (or, if you wish, a multicentre) organization that reduces hierarchy and places critical decision-making in peripheral units across the world.

The problem with global matrices and networks

In practice, both global matrices and networks have been found to be problematic. The biggest advantage of the matrix structure is that it facilitates the multinational firm's need to be global and local at the same time, yet there are also major shortcomings. Dual (or triple) reporting and profit responsibilities frequently lead to conflicts or confusion, for example, role ambiguities, dilution of responsibilities and turf battles. Matrix structures might also lead to bureaucratic bloat in that decision-making processes get bogged down and flexibility is lost. Similarly, the structure might lead to cost inefficiencies and nongoal-oriented compromises.

Interestingly enough, the transnational network, which was intended as an organizational response to overcome the shortcomings of the global matrix, does not fare much better. In principle, managers do not always like the fact that there is no clear hierarchy and line authority. If a subsidiary head leads the firm's worldwide operation in terms of marketing and sales but has to follow other rules when it comes to global product policy, conflicts of accountability and control arise. This frustration about shared accountability was also echoed by one senior manager we interviewed: "I don't like it when people tell me they share accountability. The reality is, if more than one person is accountable, in the end, when things turn bad, no one is accountable." Furthermore, two decades after Bartlett and Ghoshal popularized the terms "Network MNC" or "Transnational Solution", empirical research has found rather few firms that clearly adopted a transnational structure.[12] Research has also demonstrated that one of the assumed key advantages of the transnational network, for example, its ability to foster worldwide learning, is questionable at best. In particular, the strong focus on social control often turns out to be detrimental to knowledge sourcing and stimulating breakthrough innovation. As the company turns to stronger social control to maintain unity, it often creates a company-centric rather than geocentric culture. Yet, absorbing knowledge from local research networks requires a strong local integration, which these transnational networks find difficult to build up.[13]

In light of these drawbacks, neither of the two proposed solutions has found widespread acceptance among globally operating firms. And although many global firms often operate under an implicit or explicit matrix structure, they usually assign one of the two key dimensions, that is, geography or product divisions. As a consequence, the empirical trend of the last two decades was a clear swing towards organizations dominated by product divisions.[14] If we accept that increasing globalization along with increasing pressures to drive down costs by achieving global economies of scale and cross market coordination is favoured by a product division structure, this trend is understandable. In this book, we like to challenge conventional organizational thinking and argue for a swing towards a "new form" of geographical structure: the regional headquarters solution. Regional headquarters (and regional strategy), as we will point out in the remainder of this book, have a potential to solve critical parts of the inherent tensions faced by global organizations. Furthermore, as we will show in the next section, a regional approach to strategy is a logical and arguably the most effective way to deploy the firm's resources and capabilities.

Towards a regional view

In his analysis of the world's largest 500 companies, Rugman concludes that few firms actually pursue a global strategy.[15] Rugman defines "global firms" as those having a minimum of 20 per cent for their sales in each of the triad markets (North America, Europe and Asia). Of the 380 firms from which he was able to obtain data, only 9 firms qualify as truly global (for example, IBM, Canon, Coca-Cola, Flextronics, LVMH), 25 are "bi-regional" and the vast majority of the 320 firms are home regional. Rugman's definition has been criticized for various reasons.[16] For one, critiques have argued that the thresholds selected by Rugman to define his clusters are picked arbitrarily and that altering the threshold may change the picture somewhat. Also, sales as a measure for globalization downplay the globalization on the supply side of the business, which, in case of manufacturing firms, can be quite significant. Consequently, firms with far lower thresholds of international sales will feel the pressures and needs to find solutions to their local – global dilemma. Notwithstanding these criticisms, Rugman's analysis clearly indicates that firms apparently have great trouble being successful in more than one region of this planet. This observation raises a couple of interesting questions:

- Which factors inhibit the firm from extending its advantages beyond the home region?
- Are there limits to scale and scope that prevent firms from succeeding outside their home region?
- Or, simply, do current organizational structures prove inadequate for dealing with a multiregion strategy?

An intuitive answer for some of these questions is provided by Rugman and colleagues. Rugman and Verbeke argue that benefiting from global integration requires firm specific advantages (FSA) that are essentially nonlocation bound.[17] On the contrary, to reap the advantages of national responsiveness requires companies to possess firm specific advantages that are location bound. Individual activities of the firms' value chain vary with regards to whether they require location-bound or non-location-bound advantages. As a consequence, it may make sense to map these value-chain activities to the extent to which they require the one or the other. Figure 3.2 visualizes this relationship graphically: the relative FSAs are mapped on the vertical axis, while the individual value-chain activities are sorted on the horizontal axis and range from "pure" nonlocation-bound FSAs on the left side to completely location-bound FSAs on the right side of the diagram. The managerial takeaway of Figure 3.2 is that executives should primarily concentrate on and scale those FSAs (or activities) that are nonlocation bound. Value-chain activities that require high degrees of local adaptation will need to be performed on a local level. Thus, on a basic level, the figure suggests that a firm should untangle its individual value activities that may lead to a very concentrated product development organization and a much more decentralized sales management.

In light of the evidence that few multinationals really have a globally balanced distribution of their sales, Rugman extends his framework. Specifically, he suggests that in order to compete successfully within a region, firms may also need to develop a set of region-bound FSAs (see Figure 3.3) to complement the nonlocation-bound and location-bound advantages.[18] Wal-Mart is a case in point. Wal-Mart's success in North America can be attributed to a significant cost advantage resulting from a bundle of unique resources and capabilities. One success factor is Wal-Mart's unique management culture. More than just valuing price-conscious behaviour, greeters and singing morning songs, Wal-Mart relies on

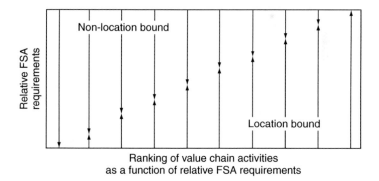

Figure 3.2 A resource-based re-interpretation of the integration-national responsiveness framework

Source: A. Rugman (2005), The Regional Multinationals – MNE's and "Global" Strategic Management p. 68, Cambridge, © Cambridge University Press.

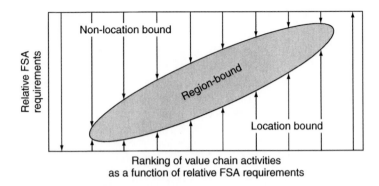

Figure 3.3   Extension of the resource-based integration-responsiveness framework

Source: A. Rugman (2005), The Regional Multinationals – MNE's and "Global" Strategic Management p. 68, Cambridge, © Cambridge University Press.

a group of middle managers from throughout the United States that meets every Saturday at corporate headquarters in Arkansas to make strategic decisions. With the same managers responsible to implement the strategy the following Monday in the field, Wal-Mart achieves an almost unrivalled strategic alignment. Like corporate culture and distributional advantages, Wal-Mart found it difficult to replicate or extend the system beyond its home region, suggesting that a significant part of its FSAs are in fact region bound. Another case where region-bound FSAs pose challenges for further internationalization beyond the home region is Inditex. ZARA's approach to fashion with fast turnaround times and a centrally located factory in Spain will make it hard for the company to extend this advantage beyond its European home region.

Rugman concludes his analysis by pointing to the gap in Figure 3.4, which indicates that firms operating in a host region often lack the region-specific advantages needed to compete in the host region. The work and conclusions of Rugman and colleagues are important. Collectively, they suggest that FSAs may indeed be region bound and hard to transfer across regions. Wal-Mart, for example, had great difficulties replicating its business model in Europe and finally had to withdraw from key markets like Germany. Furthermore, Rugman's findings and analysis suggest that the benefits of aggregation (scale and scope) may often already be achieved at the regional level. Findings by other scholars echo Rugman's findings.[19]

Rugman's analysis is also in line with Ghemawat's call for strategies in a semi-globalized world.[20] Consistent with Rugman's terminology of non-location-bound and location-bound FSAs, Ghemawat suggests that global firms may add value by aggregation (achieving economies of scale with nonlocation-bound FSAs) or adaptation (creating value by developing location-bound FSAs).

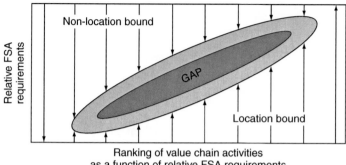

Figure 3.4 Extension of the resource-based integration-responsiveness framework: The host country case

Source: A. Rugman (2005), The Regional Multinationals – MNE's and "Global" Strategic Management p. 68, Cambridge, © Cambridge University Press.

Again, for many firms, the potential benefits of scale have already materialized at the regional level. Most car factories, for example, become viable at a production capacity of 100,000 cars per annum, thus, seldom requiring plants to cater to global markets. Similarly, adapting product offerings only to a regional rather than country level is often justified, particularly when consumers within the region behave similarly or when the same economic or institutional climate prevails in more than one market (see, for example, the many illustrations on European consumers provided in Chapter 1 of this book). Although much of this has been said before, Ghemawat enriches the discussion by introducing a third category of global value creation that he terms "arbitrage". With arbitrage, he refers to the multinational's ability to create value by transferring products, knowledge or ideas across markets and, thus, generate rents of relative specialization. The idea itself is not as novel as it sounds,[21] yet it does seem reasonable that the largest potential to leverage knowledge is in fact on a regional, not a global, level. Thus, the ability to reuse and to leverage key assets across the regional network may very well constitute another important region-bound capability. The power of region-bound knowledge transfer is probably best illustrated when considering that most innovative clusters (for example, the Italian ceramic tile industry or German automotive industry) are geographically very clearly defined. Knowledge, it seems, is best transferred within close communities and usually does not travel well into unfamiliar territories.[22]

In sum, Rugman and colleagues make a convincing point that competitive advantage is often already achieved on a regional level. And while the "region" may be a logical and practical unit of analysis, we do not gain much information on how firms actually achieve these regional advantages. Consistent with our arguments above and further extending the ideas from Rugman and colleagues, our book focuses on one of the most striking solutions to this regional management dilemma: the regional headquarters solution.

The regional headquarters solution

The increasing significance of regional headquarters

The importance of region-specific advantages to succeed in any of the world's regions triggers an interesting question: how can one obtain these advantages, particularly when venturing beyond the home region, where these advantages usually developed as a by-product of the initial success?

As the previous sections suggests, a key parameter of succeeding in a host region is to think about strategy on a regional not a global level. And as we will argue later in this book, regional strategy does not necessarily require a regional structure. Yet evidence from our survey reveals that regional strategy and structure often go hand in hand. The significance of this conclusion is not only captured in Rugman's sales data of the world's 500 largest firms, but also in the cumulative increase of regional headquarters within multinational firms over time. In fact, as our data reveal, the number of regional headquarters within Europe has increased significantly over the last decade (Figure 3.5) suggesting that regional headquarters are becoming a more important means for managing global businesses. This trend has at least two implications. First, the fact that firms increasingly structure around key regions gives further support to Rugman's claim that the world is in fact becoming more regional and less global. Second, it clearly demonstrates that regional headquarters become an increasingly important structural response to deal with the global – local dilemma.

Regional headquarters bring two types of value to the MNC. The one is strategic value; the other one is managerial value.

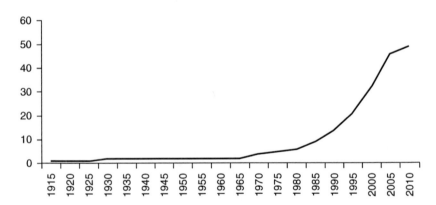

Figure 3.5   Formation of regional headquarters over time
Source: Own data, RHQ Survey.

The value of regional headquarters

In the above section, we already spelled out the strategic value of regional strategy, both in achieving economies of scale and scope as well as in dealing with some of the most pertinent pressures to locally adapt the firm's offerings. In principle, a firm's decision to follow a regional strategy does not say much about its structural approach to implement and support the strategy. Yet, as we demonstrate above, many firms do use regional headquarters to support their regional strategy. This suggests that there is a strong correlation between the development of a regional strategy and the foundation of a regional headquarters. So far, research on regional headquarters has been quite sparse and mainly focused on the Asian context. However, building on the larger stream of research on the role of corporate headquarters, a few key insights can be readily transferred to regional headquarters. In this final section of this chapter, we will summarize the potential advantages of regional headquarters. In the two following chapters, we will then elaborate on the advantages of regional headquarters in more detail.

The parenting advantage

As an intermediary located between the global headquarters and the local subsidiaries, for regional headquarters the answer to the value question has apparently two sides. On the one hand, regional headquarters organize the economic activity within the region they are responsible for. As such, they fulfil the classic role of a parent. Consequently, the advantages that the regional headquarters bring to the organization should be similar to that of other corporate parents. In this context, Campbell and Goold also speak of the parental advantage that any parent should possess.[23] In other words, to justify their position within the organization, a regional headquarters, like any other parent, should add value to the operations of its local subsidiaries that would be hard to create without the parent. According to Campbell and Goold, the parenting advantage depends on two crucial questions: Does the parent understand the business of its local subsidiaries? Can the parent contribute to the resource and capability endowment of the local subsidiaries?

Parents that neither understand the local businesses nor are in a position to contribute to local operations in any meaningful way are operating in what the authors' call "alien territory". In these situations, parents are not likely to add value. On similar grounds, a mere understanding of the local business without possessing any meaningful way to improve local operations is also likely to fail; as will possessing capabilities but not really knowing how to deploy these capabilities in local markets due to a lack of knowledge. Thus conclude Campbell and Goold, the parenting advantage requires both knowledge of the local context as well as capabilities to add value to the local units. The examples quoted above indicate that regional headquarters often do possess these two advantages within the MNC. By pooling resources and achieving scale economies and leveraging knowledge within the region, regional headquarters can, in fact, add tremendous value to the individual local subsidiary. Thus, in this respect, regional headquarters do indeed fulfil similar functions for local subsidiaries as any other parent. The interesting question that remains is whether regional headquarters fulfil these functions better than any other parent. We will dig deeper into this question in the succeeding chapters.

The knowledge advantage

From the perspective of the parent, regional headquarters may be viewed as a bundle of unique capabilities that may create superior value for the MNC. Thus, in addition to the strategic impetus dictated by limited economies of scale and scope mentioned above, regional headquarters have also been found to add tremendous value in their own right. In fact, the knowledge advantage of regional headquarters within the region is consistent with the criteria for the parenting advantage spelled out above. To this end, one could easily make a case that regional headquarters are, in fact, the unit with the *largest potential* to add value because they possess the most relevant knowledge and capabilities to govern the local subsidiaries within a region.

Possessing relevant knowledge is crucial. As already indicated in the previous section, much of the knowledge needed to operate globally is local, or regionally bound. Thus, making informed decisions from a distance becomes quite difficult for corporate headquarters. In this respect, regional headquarters fulfil the important mission of translating global headquarters' targets into successful strategies for local markets. Regional headquarters may serve as important competence centres within the corporate network that provide valuable services to local operations. Figure 3.6 illustrates the role of regional headquarters as a knowledge bridge. On the one hand, the regional headquarters receives valuable knowledge on the global operations from the global headquarters and filters and channels this knowledge to the individual subsidiaries within the region. On the other hand, the regional headquarters takes information from local markets and provides the global

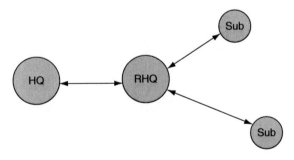

Figure 3.6   The regional headquarters as a knowledge hub

headquarters with accurate information on the region, which enables the latter to make more informed decisions. Finally, the regional headquarters may add value by transferring knowledge from subsidiary A to subsidiary B and, by doing so, increase the performance of all actors within the region. To illustrate this last option of value-creating knowledge flows, consider the case of Unicredit's regional headquarters in Vienna. The regional headquarters controls a total of 19 individual country markets within the region. The development of the individual markets is quite diverse, thus making product standardization across the region difficult. However, as many of the markets go through similar stages in their development, the regional headquarters adds value by transferring knowledge from one market to another and, in doing so, enhances the value for the whole group.

The organizational advantage

As Asakawa and Lehrer[24] pointed out, the intermediary role of regional headquarters may also help to alleviate the tensions between global needs for integration and local needs for adaptation. In this sense, a regional headquarters may function as an organizational pressure valve: on the one hand, managing the tension between global integration and regional adaptation with its global vis-à-vis the corporate parent and, on the other hand, managing the dual pressures of regional integration and local adaptations with the local subsidiaries within the region (Figure 3.7).

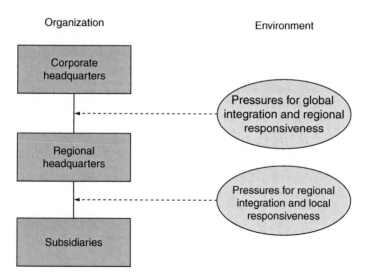

Figure 3.7   Regional headquarters as pressure valves within the region
Source: Lehrer and Asakawa (1999).[25]

In addition to relieving tensions, the intermediary role that regional headquarters play also helps reduce the span of control for the corporate parent. In doing so, the regional headquarters helps the organization direct its attention to directions that are most useful for the whole group.[26] In large multiregional organizations, this becomes important as managerial attention becomes a scarce resource that needs to be optimally managed to avoid dysfunctional priority setting.

Although this section provides only a brief summary of the potential advantages and benefits of regional headquarters, we argue that regional headquarters possess some unique characteristics, enabling them to add value to the whole MNC. This holds true with regards to the subsidiaries they supervise and the global parent for which they act as agents. The following chapters will provide more detail on how regional headquarters achieve these benefits. In light of an increasing regionalization of the world's main markets and the resulting pressures for regional strategies, understanding how to manage a regional operation seems to be more pertinent than ever.

Conclusion

In this chapter, we undertook a more detailed look at the integration responsiveness dilemma as experienced by many multinational firms today. We then outlined the common organizational responses to manage this dilemma. Based on this debate, we introduced and discussed more recent evidence suggesting that the quest for superior performance may be determined at the regional level. Few of the 500 largest firms are truly global. In fact, most of them predominantly concentrate their sales activities in the home region or within only two of the world's main trade blocks. Based on this discussion, we suggest that firms venturing beyond the home region may gain by tilting the global matrix towards a more regional approach that is consistent with regional strategy.

4
Developing Regional Structures

Let's forget for a moment that there are borders in Central America. How would we operate, if the market would just continue South from Mexico, when everything would be districts of Mexico and not separate nations? Nobody would dream of having someone separately in charge of Central America. And that is why we decided to steer these countries from Mexico – no separate campaigns any more. What we are doing in the domestic market in Mexico, we will also do in Central America. We have nearly standardized our product portfolio. We not only have the same products, but also the same packaging and instructions. Nearly everything is standardized for Mexico and Central America. And we advertise our products in Mexico the same way as we advertise in Central America.

Mr Hülse, President, Boehring Ingelheim,
Latin America

Developing regional strategies and structures

From the preceding chapters, we learned that many multinationals today are better off developing a regional strategy than going for a pure global or multidomestic strategy. The bare necessity, however, does say little about how managers can actually build successful strategies for a region such as Europe. This overarching question will guide us through the remainder of this book.

By deciding to develop a regional strategy, top management has to consider a variety of issues: Which countries should be combined into a region? Should we build up a regional headquarters or manage the region virtually, or from the home office? How should we structure the region once we decide to build up a regional headquarters? Finally, how should we manage the regional operations? In this chapter, we will focus on the structural and strategic questions involved in developing a regional strategy and corresponding organizational architecture. The next chapter will then deal exclusively with the issue of how to manage your regional operations.

Defining your region

Throughout our conversations with managers in headquarters, regional offices and local subsidiaries, no single question triggered as much interest as how to figure out what should constitute an optimal region. If nothing else, the managerial interest in this "seemingly obvious" question clearly indicates that the common practice to divide the world into three triad markets (North America, Europe and Asia) does not do justice to the managerial problems at hand.[1] As we outlined in Chapter 2, even within Europe a large variation in consumption patterns, attitudes and preferences does exist. On the other hand, firms do not necessarily stick to geographical boundaries or consumer-centred market segmentations. The mandate of Puma's regional headquarters in Salzburg, Austria, for example, extends far beyond the Central and Eastern European (CEE) region and includes countries like Brazil, the Emirates and South Africa. Quite a few US MNCs bundle their African and European business into a so-called EMEA (Europe, Middle East and Africa) region. What constitutes a region to the individual MNC, and which countries are managed by the individual regional headquarters, is therefore not as clear-cut as it appears.

Our research and discussion with many managers reveal five defining factors for the scope of a regional headquarters: geographic proximity, market similarities, managerial consideration, political consideration, and cost efficiency. In reality, many of these factors are interlinked, and firms take more than one of these factors into consideration when building up their region. However, for sake of conceptual clarity, let us present them one by one.

Geographic proximity

Few managers we talked to actually organized their regions on a purely geographical (continental) basis. This is not to say that geography does not matter – quite the contrary. Grouping geographically proximate markets eases transportation and logistics, which is particularly an issue for firms that sell similar products in multiple markets, because setting up a joint distribution centre saves costs. Honda, for example, has built up three sub-regional headquarters in Europe (London, Paris and Frankfurt). Each of them takes care of a separate region, supplying the markets with appropriate products: diesel engines and dark colour schemes for Germany, Austria and Switzerland; lighter colours for Iberia (Spain and Portugal). Geographic "proximity" of a somewhat different kind has led many US and Canadian firms to group Africa, the Middle East and Europe into a so-called EMEA region. For example, Norsat International, a Vancouver-based firm that designs, engineers and markets intelligent satellite solutions, built a regional headquarters in Lausanne, Switzerland, to oversee its business in Europe, the Middle East and Africa. As CEO Amiee Chan states: "Sustaining regional growth requires strong regional presence. The EMEA headquarters will provide the support needed to meet today's initiatives while ensuring Norsat's ongoing growth and future developments in the region across all business units."[2] Grouping countries along the same geographical latitude into one region does make particular sense if, for example, global headquarters is some nine hours away, which makes it virtually impossible to communicate via telephone during normal business hours.

Market similarities

It seems obvious that market similarity should constitute a main driver in deciding which markets to group. It has become custom to define market similarity by its antonym distance.[3] Ghemawat, for example, talks about cultural, administrative, geographic and economic distance and relates these distances (or the lack of them) to the optimal scope of the firm.[4] As we outlined in Chapter 1, European consumers are not all alike in all respects. Important cultural differences and practices lead to different product offerings. For obvious reasons, athletic shoe manufacturers, for example, find it difficult to sell green and yellow, the national colours of Brazil, in Germany, because the two countries are usually archrivals in the soccer world cup. On the other hand, where consumer preferences align, a similar marketing approach and penetration of the region makes a lot of business sense. The existence of common administrative bodies constitutes another reason for grouping similar markets. Within the pharmaceutical industry, for example, jurisdiction and drug approval processes have become vital parameters for firms' considerations on how to structure their global operations, leading to a more-or-less triad structure around the Federal Drug Administration (FDA) approval in the United States, the European EMEA, and the Japanese authorities in Asia. Finally, as pointed out in Chapter 1, similarities in the economic development of countries may constitute other grouping criteria for firms seeking similarities within their region. Fast-moving consumer goods manufacturers build their grouping decisions in part on the relative purchasing power of the consumers in the respective markets. This argument holds also for the banking sector, where many banks bundled their CEE operations in one emerging market segment. Nike Austria is also a case in point. Within the European organization, Nike Austria originally reported to CEE Markets. However, for the local manager, this official grouping proved dysfunctional, because most other countries in this region need emerging market support whereas Austria and Slovenia are quite mature markets. Thus, the manager felt that she would fare better by joining with Germany and Switzerland (this despite the fact that few Austrians love to render authority to Austria's much larger neighbour to the west).

Managerial considerations

One important factor that is often downplayed by studies looking at distances to define the optimal scope of a region is the role of management. Although limited span of control, information-processing capabilities and the ability to reconcile conflicts already help to explain why regional headquarters exist, they arguably reveal only a little about how to structure the regions they create. Managers, however, also use structure to devote attention to specific issues. In this sense, the grouping of markets is very often a reflection of the relative importance or attention headquarters wants to devote to individual markets.[5]

Nearly all big pharmaceutical companies in Europe maintain direct reporting lines to the big five consumer markets (Germany, France, Italy, Spain and the United Kingdom), while often grouping the other markets into one or two other subregions. To quote one senior Pfizer manager: "It makes sense that the countries with similar sales volumes in a region are grouped together in a region just like the Big 5. This is very important for the benefit and interest of the smaller countries."

This approach has several advantages for the firm. First, building subregions reduces the span of control to a manageable level. Second, information-processing capacities of the firm are better leveraged. Third, the more important markets get more and quicker market attention, while less important markets do not block the corporate communications channels. As the following quote reveals, such grouping is not necessarily always negatively perceived by the smaller markets. Outlining the benefit of a regional grouping structure, one country manager of a large Japanese pharmaceutical company stated:

> I am not in favour of being in the same group as Germany per se, because Germany has always the larger voice...which means that our interests are not always visible. When the German Business Unit Manager says, "I need 100 million Euros," and then I come and say, "I need 10 million Euros," it is not counted. The regional headquarters helps in this respect, as we now belong to the same group and our voice is heard.

Political considerations

Not all groupings we saw were based on geographic, managerial or market reasons. In some cases, the grouping and allocation were merely a matter of political considerations. Consider the case of Unicredit, a large Italian bank. In 2005, Unicredit acquired HBV Group, a German bank with large operations in CEE that were coordinated and managed from the bank's regional headquarters in Vienna. After the acquisition, Unicredit left the regional reporting structure and responsibilities of the Vienna office largely unchanged with the exception of one market: Poland. National pride on the side of the Polish subsidiary and interventions by the Polish government forced Unicredit to establish a direct reporting line to the Italian headquarters, bypassing the regional hub located in the much smaller Austria. Political groupings may also become a driving force if trade blocks or political coalitions force countries into or out of otherwise logical groupings. Being part of North American Free Trade Agreement (NAFTA), Mexico, for example, is quite often integrated into the North American operations of firms, whereas a grouping on language or cultural similarity would probably result in a cluster around and along Central American countries.

Cost efficiency

Even when firms realize that consumer preferences favour a further fragmentation and adaptation of marketing activities within a region, cost considerations may render such approaches infeasible. McDonald's, for example, stopped adapting its bread-crumbs formula on its Chicken McNuggets (which used to be coarser in the alpine region) and went back to a worldwide standardized product, purely for cost-efficiency reasons. Many firms use the same copy of television advertisements in multiple countries despite the fact that subtle language differences may cause some animosity among local consumers.

To sum up, the decision about what constitutes an optimal region depends to a large degree on the firms' idiosyncratic factors. Few firms, if any, make their choice based on purely geographic boundaries of a continent. If a unified European market strategy exists, it is usually driven by cost efficiency considerations or economies of distribution. However, as this section demonstrated, other criteria such as market similarity, managerial considerations and political factors also strongly influence what is in or, probably more importantly, which markets are out of the regional scope of a specific regional headquarters.

Table 4.1 provides a summary of the key points to consider.

Does regional strategy always imply a regional structure?

The short answer to this question is, of course, no. There are many examples of firms that manage their regional business successfully without developing a clear supporting structure within the region.[6] Samsung, for example, has achieved fairly balanced global sales within its memory chip division without a designated regional headquarters structure.[7] The same holds true for many of the renowned Swiss watch manufacturers, which penetrate regions without a large supporting regional structure. However, looking at these firms' product offerings, little of the strategy actually has to be adapted on a regional basis anyway. Although the above categories of firms primarily rely on exporting and independent vendors to broaden their global outreach, firms may also decide to manage their host regional operations from

Table 4.1   Decision criteria for defining the boundaries of the region

Grouping factor	Dominant logic	Example
Geographic proximity	• Minimize distribution costs within the region • Short travel time of regional managers to individual markets • Time zones	Honda
Market similarity	• Grouping of countries with similar consumer preferences • Grouping of countries falling in the same or similar legal or institutional environment • Grouping of countries with similar stages in their economic development	Nike
Managerial	• Grouping of countries to reduce span of control to a manageable level • Grouping of smaller countries to give them an equal share of voice	Pfizer
Political	• Singling out countries that need specific political attention • Grouping countries along boundaries of economic trade blocks to reap benefits of membership on economic zones	Unicredit
Cost efficiency	• Trade off adaptation benefits against scale economies of regional grouping	McDonald's

their traditional home base. Helmut Schütte calls this form of regional management a *regional headquarters for the region* (as opposed to the alternative, which, in his terminology, would be a *regional headquarters in the region*).[8]

Building on a regional headquarters for the region

In this setting, the MNC does acknowledge the importance of a regional differentiation; however, the managers responsible for the region sit at global headquarters. Thus, regional management is simply added as a global headquarters function. In contrast, a regional headquarters in the regional actually has an organizational structure in the region. A headquarters for the region has a set of advantages for firms. The most obvious is that firms do not need to duplicate many of the supporting functions in a second physical location. Key functions like human resources, IT and other internal services can be shared with global headquarters operations. Co-location with the strategic apex of the firm also usually ensures a smooth knowledge flow between headquarters staff and regional management. Pfizer is a case in point. Pfizer maintains a large group of managers in Europe, however, functionalities are not bundled within a central location but split between

Germany, the United Kingdom and France. In certain therapeutic areas, the United Kingdom has a broad responsibility and support role across all countries, while the same holds true for Germany in other therapeutic areas. Although these managers deal with the operational business, the VP Europe, like all other vice presidents, is located at Pfizer's global headquarters in New York. Pedro Lichtinger, Area President Europe, describes the logic of this structure as follows:

> If I lived in Europe, I would have to travel 50 per cent of my time to the US. Why – because I interact with the management on providing input into new customer needs and our prioritization process on where to make investments in research, I interact very strongly with manufacturing and with many functions of the company – and as a senior member of the team, I also participate in the alignment of our policy decisions, and with that I don't mean internal, but relative to health care and what's happening in our industry. So I have a lot of interactions in the US, representing Europe, that I believe are very particular to the pharmaceutical industry and that need to happen. On the other hand, of course I need to be in Europe as well. So there is no easy solution. I don't think it matters; I'd have to spend 50 per cent of my time there and here, on average – some months 70 per cent here, other months 70 per cent there. So I don't think it matters where I say I officially am, because I'm going to be in both.

A latent risk of a headquarters for the region is the apparent lack of market embeddedness that is often closely tied to market knowledge.[9] Thus, even companies like Pfizer operate a large share of their operational business in the region and not for the region. As customer intimacy becomes important, or competitive pressure requires a quick reaction, a physical presence in the region becomes a necessity. In hindsight, one senior manager in Detroit explained the need for a local presence for Ford's Asian operation in Thailand:

> I got to feel Thailand in order to be effective in Thailand. But I cannot feel Thailand when I am here in Detroit. I mean the government is exploding in Thailand right now, the prime minister quit and the king is not amused. I got to have a strong person in that market that can sense and feel that, because that is going to direct our strategy and how we present Ford. Whereas when I am over here on the other side of the world, in the wrong time zone, I am not even awake when things are happening.

Building a regional headquarters in the region

Building up designated structures within the region can help the firm achieve a range of objectives within its regional strategy. Figure 4.1 lists the

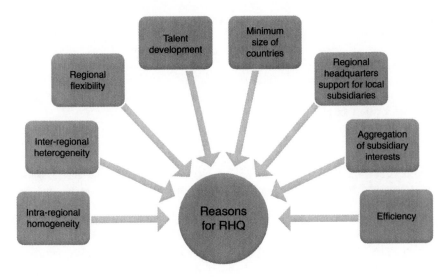

Figure 4.1   Reasons for RHQ in the region

most common factors managers suggest for supplementing their regional strategy with a designated regional structure.[10] As one can easily see, many of these motives go hand in hand with the preceding considerations of what should constitute an optional region. This clearly indicates that regional management and regional structures are closely interlinked (at least in the minds of the managers).

Intraregional homogeneity and interregional heterogeneity

Homogenous consumer preferences within the region make it feasible to centralize many core activities within a regional hub to reap economies of scale. Similarly, interregional heterogeneity requires these activities to be carried out on a regional and not on a global level.

Regional flexibility

A regional headquarters increases the strategic flexibility of the firm to cater to local or regional differences and, thus, achieves a higher degree of local adaptiveness than a global structure.

Talent development

Another point that was mentioned by managers at all levels was the ability of regional headquarters to scout talent within the local subsidiaries and to further develop these managers to take on more important functions within the organization.

Minimum size of countries

From a headquarters perspective, regional centres also reduce the span of control and thus make regions with a high number of small country markets more manageable.

Regional headquarters' support for local subsidiaries

Regional headquarters are also used to fulfil valuable support functions by pooling and grouping expertise that would be too expensive for local markets to maintain, such as basic research on consumer habits, economic trends, new product development or legal services.

Aggregation of subsidiary interests

Regional headquarters may also play a vital role in aggregating local subsidiary managers' interests, thus increasing the voice of the region vis-à-vis the global operations.

Efficiency

Finally, efficiency-related motivations trigger the establishment of a regional headquarters. As indicated in the previous section, these efficiency gains can be achieved not only through regional economics of scale and scope, but also as the result of a compromise beyond which further local adaptation is feasible on economic grounds.

Mapping the organizational structure for the region

In the section on "defining your region," we already mapped out the dimensions that firms should consider in defining the broad boundaries of their region. The definition of a region does not solve, however, all the structural issues a firm has to consider. In particular, when multiple defining dimensions overlap, firms are challenged to find an appropriate structure for the market. A common outcome of the analysis above may be that a region should encompass Germany, Austria, Sweden, Finland and Norway from a market development point of view. Distribution and logistical considerations, however, would suggest splitting the three Nordic countries from the two Germanic nations, while managerial considerations would yet again imply a separate reporting for Germany, while grouping the rest into one subregion.

In our research, we found that managers deal with these challenges by selecting a structural option that caters to their specific problem best. We call the different structures the single country market approach, subregional approach, mixed approach, and virtual network. Figure 4.2 gives a graphical account of each of the four approaches. Each of these four approaches has its own set of advantages and drawbacks.

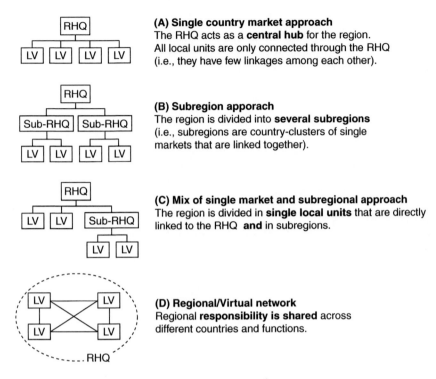

(A) Single country market approach
The RHQ acts as a **central hub** for the region.
All local units are only connected through the RHQ
(i.e., they have few linkages among each other).

(B) Subregion apporach
The region is divided into **several subregions**
(i.e., subregions are country-clusters of single
markets that are linked together).

(C) Mix of single market and subregional approach
The region is divided in **single local units** that are directly
linked to the RHQ **and** in subregions.

(D) Regional/Virtual network
Regional **responsibility is shared** across
different countries and functions.

Figure 4.2   Four different approaches to structure the region

Single country market approach

In a single country market approach, all country markets report to one regional headquarters. We found that firms favour a single country market approach when the span of control was relatively small, the markets were of equal importance or consumers were quite homogeneous across the whole region. Asics, for example, sells a set of very standardized products in Europe: running shoes and sports apparel. Given the size of Asics's operations in the market (many European countries are still serviced via independent distributors), a single European headquarters, located in Amsterdam, seems most feasible for the operations at hand.

Subregional headquarters

In a subregional headquarters structure, country markets are separated and grouped together in homogenous subgroups that then report to a regional headquarters. We found this approach to be most common in firms with large operations within an otherwise heterogeneous region. Nike, for example, further segments the market into coherent consumer markets (as, for example, with Austria, Germany and Slovenia). In a similar fashion,

Honda has divided the European market into three subregions. The objective of these approaches is to eliminate variation within the region by grouping subsidiaries with different needs into different subregions. Thus, the logic of this approach does not differ much from the single country market approach, despite the fact that the degree of coherence achieved is somewhat higher than in the previous approach.

Mixed structure approach

In the mixed structure approach, firms place some units into subregions while other units maintain a direct reporting line. We found this approach to be the predominant one in unbalanced firm portfolios or in situations where a few markets require special attention, either due to their impact on the bottom line, special development (growth) goals or interests of political stakeholders. In our study on European management, almost all pharmaceutical companies followed this approach. As previously indicated, Pfizer clusters all smaller European markets into one subregion, but maintains direct reporting lines with the big five consumer markets: Germany, Spain, France, Italy and the United Kingdom.

(Virtual) network structures approach

In the virtual network structure, firms do not physically assign a regional headquarters function to a specific location. Instead, the regional management tasks are divided and carried out by the individual subsidiaries in a shared manner. Thus, the headquarters is a mere virtual concept to which the competencies and functions of individual units contribute. The primary benefit of this approach is to ensure a higher engagement of individual subsidiaries, given that the structure tries to achieve some degree of regional specific management without adding another layer of hierarchy to the organization. This might be a particular asset for firms with relatively mature country operations, where the establishment of a designated regional headquarters would cause a serious dispute in the existing power structure of the MNC. The downside of this approach, as with all self-organizing systems, is high coordination intensity.

In our sample, we found only few firms that managed their regions using a pure network approach. One firm that comes relatively close to this approach is Volkswagen. Within the Volkswagen group, most important decisions are made by the so-called Verwaltungsgremien. Members of these councils enter with the goal to maximize the welfare of the whole organization. To combat political fights among members, Volkswagen has implemented a system to give each senior manager dual (or triple) accountability. For instance, the president of SEAT is not only accountable for the SEAT brand and brand sales, but also for factory utilization in Barcelona, Spain. In product portfolio disputes, that is, whether a particular model should be developed for the Audi, Skoda, Volkswagen or SEAT brand, he has to make an organizational as well as internal trade-off to determine whether to maximize factory utilization, for example, going for an Audi model that can be produced in Spain and would increase his factory utilization, or a SEAT type, which helps his brand but not necessarily his factory utilization (unless of course both cars can be produced on the same platform, that is, in the same factory).

Figure 4.3 graphically summarizes the replies of regional headquarters managers in response to the following question: "With regard to the selected structure (single country, subregional headquarters, mixed structure, network structure), please indicate the extent to which you agree with the following criteria were driving your decision."

Despite the points that we mentioned above, an examination of the graph suggests that network structures are most applicable when a region scores relatively high on all questions, suggesting further that a distributed approach plays out its benefits when no clear location advantage for a regional headquarters exists. Moreover, a look at the overall (average) score indicates that managerial and market-based criteria play the highest role in grouping countries within a region, whereas the ability to minimize the tax burden or the physical location of production facilities does not play a major role in deciding which countries to group.

Figure 4.4 shows the relative distribution in our sample of European regional headquarters. With 46 per cent, a single country market approach

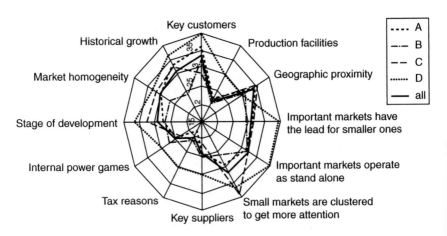

Figure 4.3   Criteria for structuring the region

Notes: A: Single Country Market Approach; B: Subregional Approach; C: Mixed Structure Approach; D: (Virtual) Network Approach.

Source: RHQ Survey.

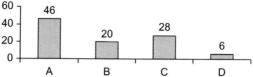

Figure 4.4 Popularity of structural approaches

Notes: A: Single Country Market Approach; B: Subregional Approach; C: Mixed Structure Approach; D: (Virtual) Network Approach.

Source: RHQ Survey.

surfaces as the most dominant form, followed by a mixed structure approach (28 per cent), the subregional approach (20 per cent) and finally the network approach (6 per cent).

The dominance of the single country market approach is not surprising. In particular, in firms with small European operations, a further fragmentation of the region is often not feasible on economic grounds. More interesting though is the high percentage of subregional structures and lead country approaches, together accounting for more than 48 per cent. In other words, for a majority of firms in our sample, a uniform market approach in Europe seems ill-suited to cater to European markets. In direct comparison of the two approaches, a mixed approach, in which some countries have direct reporting to the regional headquarters while others report to a subregional management function, seems to be more popular than a pure subregional structure. The least popular structure seems to be the network structure.

Where to locate your regional headquarters

The initial location decision

A final pertinent structural question that was brought up in almost every discussion we had with managers at regional or global headquarters was the issue where to physically locate the regional headquarters. Economists usually suggest that location of economic activity within a region can be determined by looking at a discrete set of hard (for example, taxation) and soft (for example, quality of life) determinants. Looking at regional headquarters within Europe, such a relationship does not hold. In fact, the rank-order correlation between location of regional headquarters in Europe and country attractiveness, as measured by key indicators of the IMD World Competitiveness Index, is close to zero![11] This lack of relationship made us curious to find out what drives decisions determining locations of regional

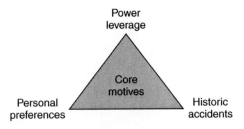

Figure 4.5   The location of regional headquarters

headquarters. In total, our interviews revealed three different motivations: power leverage of individual managers, personal preferences of senior managers and historical accidents (see Figure 4.5).

Power leverage

For most of the multinational firms we studied, the regional headquarters did not constitute their first engagement in Europe. Thus, with many national subsidiaries already in operation, the foremost concern when making a decision about where to locate the regional headquarters was not to select a greenfield site but to choose one subsidiary within the region to assume a leadership role and host the regional headquarters. Winning the regional headquarters mandate becomes a contestable charter. This background might help explain why power leverage of individual subsidiaries turned out to be one of the most prominent location drivers. Limiting the location choice to a set of established subsidiaries, competence profiles, unit or market size, relationships to global headquarters and other power levels became more important than pure economic drivers.

Puma's regional headquarters in Salzburg provides a nice example to illustrate this point. The former general manager of the regional headquarters in Salzburg, Mr Erwin Kaiser, revealed in one interview, "When Germany reunited in 1990 and CEE regimes opened up, I went to the HQ and demanded market control for the old Austrian empire states."[12] Puma at that time was facing heavy weather and found good reasons to assign this mandate to a manager and market that maintained black numbers in times of relative turbulence, in particular, because Austrians traditionally maintained good relationships with their former regions. Equipped with the regional mandate, Puma Salzburg further broadened its skill level doing business in emerging markets like CEE, Dubai and South Africa. As Mr Kaiser recalls:

> Over the years we have developed a competence in building up difficult markets. It's all about people and competences, which we have developed, and which are rooted here. There is no other reason behind the

strategy to establish a regional headquarters here in Salzburg – 300km away from our corporate headquarters in Germany.

Personal preference

A second common driver we found among firms when deciding where to locate their regional headquarters were so-called soft factors or pure personal preferences of top management. As one senior sales manager at the European headquarters of a large Japanese multinational revealed to us in privacy:

> We originally planned to set up our European regional headquarters in Germany. The decision to go to Amsterdam is often justified with looser labour and favourable tax regimes. But a major decision factor was that the CEO happened to be the son in law of our founder – and Amsterdam had the best Japanese kindergarten.

Looking at the sheer number of Japanese regional headquarters located in London or Amsterdam, the firm in question did not seem to follow a very unconventional location strategy. The importance of quality of life is also emphasized in the decision by Ecolab, a global leader in the cleaning and sanitary business, to locate its regional headquarters in Zürich, Switzerland. As Jim White, president of the regional headquarters remarks:

> After undergoing an extensive evaluation process to find the ideal location for Ecolab's EMEA Headquarters, we are pleased to have our home in Zurich. Zurich was chosen because of its consistent ranking as one of the best business locations in the world, as well as the outstanding quality of life it offers our associates.

To elaborate further on the importance of quality of life for attracting and retaining talent, White continues: "We are striving to attract, develop and retain world-class talent consistent with our strong company culture of growth and our global leadership position in the markets we serve."

Historical accidents

Although personal preferences and power leverage do often play a role in the initial location decision, managers also quite often revealed to us that the initial location decision was nothing more that a historical accident. Take, for example, the case of Ford of Europe. When Ford started in Europe, the company established its first regional headquarters close to London Stansted Airport. As one vice president at the regional headquarters pointed out: "There was no particular reason for establishing our first regional headquarters in the UK. We have been there for more than 40 years before we decided to move the RHQ to Germany."

Similarly, the CEO of Boehringer Ingelheim's regional headquarters in Vienna concludes on the location decision:

> Today, probably nobody in Ingelheim would see any strategic reason to establish a regional headquarters [for the CEE Region] in Vienna. The reasons are historical... Thirty years ago, we saw that we can enter Eastern Germany much more easily from Vienna than from West Germany. Our philosophy was then to see Vienna as a kind of "midwife" from which to conquer the Eastern European markets.

Relocation of regional headquarters

Although the initial decision about locating a regional headquarters seems to be driven by many unpredictable and often firm-specific factors, our data also revealed some kind of sense behind the decisions in the long run. In fact, a large proportion of the regional headquarters changed their original location during the course of operation. In principle, we found firms to follow one of three trajectories over time (see Figure 4.6):

- The headquarters stayed in its original location.
- The headquarters was relocated into a lead market.
- The headquarters was relocated to mirror structural changes.

Of the three identified drivers that resulted in the initial location choice, power leverage tended to be the one that was most change-resistant. The mere fact that these regional headquarters gained their charter through an internal process of political alliances and demonstration of strength helped these units to keep the edge.

Relocation into lead markets

Headquarters that relocated into lead markets within the region did so primarily for access-seeking motivations. As indicated previously, after operating 40 years from its British base, Ford responded to crystallizing trends in the European automotive industry and relocated its regional headquarters operations to Cologne, Germany. As Ian Slater, VP Public Relations of Ford

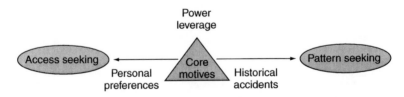

Figure 4.6   Changing location decision over time

of Europe, explains the rational:

> British people tend to think of Ford as a British company. Ford never achieved that in Germany, even not to the same extent as Opel. Secondly, we came to regard Germany increasingly as the real bellwether for quality in the automotive industry. I think the third reason was that Germany in many ways is seen as the California with respect to environmental attitudes. We were relatively slow to react to the big push, which came from Germany to mandate catalyst converters in cars. And, part of our assessment later on why we were relatively slow to react was that we haven't been sensitive enough to German opinion.

Access seeking also played a role in the decision of Astellas Pharmaceuticals to relocate its dual headquarters in Munich and Amsterdam to London. As the director for corporate planning summarized:

> [We relocated our RHQ in London] because of the talent. I mean it's easy to hire educated people, and for us Japanese it's an English country – an English speaking country. Another big reason is that the EMA – the European Medical Association for drug development processes – [is located in London].

Relocating to mirror structural changes

Multinational firms also reconsidered the original location decision when structural changes in the regional setup favoured a different location decision. As one VP vice president at Honda's corporate headquarters in Tokyo recalls the initial entry into Europe: "When planning our market entry into Europe we started by studying European Business. We went back some 500 years and tapped into the Hanse Trading League and the Fuggers. We adopted their distribution strategy."

Today, responding to different market requirements, Honda operates three regional headquarters in Europe: London, with responsibilities for the United Kingdom and CEE; Frankfurt, with responsibilities for Northern Europe; and Paris, with responsibilities for Southern Europe. Honda's new structure clearly reflects the more mature and developed business in the region, which drove the company to adapt a more fine-grained subregional structure.

Nike Europe mirrors the lessons learned from Honda. Like Honda, Nike's market approach became more fine-grained as the European business became more mature. As Hubertus Hoyt, President for Germany, Austria and Slovenia explains:

> Today, Nike's European Operation is subdivided in regions. Germany for example is responsible for marketing and distribution in Germany, Austria and Slovenia. CEE markets are grouped in a similar fashion.

The key driver for a region is similar customers (retailers) and consumption patterns. This is the reason why Slovenia goes along with Austria and Germany, not CEE.

Go for the lead country or a neutral location?

In cases where the business necessity does not dictate a location (as in the case of Ford or Astellas), managers need to consider whether to locate the regional headquarters within the region's lead country or opt for a neutral country in the region. Both approaches have their advantages and drawbacks. Locating the regional headquarters in the lead country usually has certain advantages with regards to skill levels and expertise.[13] However, other markets within the region may feel suppressed by assigning the lead to the dominating national operations. In these situations, choosing a neutral country to host the regional headquarters may be a sensible compromise. In fact, many multinational firms have, for this and other related reasons, opted for a regional headquarters in Switzerland (GM, P&G and so on), rather than in their most important European market (Germany). Strikingly enough, this motivation also holds for firms that cannot use the Swiss location to reap tax benefits.

Policy implications

Given that regional headquarters bring high value-added activities (and jobs) to a location, attracting regional headquarters has also been high on the agenda of many politicians. Our data show that tax dumping and building on other macroeconomic structures seldom leads to success in attracting a regional headquarters. At least in our sample, soft factors, like international schooling, quality of life and the existence of a large expert community play a much more pronounced role. Furthermore, as in many firms, the question about where to locate the headquarters is not a greenfield decision but one between the existing set of subsidiaries. Supporting subsidiary managers in their internal competition may be a much more viable strategy than to recede taxes for all firms. In other words, if you want a regional headquarters function in your city/country, support the local managers in winning the intracompany battle.

Conclusion

In this chapter, we looked at some of the most pertinent questions when deciding for a regional strategy. What constitutes a region? Should we manage the region with a regional headquarters or without? Which regional structure is most appropriate for our business? And finally, where should we locate the regional headquarters? As we have shown, the answers to these questions are in large part firm-specific. Nevertheless, some general rules seem to surface that managers need to follow in order to make these important decisions. Overall, our data show that, next to market similarities, managerial considerations constitute the main drivers for the grouping of individual markets. Given the prevailing dominance of geography in organizing global business, this finding is important and deserves more attention when making structural decisions. The structure that multinational firms adopt to manage the region to a large extent reflects the grouping logic. More developed and mature organizations usually adopt a more fine-grained subregional or mixed market approach within Europe, while smaller organizations go for a single regional headquarter structure. Our analysis in this chapter also shows that, as the organization matures, firms often reconsider the original location of the regional headquarters. Interestingly enough, soft factors and internal resource and power considerations have more impact on this decision than economic factors like tax benefits. Thus, given the prevalence of internal and managerial factors, managers of multinational firms are well advised to take a closer look at the organization's resources and capabilities when making decision about regional headquarters and regional management.

5
Managing Regional Headquarters

The managerial challenges at hand

Managing a regional headquarters is not an easy task. In this chapter, we will draw attention to a few factors that are germane in managing a regional headquarters. These issues include managing the dual tension between subsidiaries on the one hand and corporate headquarters on the other hand. Furthermore, we will explore how much autonomy regional headquarters need to fulfil their tasks. We will then take a look at the roles and responsibilities that regional headquarters fulfil and how firms distribute their value-added activities across the network.

Managing the dual tensions

As the dividing layer between global headquarters and local subsidiaries, managers at regional headquarters potentially have to deal with severe tensions. Local subsidiaries often challenge the regional headquarters' charter, insisting that they do not need an additional layer of hierarchy that dictates what to do. Global headquarters will ask for justification of the performance of a whole region, thus putting regional headquarters under pressure to deliver on their performance expectations. In the following section, we make an attempt to spell out these managerial pressures and provide some suggestions on how regional managers can best cope with the dilemma.

The relationship to local subsidiaries

In managing the relationships to local subsidiaries, regional headquarters managers face some of the classic challenges that are common to units that have a supervisory function for other units in the network. The tension to some degree will depend on how local managers perceive the value they gain from their superior unit as well as how much the local subsidiary feels controlled and regulated by the parent organization. The latter point is interesting, because recent studies have shown that subsidiaries do not always perceive headquarters' intervention as a challenge to their auton-omy.[1] Asakawa calls this situation a "relaxed perception gap." A relaxed per-ception gap exists when the parent thinks that the control exercised in the region is sufficiently tight, whereas the local subsidiary believes it has more than enough autonomy to fulfil its task. A tight perception gap, in turn, exists when the parent, for example, thinks it does not control enough, whereas the local subsidiary feels the contrary. Perception gaps are import-ant, because they have been repeatedly linked to subunit performance.[2] Thus, with regards to regional headquarters, a crucial question becomes whether local subsidiary managers see the value added of the regional head-quarters as laid out in the previous chapter. Looking at the data we col-lected on local subsidiaries casts doubts on whether they do (see Figure 5.1). When comparing the perception of value added of subsidiary managers that reported to a regional headquarters to those that report directly to global headquarters or divisional headquarters, managers almost always attribute more value added to the global or divisional headquarters.[3]

Given that many subsidiaries reporting directly to global headquarters GHQ belong to much smaller groups than the ones reporting to divisional DHQ or regional headquarters RHQ, the bars in Figure 5.1 are not directly comparable. However, what the graph does suggest is that subsidiaries that report to regional headquarters generally see less value added by their par-ents than in the other two cases. This finding clearly indicates that there are severe tensions within these regional headquarters organizations. The

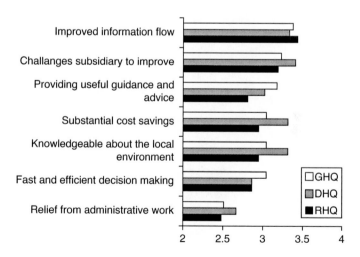

Figure 5.1   Perceived value added of parents: Regional vs divisional and global head-quarters

Note: 1 = strongly disagree; 5 = strongly agree.

Source: Subsidiary Survey.

only dimension where regional headquarters score higher than divisional or global headquarters is with regards to improved information flow within the region. This finding supports our earlier notions that sharing and transferring knowledge is probably one of the key advantages that regional headquarters bring to the firm. Collectively, all three types of headquarters also score relatively high when assessing the parent's function to challenge the status quo and to foster innovation and improvement in the local operation. Thus, while regional headquarters do not score higher than global or divisional headquarters, the graph does again suggest that, by and large, regional headquarters have their highest perceived value in fulfilling their entrepreneurial role, rather than their administrative one (see also the following section). Finally, Figure 5.1 also suggests that none of the three parents receives high marks with regards to effective decision-making and relief from administrative work. This indicates that, at least from a subsidiaries' point of view, none of these issues is sufficiently addressed by the parent.

To probe further into the questions why subsidiary managers fail to see the value provided by regional headquarters, we analysed our interview data with regards to the challenges and tensions perceived by regional as well as local managers. Figure 5.2 visualizes the main results from this analysis.[4]

One big problem when introducing a regional headquarters structure is often the ambiguity about roles for regional and local management. Thus,

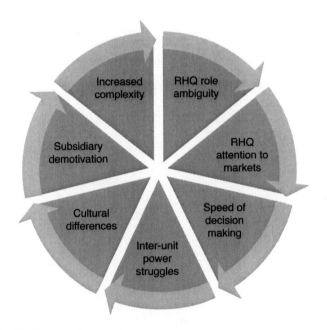

Figure 5.2   Challenges of regional management

management has to be crystal clear on what responsibilities go to the regional headquarters and which go to local units. Although this point may sound obvious, in the firms we studied, it is particularly this role ambiguity along with a headquarters' commitment not to micromanage the region that caused tremendous problems. As one regional executive revealed to us in an interview:

> A lot of discussions that we have are "should we allow this country to do this and this and that", but [...] we feel it is the best to do so but we think it is better if you do not because it could have a certain effect either on the long term or an effect on business in other countries. It is always a very difficult discussion because there are no black and white answers. In our case where the role of the European headquarters is not made clear for ourselves but also not for the countries, it is very sensitive sometimes and especially in the execution role that both myself and my colleague sit in and not being 100 per cent backed up by Japanese top managers who have a clear direction in management [...] and sometimes it is a bit unclear what is the best way.

Splitting responsibilities and clearly aligning duties are the first steps towards preventing potential tensions. However, local resistance may often prove hard to overcome. In particular, larger subsidiaries that control valuable assets and, thus, possess a certain bargaining power within the MNC often utilize their power to bypass regional headquarters and turn directly to the managers at global headquarters to seek support for their agendas. As another manager of a different firm revealed:

> But then again, the regional structure that we are currently building up, need to be built in a way that is accepted by the local subsidiaries. The country managers who are used to communicating with the headoffice are saying, "Wait a minute, used to talk to discuss my issues directly and I made my own decisions. Now there exists another level with whom I have to discuss my decisions with." At the moment, the largest cross is that the quality and the communication to the higher level (through this in between level) is not lost.

Similar statements by two other senior managers reflecting on the implementation of their new regional structures reveal a similar picture:

> That is what we have now done with the different areas I just listed...because that is one of the biggest questions – "What are you doing? and what will we do?" We started this in 2004. It does not work yet as we had foreseen because the local subsidiaries are still testing how far they can go.

That is a long process and what was written in paper is not what it turned out to be. I think the relationship and in particular the emotional aspects of this relationship between head office, the other regional headquarters is very often under pressure.

In sum, one of the largest challenges in managing the relationships with local subsidiaries in the region is to eliminate role ambiguity and clearly define the responsibilities of subsidiaries. To accomplish this objective, firms need to spell out clearly the roles and responsibilities of regional headquarters and leave no doubt which organizational unit is in charge of which process. We will return to this point in more detail later in this chapter. Managers at regional headquarters also need to actively seek support of the global parent. Quite a few firms we spoke to established clear policies stating that global headquarters would refuse to deal directly with local subsidiary requests, but would redirect every request back to the responsible regional headquarters manager. Although such policies may sound bureaucratic to some readers, they serve as valuable tools reinforcing the regional headquarters' charter. This is particularly important in cases where the regional headquarters is a relatively new addition to the organizational chart and established and powerful subsidiaries continue to test the boundaries of their power by bypassing the regional headquarters.

The relationship to global headquarters

In addition to managing the relationships with local subsidiaries, regional headquarters also need to manage the relationships with corporate headquarters. Given the regional headquarters' dual role, the relationship to global headquarters may vary from situation to situation. As an agent of the corporate parent and with its own headquarters mandate themselves, regional headquarters managers often have little trouble seeing the bigger picture that global headquarters is trying to sketch. In quite a few firms we studied, the head of the European operations also had a seat on the board of the multinational firm and thus was well able to represent and articulate the interests of the region. Close relationships between regional management and corporate management further enhance trust and often facilitate a smooth relationship. The CEO of Boehringer Ingelheim's regional headquarters in Vienna summarized the regional headquarters relationship to the global parent as follows:

But we want more money from corporate as well, because again, one of the key things there was that the people involved know the people in Ingelheim and have their trust and respect that they won't reject the problem. And that's I think what they look for. From the corporate point of view, when we present something, they take it serious. They trust everybody in the organization, as we have a history of doing things in a particular way.

However, even the tight integration of regional headquarters managers into the global operation is not always a guarantee for a smooth relationship. Whereas the key challenge for managing the relationship to local subsidiaries was to ensure a uniform chain of command (get acceptance for the leadership of the regional headquarters), the tensions with the global parent primarily centre on budgets, getting acknowledgment and approval for regional specific solutions rather than a uniform approach. In other words, the challenge between the global parent and the regional headquarters is essentially about the degree of autonomy and uniformity that all regions need to follow.

Influence, autonomy and performance

Given that autonomy constitutes a crucial variable in defining the relationship between global and regional headquarters, a more detailed analysis of regional headquarters autonomy is necessary. To assess the degree of autonomy granted to the regional headquarters, we asked regional headquarters managers to rate the relative autonomy vis-à-vis the global headquarters on several decision parameters (Figure 5.3). As the bars in Figure 5.3 reveal, the average degree of autonomy granted to the regional headquarters is quite high. Regional headquarters receive the most freedom with regards to local manufacturing, for example, switching from one manufacturing process to another or investing in new production capacity. Global headquarters, in turn, remains somewhat more reluctant to leave key personnel decisions as well as organizational questions solely within the hands of the regional headquarters managers. Global headquarters managers also kept a tighter-than-average control on pricing decisions for major products or product lines.

Our data show that there is some variation with regards to the autonomy levels across the regional headquarters we surveyed. In general, we found that more influential regional headquarters had more autonomy and usually also performed better than less influential and less autonomous regional headquarters. Influential regional headquarters were able to influence corporate marketing strategy (for example, the global product pricing). They were also usually able to influence the global product offerings, the direction of corporate R&D and also participated in setting long-term corporate objectives. Whether influence and autonomy lead to higher performance or whether higher performance leads to higher autonomy is hard to tell due to the cross-sectional nature of our data. However, the data at least suggest that successful regional operations get a strong voice within the corporation and a high operational autonomy in fulfilling their role.

Roles and responsibilities

At the beginning of this chapter, we discussed the idea that role ambiguity and role conflict turn out to be key challenges for regional management.

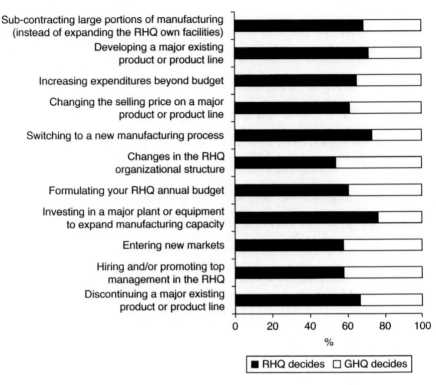

Figure 5.3   Who decides: Global headquarters vs regional headquarters
Source: RHQ Survey.

Thus, in this section, we will take a closer look at the roles that regional headquarters' fulfil for the network. Like the role of any headquarters (corporate, divisional), the regional headquarters' mission can be usefully mapped along two primary dimensions or charters: its entrepreneurial and its integrative charter.[5] As with any such typology, some regional headquarters are heavily concentrated on the entrepreneurial mandate and some on the integrative charter, while others try to balance both charters simultaneously.

The regional headquarters integrative charter

As the term *integrative* implies, a regional headquarters' integrative function within the region is to coordinate the MNC's activities across the individual markets and to further achieve synergies by pooling resources and certain value-added activities.

Coordination

The regional headquarters ensures that synergy potentials are realized and that corporate policies are implemented consistently throughout the region. Coordination of value-added activities becomes important when value creation happens in a dispersed manner throughout the region, for example, when sales subsidiaries located in one market depend on the marketing support or production facilities in another market. It also becomes important when product roll-outs do not happen simultaneously or when large pan-European customers want to use the concessions they receive in one market, only to sell products at a discount in another (a special form of grey imports). The former case is common in consumer goods industries, where the international rollout of products generally does not happen simultaneously. Take, for example, the Apple iPhone, which was introduced by T-Mobile into the German market more than half a year earlier than into the Austrian market.

A particularly challenging issue for multinational firms operating in Europe is to coordinate prices to avoid profit erosion due to grey imports from other regions or other countries within the region. Grey imports arise as a result of different price points within the region, which usually reflect different levels of purchasing power, taxation policies and the firms' abilities to skim individual markets. The European Union sets limits to which firms can actually prohibit independent vendors or consumers to shop or sell the companies' products abroad to make an arbitrage. Yet the grey imported goods can significantly hurt the overall performance of the group. Take, for example, the pharmaceutical industry, where prices for prescription drugs in many countries are regulated by local governments. This provides incentives for buyers to export goods to markets where they can reap the highest arbitrage. Similarly, as one industry insider told us, due to the high price markups in Europe for athletic footwear, all significant overcapacity in the Unite States will ultimately end up in Europe. Combating these grey imports is tricky, particularly within a common economic area. In these situations, the only two options left for firms are to manage supply to avoid large overcapacity to build up in low price markets or to find ways to differentiate the product to a degree that it becomes hard to sell in the other market, for example, by introducing different forms of packaging and adding service functions that are not transferable across borders, including service checks, software updates and so on.

As stated in Chapter 2, leveraging synergies, especially knowledge, across markets has become a key concern for every multinational firm. Although, in principle, a subsidiary can share knowledge across markets, regional headquarters often play a vital role in this process.[6] Thus, the regional headquarters also assumes a prime role in coordinating and sharing knowledge throughout the region.

Achieving and maintaining control

To achieve coordination, the regional headquarters has to exercise a certain level of control. This is necessary to ensure that local units follow common objectives and do not come up with divergent solutions to common problems. This is often particularly important to maintain the overall corporate identity or to establish common service policies. Audi, a division of Volkswagen AG, for instance, uses its general importers to ensure a set of consistent policies for both company-owned and contractual dealers. These service policies include a common corporate identity: separate showrooms as well as the policy that patrons shall not see a collision vehicle while visiting the dealership.

Pooling of resources

A third integrative function of regional headquarters is the pooling of resources to manage certain key functional activities across the region. Resource pooling is common for back-office and support functions like legal services, marketing research and product design, but also takes place in areas like joint distribution centres or in taking over pan-European key accounts from local units. Asics, for example, maintains a main distribution centre in Germany to cater to the entire European market. Similarly, banks like Unicredit bundle IT services on a regional level. Although pooling of resources at the regional level makes sense, the cases of Unicredit (IT in Romania, regional headquarters in Austria) and Asics (distribution centre in Germany, regional headquarters in the Netherlands) suggest that these functions do not necessarily need to be co-located.

The regional headquarters entrepreneurial charter

A regional headquarters' entrepreneurial charter describes its role to scout and explore new business opportunities, initiate new ventures across the region, stimulate and assist the local subsidiaries in understanding the changing nature of the regional business environment and help them integrate these changes into their business strategies. Finally, regional headquarters may be used by firms to signal commitment to the region.

Scouting and exploring

One key entrepreneurial function that regional headquarters fulfil is to explore new business opportunities within the region or even beyond. As new market opportunities open up, the regional headquarters is chartered to evaluate these opportunities and prepare adequate action plans. McDonald's CEE headquarters, for example, fulfilled such a role when expanding the company's business into the eastern European markets. A team of experts at the regional headquarters carefully examined the market readiness of individual markets and prepared decisions to either go into the market or wait on the sidelines when the business climate did not yet appear ready for market entry.

Stimulating and assisting

A second key function of regional headquarters is to assist local subsidiaries and push them to higher goals. Assisting can take the simple form of providing service assistance and to help spread best practices across the group. In global matrix structures, this may include serving as a switchboard between product divisions and country managers. Puma's regional headquarters in Salzburg, for example, gained considerable experience doing business in markets with underdeveloped banking systems, such as Romania. The regional headquarters utilized this expertise to consult with and assist other subsidiaries in its network that share similar market environments, such as those in Brazil and South Africa.

Signal commitment

Finally, regional headquarters sometimes fulfil the more symbolic function of signalling commitment. This issue is particularly important in developing country markets where governments want to see a sustainable investment of foreign multinational corporations. Thus, within the European context, this issue is probably not quite as important.

Figure 5.4 displays the degrees to which regional headquarters fulfil various roles. As the chart indicates, regional headquarters indeed pursue a mix

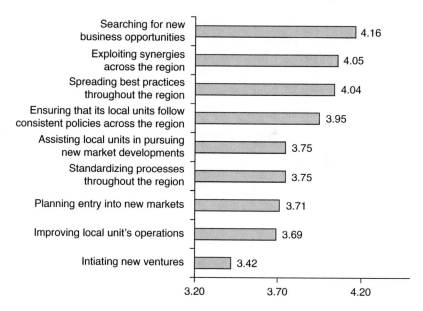

Figure 5.4 Comparing the frequency of various regional headquarter roles

Note: 1 = not carried out by RHQ; 5 = carried out to a very great extent.

Source: RHQ Survey.

Table 5.1 Common functions performed by European regional headquarters

Function	Objective	Company Example
Pooling of Activities		
Regional Distribution Management	Joint warehouses to cater to the region or a subregion	Asics European distribution centre in Amsterdam
Regional Marketing	Joint marketing for the region	P&G DACH region
Key Account Management	Central management of key or pan-European customers	Unicredit Banca, for corporate customers in the region
Regional Product Development	Shared R&D Centre to adapt or develop products for the European market	Ford's European R&D centres in Germany, Spain and the United Kingdom
Back-office Management	Joint human resource and legal services	Henkel's CEE headquarters in Vienna
Regional Manufacturing	Buildup of central plant to cater to multiple markets	Toyota's manufacturing plant in Wales
Regional IT Management	Managing a joint IT platform for the region	Tiffany's & Co. IT centre in Munich
Coordinating Activities		
Budget Allocation	Financial control and management of budget allocation process	Puma RHQ in Salzburg
Control of Subsidiaries	Ensuring compliance and control within the region	Boehringer Ingelheim, CEE
Regional Strategy Development	Developing and adjusting the market strategy for and within the region	P&G European headquarter in Geneva
Regional Benchmarking	Performance and best-practice benchmarking across the region	Boehringer Ingelheim, CEE
Entrepreneurial Role		
Regional Issue Selling to Global HQ	Representing a regional voice in the corporate governance councils	Honda's VP Europe sits on the board in Japan
Intra-regional Knowledge Sharing	Sensing useful practices in one national market and transferring them to another within the region	Unicredit Banca. Transfer of practices across the CEE region
Regional Opportunity Seeking	Development of new markets within the region, introduction of new brands/products into the European markets	Henkel CEE. Development of new markets in Asia (that is, detergent business in Kazakhstan)

of both charters, entrepreneurial and integrative. The highest rated function is searching for new business opportunities (part of the entrepreneurial charter) followed by exploiting synergies across the region and spreading best practices throughout the region (part of the integrative charter). Initiating new ventures, planning entry into new markets and improving operations of local units, in turn, rank last in the hierarchy of roles. Our findings further underline that the mandates of European regional headquarters differ somewhat from what Lasserre observed in his sample of Asian regional headquarters. None of the firms surveyed by us indicated that they established a regional headquarters to signal commitment to the region, a motivation often mentioned in Asian studies.[7]

Table 5.1 provides a set of examples of how and in which way regional headquarters fulfil the above outlined roles along with examples of firms.

Changing roles over time

Philippe Lasserre argues that regional headquarters' roles are likely to change over time (see Figure 5.5). At the entry stage, it is likely that a regional headquarters takes on a more entrepreneurial role. As the company becomes more established in the region during the development phase, it will augment the entrepreneurial role and add the integrative role to its primary functions. When the regional operation reaches maturity, it starts to consolidate and, in this process, shifts the emphasis entirely from the entrepreneurial

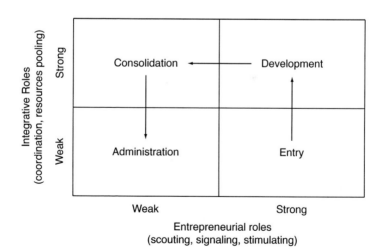

Figure 5.5 The life cycle of a regional headquarters

Source: Lasserre, P. (1996) "Regional Headquarters: The Spearhead for Asia Pacific Markets," *Long Range Planning*, 29, pp. 30–7. Figure reprinted with permission of Elsevier.

function to the integrative functions to concentrate on leveraging synergies within the region. In the final administration stage, the full responsibilities of carrying out various tasks by the headquarters are taken over by the local country markets.

Although there is some intuitive appeal in Lasserre's attempt to map out dynamics of regional management, some caution is warranted when transferring this model into the European context. Lasserre developed his model by looking at Asian regional headquarters. With this in mind, the entry for many MNCs into the Asian market indeed happened through a regional bridgehead, mandated to enter the region, develop business and, eventually, become redundant, as national markets became mature enough to take over the tasks provided by the regional headquarters. For many European operations, however, this trajectory does not apply. In the overwhelming majority of cases we investigated, the regional headquarters was not established as the first unit in the market but much later after local subsidiaries were up and running. Indeed, even for mature and large organizations, the current location and establishment of a regional headquarters is a fairly recent phenomenon (take, for example, Procter and Gamble or Ford, which both established their current structures in the mid-1990s, despite a European presence for more than half a decade). This difference is important because it highlights not only the different starting points and challenges faced by MNCs in their European operations, but also demonstrates once more that the objectives to set up a regional headquarters are much more deeply embedded in a general strategic belief that regional headquarters are not a temporary structure, but indeed help the firm to better manage its international operations in the long run.

Thus, the challenge for many firms in Europe was to establish rapport by initially taking on some support functions and providing value to the group. Subsequently, regional headquarters proceeded to integrate the activities, materialize resource-pooling opportunities and increase the consistency of firm strategies across all markets. Only later did firms try to balance their integrative efforts with a more entrepreneurial mission. As a consequence, the sequence of regional headquarters' roles in mature, developed markets may be more accurately depicted by the following figure (see Figure 5.6).

Allocation of value-added activities across the firm

Beyond the overall charter of the regional headquarters, a crucial point for firms operating with a regional headquarters structure is to allocate responsibilities for individual value-added activities across the three levels: global headquarters, regional headquarters and local subsidiaries.

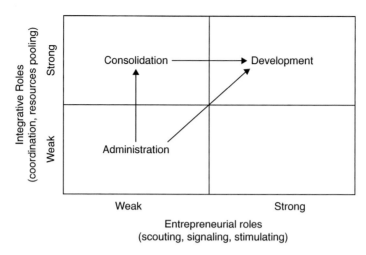

Figure 5.6 Dynamic roles for regional headquarters: A European perspective

An examination of the distribution of value-added activities within our sample of firms revealed the following picture. The two most localized functions within the MNCs are sales and distribution, for which responsibility remains predominantly at the local level. In turn, the three most centralized functions at the global headquarters are manufacturing, research and development and IT support. As Figure 5.7 illustrates, regional headquarters take a middle role for most functions, taking responsibility for about 15 to 40 per cent of the total value added in a given function. However, with the exception of sales and distribution (which largely remain the responsibility of the local subsidiaries) and manufacturing (which tends to be either in the hand of global headquarters or the local units), regional headquarters play a more important role than local units when it comes to distribution of responsibility. Another interesting observation from looking at Figure 5.7 is that regional headquarters hold the most responsibility in the allocation and consolidation of finances and purchasing.

Our findings nicely relate to previous work by Michael Enright, who examined the strategic role of regional headquarters and offices in Asia Pacific.[8] His research stresses the important coordination function of regional headquarters at nearly all steps in the value chain, except customer service support, manufacturing quality control, basic research and applied research. However, Enright concentrated on the importance of the function performed by local subsidiaries and regional headquarters, respectively, and not, as we do, on the distribution of work. Results of both our surveys – that is, the subsidiary survey and the regional headquarters survey – suggest that

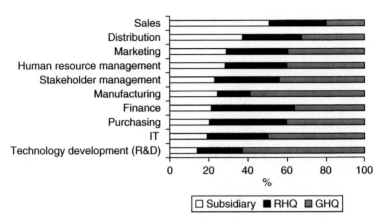

Figure 5.7   Division of work between subsidiaries, RHQs and GHQs along the value chain

Source: RHQ Survey.

the above-mentioned functions are, in fact, not the prime focus of regional headquarters.

Figure 5.7 also relates back to Rugman's framework that we presented in Chapter 2. The framework suggests that globally operating firms need to develop location-bound, nonlocation bound and regional-bound firm-specific advantages in order to be successful. If we assume that firms allocate the responsibilities on a rational basis, Figure 5.7 gives us some indication as to where these advantages lie. With reference to what we said above, sales require predominantly location-bound advantages, a finding that makes intuitive sense, particularly if the firm in question sells its product through a local distribution system and few pan-European customers exist. On the other extreme, R&D seems to rest largely on nonlocation bound advantages in most firms. Thus, multinational firms tend to assign responsibility for this function to the global headquarters. Production, our data suggest, can be organized locally or globally. No matter for which strategy the multi-national firm opts, regional headquarters do not seem to add much value to this function either way. For most of the remaining functions, regional specific advantages enable the regional headquarters to add value to the network and thus take over a larger share of the value creation within the network.

Conclusion

Managing a regional headquarters is not an easy task. Being the intermediary between global and local interests, regional headquarters often serve as the main pressure point in the organization. To relieve some of the tensions present in the organization, clear roles, responsibilities and reporting lines are essential. Successful regional headquarters are usually equipped with wide-ranging degrees of autonomy and have an important say in corporate strategy development. If managed well, regional headquarters fulfil a series of crucial roles for the multinational firm, which can be usefully summarized in its entrepreneurial charter and its administrative charter. From the data we analysed, it seems that the entrepreneurial charter seems to gain momentum, and not lose it, over time. Furthermore, it is here where subsidiary managers perceive that regional headquarters add the most value to their operations. Our findings also suggest that it would be wrong to view regional headquarters merely as administrative centres that lose in importance as the organization matures. Quite the opposite is true: As the firm becomes more established in the European market, the regional headquarters usually gains, rather than loses, importance.

Part II
Strategies for US and Japanese Firms

6
US Companies in Europe: Going East

In the last four chapters, we have looked at the structural and managerial challenges firms face in setting up their regional operations in Europe. In this and the succeeding chapter, we take a closer look at how US and Japanese firms set up their regional operations, how they configure their global value chains and which managerial challenges they face in coming east or westwards. We start by looking at the case of US firms, notably by investigating how Nike, Ford and Pfizer built up their regional presence in Europe.

Organizational structure

The three US multinationals structure their European business in different ways. Ford has an autonomous and regional-focused approach in Europe. It has established a formal subregional approach by setting up two separate product-based operations in Europe that operate independently from each other. In Ford of Europe, this is further augmented by a regional headquarters structure in Germany that shares functional specialities with a well-established subsidiary in the United Kingdom. The national organizations in each country then interact in a matrix format with these two regional units.

Nike centralizes its non-European regional operations in its home base in Oregon. Europe, with a regional headquarters in the Netherlands, is the only exception to this rule. Still, through so-called product engine groups and other personnel, Nike Europe is also well represented at the headquarters in Oregon. A product engine group, as defined within Nike, is a global product group responsible for the continuous development of a product. Its informal, open but complex matrix structure provides the flexibility for team-driven communication in a dynamic environment. "Off the line" teams are formed as product engines and provide a platform by which the subsidiaries from Europe can voice their opinions on product adaptation and innovation.

Pfizer uses a mix of single market and subregional headquarters on two levels. Because of several mergers and the need to protect its medicines from counterfeit drugs, Pfizer has centralized key business functions at the global headquarters. However, the diversified regulatory infrastructure of the pharmaceutical industry has led Pfizer to set up an extensive network of national sales organizations across the European region. This has resulted in a two-layered subregional structure in the smaller and/or developing markets for the CEE.

Below is a more detailed description and analysis of the organizational structure and the regional headquarters of the three US multinational companies.

Ford Motor Company, headquartered in Dearborn, Michigan, is one of the "Big-3" US automobile manufacturers. The company was present in more than 200 markets and operated more than 95 plants globally in 2008. Total sales in 2008 stood at USD146.3 billion with a consolidated net loss of USD14.7 billion. The car company has been facing losses during the last few years due to competition from Asian car manufacturers and a deteriorating saturated market in selected mature geographic areas.

Ford's core business segments are the automotive division, currently contributing roughly 89 per cent of total revenues, and the financial services division, with 11 per cent of revenues. The automotive business includes both distribution and manufacturing operations for a range of vehicles from passenger cars, trucks, vans and SUVs. The financial services division provides the credit financing for the vehicles purchased by customers. After-sales customer service, repair and spare parts are extended services offered by Ford (see Figure 6.1).

In 2007, Ford aimed to work as one global company with the goal "to build more of the products that people really want and value with striking designs that are safer, more fuel efficient and offer greater value."[1] A commitment to small cars, more crossovers, and more capable, efficient trucks was an important part of this goal. By 2007, Ford's operating strategy focused on reducing operating losses, realigning production capacity and upgrading and strengthening product development. Such improvements were possible through an organizational realignment with a defined focus on markets and customers.

The new structure still has two main product groups but the automotive division is organized under a Consumer Business Groups (CBG). The CBG is a business organization that is built around diverse regions or brands and has responsibilities for running day-to-day operations. The products were differentiated by pushing different brands into specific targeted segments. Each brand is then limited to core models. Customers have to switch brands if they opt for another product type.[2] In addition, Ford's Global Centres of Excellence, for example, Global Product Development or Global Marketing, support CBGs to gain economies of scale.

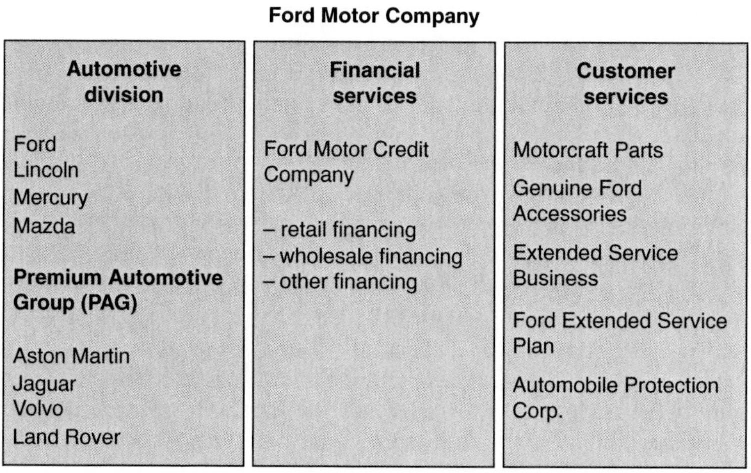

Ford Motor Company

Automotive division	Financial services	Customer services
Ford Lincoln Mercury Mazda **Premium Automotive Group (PAG)** Aston Martin Jaguar Volvo Land Rover	Ford Motor Credit Company – retail financing – wholesale financing – other financing	Motorcraft Parts Genuine Ford Accessories Extended Service Business Ford Extended Service Plan Automobile Protection Corp.

Figure 6.1   Global corporate structure of Ford Motor Company, 2007
Source: Ford Annual Report (2006).

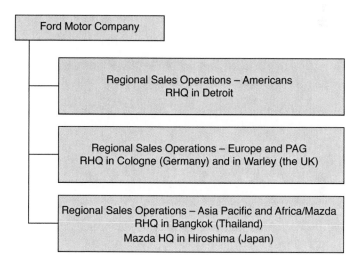

Figure 6.2   Regional headquarters of Ford Motor Company

Ford's CBG structure was regrouped into three regional groups reporting directly to the CEO at headquarters in Michigan. Ford of the Americas is responsible for North America including Canada, South America and Mexico. These operations include design, engineering, production, marketing, sales, after-sales customer service and financing of the Ford brand. In Europe, there are two autonomous operations. There is the Ford of Europe organization, which is the CBG operation for Ford brands such as the Focus and the Mondeo vehicles. It handles Western and Eastern Europe, Scandinavia, Benelux, Turkey and Russia. In addition, there is also the Premier Automotive Group (PAG), which is an autonomous operating arm serving as the umbrella for the European luxury car brands such as the Aston Martin, Jaguar, Land Rover and Volvo. Lastly, Ford of Asia and Africa handles Japan, China, Australia, New Zealand and the emerging markets of South East Asia, the Indian subcontinent and South Africa. Mazda is also included as separate operating units. Figure 6.2 illustrates Ford's global structure.

For over 40 years, the first European regional headquarters of Ford was located in England. In 1986, Ford of Europe was formally established and then relocated to Cologne, Germany, in the 1990s. There were several reasons for this strategic move. Ford Motors wanted to reposition itself and be identified as a leading manufacturer of top-quality automobiles. During this time, Germany had the largest sales volume for Ford.

> We came to regard Germany increasingly as the real bellwether for quality in the automotive industry. Our management at that time felt, unless more of our management was located in Germany we would not be sensitized to German attitudes of quality, which are arguably much more demanding than for example British attitudes towards quality. (Ian Slater, Vice President for Public Relations, Ford of Europe)

Although Cologne is the official regional headquarters, the value activities are split between Warley in the United Kingdom and Germany (see Figure 6.3). The staff shuttles to and from the two locations via a private air transport. The marketing, sales and service functions, information management and public affairs are based in Warley. The operating functions, pricing and communication (internal and external) are based in Cologne. Both locations have a product development function for certain car models. In addition, Ford of Europe has a regional presence based in Budapest, Hungary. It is responsible for covering the Eastern European countries.

> Ford of Europe is a stand alone, full service business entity which is primarily producing European cars for Europeans. (Ian Slater, Vice President for Public Relations, Ford of Europe)

> We develop products for Europe, we produce them and we market them and we sell them and we service them in Europe. (Hans Schlep, Marketing Manager, Ford of the Netherlands)

In Europe, most of a country's operations are national sales organizations, which are 100-per cent-owned subsidiaries of Ford Motor Company. The subsidiaries are responsible for local sales, dealer network and customer service.

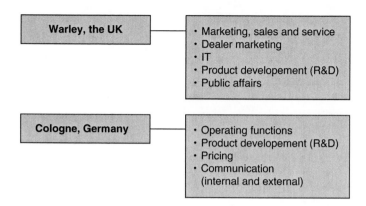

Figure 6.3   Ford of Europe distribution of functions

"Locally, there is no significant management of anything like manufacturing, purchasing or product development," according to Ian Slater, Vice President for Public Relations, Ford of Europe.

Nike is the largest manufacturer of sports footwear, sports apparel and equipment in the world. The headquarters is located in Beaverton, Oregon, and continues to be the heart of Nike's global operations. In addition to the Nike brand, the other well-known brands are Cole Haan, G Series, Converse, All Star and Jack Purcell to name a few.[3] Nike products emphasize action and experience in a variety of sports such as soccer, golf, tennis, running, fitness and training as well as basketball.

In 2008, total net sales amounted to USD18.6 billion for Nike. Net income during the same period stood at USD3.8 billion. With its long-term strategy to maintain market leadership of its major brands, total sales are expected to grow to USD23 billion by 2011.[4]

Nike's corporate culture is identified with growth and timely innovation within a communication-driven, team-driven organization. As such, it is important for Nike to be close to the ground and to have a presence in the main epicentres in each region.

> We always believed that it was very important for us in terms of being able to stay very close to the ground, in the market, and understand what's going on. Europe in particular was instrumental in helping us to understand soccer football, so that we could grow in that sport and create a significant halo for us in terms of the brand and the credibility we've had in the sport there....And we remained under a belief system over time that we need to have strong on the ground knowledge about what is occurring in different markets and need to aggregate that at least one level before it gets to here (Oregon). (Mr Peter Ruppe, Vice President for Global Equipment, Nike Oregon)

Nike has four main regional groupings worldwide. Although the company generates more revenues outside its home base, the US market continues to be a major contributing area for Nike in terms of sales volume. In 2008, the United States accounted for 34% of total sales. Europe, the Middle East and Africa are grouped as the EMEA region. This group contributed about 30% of total net sales. The Asia Pacific region brought in approximately 15% of total net sales, the Americas Region stood at 6.19% and about 14% of total net sales were from other sources.[5]

The regional headquarters for Asia Pacific and for the Americas are centralized in Oregon. Thus, these are regional headquarters for the region and not in the region. Only the European regional headquarters is based in the region, in Hilversum, the Netherlands. It is responsible for covering not only the main countries in Europe, but also the Middle East, Turkey, Russia and South Africa.

Because innovation is key for Nike, top management feels that, by and large, the flow of communications is better when the regional headquarters are kept in one location. The exchange of information about the ongoing changes within and among the different geographic groups is better managed. Response is immediate, especially for an industry where trends change seasonally and where there is a high product turnover.

The only exception is the EMEA regional headquarters (see Figure 6.4), which is the largest unit within Nike in terms of land area and country coverage.

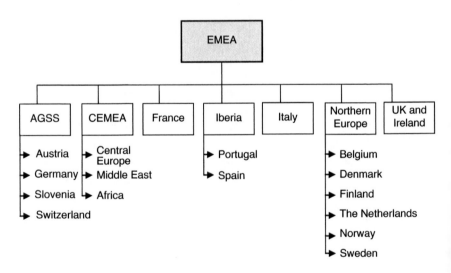

Figure 6.4   Nike's EMEA regional group

Nike's approach for this region is a clustering system based on the geographic distance and market development. We would identify this as a mix of single market and subregional structure. The subregional groupings were created due to similarities in consumer preference and business practices.[6]

> [We] built one structure that can oversee all that, keep the selling activities at the country level and try to aggregate as best as we can there. Same type of philosophy.... That even though they have different cultures, they are geographically reasonably together, from a management scope and scale comparable to the size of the business. (Mr Peter Ruppe, Vice President for Global Equipment, Nike Oregon)

The EMEA regional headquarters is responsible for setting the regional strategy and identifying synergies in the supply chain, financial and general business operations. Although it acts as a coordinator, the EMEA regional headquarters plays an intrinsic role in stimulating the entrepreneurial initiatives of the country subsidiaries. A loosely defined matrix structure (see Figure 6.5) was set up to facilitate this. The matrix is defined by functions and product groups.[7]

In the near future, Nike intends to change the matrix structure by defining sports categories according to functions. For example, there will be golf, tennis and running instead of the product categories of sports footwear, apparel and equipment.

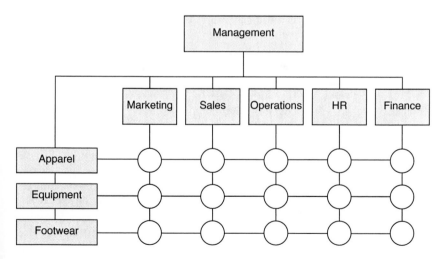

Figure 6.5   Regional matrix structure

The country operations of Nike concentrate on the marketing and sales functions. They play a critical role in providing data on consumer tastes and market trends for all core products of Nike.

The Netherlands was chosen as the location for the regional headquarters due to tax incentives, economic reasons and the easy access to various types of transportation. Another reason was the Dutch population. The extensive pool of English-speaking talent allows for easy communication for Nike managers and staff.

Pfizer is one of the largest pharmaceutical companies worldwide and is based in New York. Pfizer acquired Warner-Lambert in 2000 and Pharmacia in 2003, resulting in many years of corporate restructuring. Pfizer's global net sales stood at about USD48.3 billion in 2008 with net income of USD8.1 billion.

Pfizer specializes in human prescription drugs and animal health. Pfizer focuses on nine major therapeutic areas, including cardiovascular and metabolic diseases as well as central nervous system disorders.

The global trend in the pharmaceutical industry has led Pfizer to integrate and consolidate key business activities. There is an executive leadership team that is divided according to functions such as medical, human resources, legal and public affairs. Research and development is centralized and managed out of the headquarters under Pfizer's Global Research & Development Group (PGRD). Similarly, Pfizer Global Manufacturing (PGM) is responsible for the worldwide operations of production and is directly handled by the vice chairman. The commercial activities are under the Pfizer Worldwide Pharmaceutical Operations (PWPO).

Pfizer has had an international presence since the 1950s. The United States, however, continues to be the dominant market for the company. Pfizer's pharmaceutical organization is subdivided into five US-based business units and three key international business segments (see Figure 6.6).

All regional headquarters management teams are located in New York. Pfizer Europe is the largest international area and is responsible for all European countries, Turkey, the former Commonwealth of Independent States (CIS) and Eastern Europe.

The objective of Pfizer was to achieve strong embeddedness in its local operations. Therefore, the strategy of the European regional headquarters is to facilitate national organizations in establishing a stronger presence in their respective markets. As such, Pfizer Europe serves as a coordinating body for setting the benchmarks for the region, sharing best practices, streamlining back office functions and financial responsibility.

In 2007, Pfizer underwent another wave of restructuring. Similar to Nike, the European headquarters of Pfizer utilizes the single market and subheadquarters regional approach. The continent is divided by market size, geographical proximity and the development stage of the market. The largest

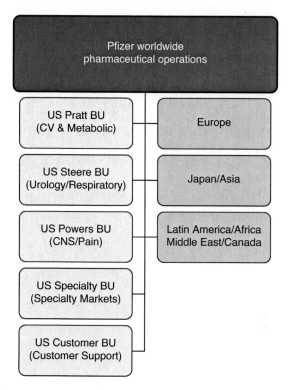

Figure 6.6   Pfizer's global pharmaceutical operations

"Big 5" markets are France, Germany, Italy, Spain and the United Kingdom, and they directly report to the Area President for Europe. In addition, there are two subregional headquarters that are responsible for a cluster of smaller markets. The Nordic subregional headquarters is responsible for Belgium, Denmark, Finland, the Netherlands, Norway and Sweden. The Central Southern European subregional headquarters manages countries such as Austria, Greece, Portugal, Switzerland and Turkey together with the Baltics, Eastern Europe and the Middle East. These subregional headquarters report to regional vice presidents who are the same level as the country managers of the Big 5. The less-developed markets of Eastern Europe and the Baltic countries are further grouped into geographic and political clusters under the CEE subregional headquarter. The vice president for the CEE subregional headquarters reports to the regional vice president for the Central Southern European subregional headquarters, who is based in New York (see Figure 6.7).

The CEE subregional headquarters is based in Brussels, Belgium. This has been a long-standing arrangement due to its proximity to the European political policy decision makers.

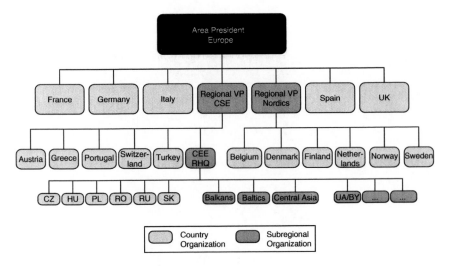

Figure 6.7   Regional structure of Pfizer Europe

The regional grouping for Pfizer Europe is primarily based on the market size or sales volume. Geographic proximity and political reasons are only secondary factors in Pfizer Europe's regional structure. In the pharmaceutical industry, products are fairly standardized and, thus, Pfizer has developed a centralized management system for the key functions while the country subsidiaries are basically marketing and sales oriented.

Similar to Nike, Pfizer centralizes its core business functions at the New York headquarters and creates synergies among its regional headquarters and headquarters management by keeping them together. The Area President for Europe has always been located in New York. As the company matures in its operating life and settles to a structure after several mergers, the advantage of being on the ground in New York and having the ability to influence policies and decisions affecting the European region outweigh the distance and time zone differences as well as the direct contact with country managers.

The regional headquarters vice presidents and area president are supported by functional teams that are located within the main European markets. These are teams that manage marketing strategy and medical strategy. The teams are located in Germany, France and the United Kingdom.

> As an example, the UK is responsible for selective therapeutic areas. The UK support team has a broad responsibility and support role across all countries. It is the same with Germany on the pain therapeutic area. (Pedro Lichtinger, Area President Europe, based in New York)

The national organizations are responsible for marketing and sales programs. The country manager is normally supported by functional staff, such as customer director, finance, human resources, legal and information technology. These functional staffs have a dual reporting line to their country manager and the regional functional manager at the regional and/ or subregional headquarters.

In summary, the US multinationals differ in their rationales for establishing a regional headquarters in Europe. Ford exercises an autonomous and fragmented style in managing its regional headquarters. It has a regionally consistent brand strategy. Nike, with its dynamic strategy for growth and communication, requires a structure that allows centralized information and coordination. Its regional headquarters for Europe, though, needs to be close to the consumer due to industry dynamics. A matrix organization is overlapping with its European regional structure. This facilitates better coordination and flexibility in decision-making strategy. Postmerger events have resulted in Pfizer maintaining a more centralized function-based structure as well as keeping key regional managers close to headquarters in New York.

Value activities within and across the region

Research and development

Ford's European regional headquarters has two research and development centres. In the 1960s, it was decided to draw on the strengths of both German and British engineering skills. The R&D group in Cologne, Germany, is in charge of vehicle engineering, while the R&D group in Dagenham, United Kingdom, is responsible for power trains and commercial vehicles. It is a European business group responsibility. "We try to keep a balance between the two centres – it works remarkably well. We have been able to accommodate both," said Ian Slater, Vice President for Public Relations, Ford of Europe.

The R&D activities of Ford of Europe are split evenly between the two locations.

The R&D operation for Ford of Europe was preconceived as a global product development centre for small and medium vehicles. The United Kingdom has a design centre for the small cars, and the medium to larger cars are in Germany. By centralizing these development functions, sourcing of component parts is more efficient and costs are better controlled.

> We are very cost intensive in terms of R&D and our investments are significant. What drives this business is that our costs are geared towards producing these high class items that we need to sell efficiently. And we do have to centralize the thing, we have to save the costs by centralising them, by volume and whatever. (Public Relations Manager, Ford of the UK)

Ford Motors has what is referred to as "shared technologies," which is a way of leveraging global economies of scale. About 40 per cent of technologies are shared.

In the late 1990s people talked about virtual platforms – some were global platforms and some were regional platforms. We have now moved on to shared technologies and architectures. So rather than developing a one size platform you have a set of technologies, which come together in different forms to make different vehicles. For example, the new generation "Focus" had a lot of technologies common with the Volvo S40. But if you look at the two vehicles they have nothing in common. (Ian Slater, Vice President for Public Relations, Ford of Europe)

The research and development activities of Nike are based in its headquarters in Oregon. Given the dynamic changes in the sports footwear and apparel industry, timely market information on consumer tastes and pricing is essential for Nike to maintain its competitive edge. As such, there are designer and product engineers who are sent out to the various European subsidiaries.

The people here in Germany are responsible for important consumer insights in terms of running, lifestyle and equipment. These insights and market information is then given to the regional organization and this is further inputted to the global collection. There are several global and regional staff members who travel to the local markets and set up consumer questionnaires and analyze them. (Hubertus Hoyt, General Manager, Nike Germany)

Through the coordination of the European regional headquarters and the product engines, local trends are immediately relayed back to headquarters in Oregon. Collaborations with universities play a substantial role in keeping Nike ahead of its competitors.

In Germany, we have three global Development Centres in cooperation with universities. One is in Köln with Prof. Brückemann. One is in Hessen with Prof. Hennig and the third is in Tübingen with Prof. Grau. We have these centres in three type of sports: football (soccer), running and indoor. The global product engines work with these research institutes. Nike receives a lot of new ideas for the product attributes which are integrated into the collections. (Hubertus Hoyt, General Manager, Nike Germany)

As mentioned, Pfizer has centralized the management of research and development at its headquarters in New York. Most of its research is primarily concentrated in the United Kingdom.

> The trend in our industry and our company is to globalize most activities, e.g. research is fully global. And we try for the customer needs to be global, meaning diseases that are prevalent in large populations in the world and that we can treat. Having said that triggers are very different dynamics in research than what you would have in finance. In research, we have a process of inputting the customer needs into the discovery process, which tries to capture global customer needs and is then deployed by research. (Pedro Lichtinger, Area President Europe, Pfizer New York)

Tensions may arise within the organization as to the location of the research operations, the areas of research as well as scientific research. The Area President of Europe's role is to partake in policy decisions for R&D investment and scientific talent. Research ideas are also initiated via strong collaborations with universities such as the University of Edinburgh.

Sourcing and production

Ford of Europe does not produce any individual components in-house. It develops some integration systems and subsystems for its European car models. For example:

> The instrument panels would be potentially a commodity you would define, develop differently in terms of what the instrument clusters look for a Volvo versus a Ford product. But behind these visually different instruments are clusters that might have similar individual components or technology. (Ian Slater, Vice President for Public Relations, Ford of Europe)

In developing new vehicles, Ford tries to determine whether internally invented technical products/systems should be used or if this should be externally sourced.

> We are about to launch a new Focus which is a little bit more powerful with 225 PS, but the engine that will be in this car is actually an inline-five engine. From early on there were different options for this vehicle: we could have taken an existing Ford engine...and we had the option of buying an engine from somebody else, even from a competitor, but normally we don't want to do that if we can do it ourselves. In this case we figured out that the Volvo engine was the best combination in terms of what we wanted to achieve, and in terms of dynamics and performance of the vehicle. And we determined early on that we could package it in the shape of the existing Focus. So, in this case, we specified the Volvo engine and made sure that they could deliver it in the right time and

in the right quality levels and whatever modifications were required to package it into this process. (Ian Slater, Vice President for Public Relations, Ford of Europe)

Thus, suppliers become a core member of the sourcing and production process for the cars. Suppliers are like a partnership.

It's a balance of power... in the earliest stages of the R&D process is that you get the suppliers involved such as in sharing technology expertise, very early on defining the characteristics of the systems and subsystems that you are looking to pull into the future car model. You work with them to develop the best systems at the highest quality and lowest cost. You have to develop a long-term relationship. (Ian Slater, Vice President for Public Relations, Ford of Europe)

In the United Kingdom, Ford has a factory in Dagenham that is a world centre for diesel manufacturer, Bridgend for petrol engines, a commercial vehicle plant in Dunton and South Hampton, a plant in Leamington, which produces car items, and Halewood, a truck Ford plant which builds transmissions. Most of the car manufacturing is located in Germany and France, such as the Fiesta in Cologne and the Focus and C-Max in Saarlouise. There is also a large manufacturing base in Valencia, Spain.

In the sports footwear and sports apparel industry, most products are outsourced. Critical to Nike's global sourcing strategy is the partnership with its sources. A well-established information system across the supply chain tracks and monitors the flow of inventory till final distribution. Security and product integrity are two basic concerns for Nike. Thus, Nike is selective in choosing its source. In Nike's case, these operations for footwear are primarily located in Asia, such as China, Vietnam, Indonesia and Thailand. The apparel is produced in several countries worldwide, such as Honduras, Turkey, India and Mexico, to name a few. The partnerships are long-standing relationships controlled by tight supply agreements. Some of the manufacturers have had a 30-year working relationship with Nike and remain loyal to Nike.

You know the basic thing that we do. How we treat the sourcing base we have, how effective we are at making sure that they are really in partnership with us and they see a threat as well to their business as ours, so blueprints and designs or files are getting out of their hands too soon. We continue to make products that are hard to copy. (Mr Peter Ruppe, Vice President for Global Equipment, Nike Oregon)

It is rare that two top brand competitors are in the same outsourcing facility. The technical attributes of the Nike products are already kept confidential from the R&D stage. Thus, Nike makes sure that the manufacturer has a "separate and well contained R&D facility" in place. In addition, the manufacturers themselves face a competition for outsourcing contracts. Manufacturing is dependent on the costs savings or the technical know-how. For Europe, the apparel production is in the Far East and Europe. The shoes are mostly manufactured in Asia; but specific products are made in Europe. Top quality, high-priced football shoes are produced in Italy. In sports equipment, production is located depending on the segment. Socks are produced in Europe, and bags are made in the Far East. If production is in Europe, then Nike gains 30 to 45 days in terms of final delivery to the market or customer.

One of the concerns of Nike is distribution of counterfeit products. The company tries to maintain a good relationship with the factories to protect itself from grey imports and counterfeits. Tracking the product flow and tight inventory management are the main control processes. Innovation and speed are two ways in which counterfeiting is controlled. Staying ahead of market trends and making things that are hard to copy is another way. The supply base is kept narrow and limited. Communication lines and file transfers are tightly secured. In some cases, buildings are kept locked up.

Pfizer has centralized the sourcing and production functions at headquarters in New York. There is a separate operating entity that manages the manufacturing for Pfizer worldwide (PGM). The commercial organization (PWPO) only interacts with PGM at regional management and headquarters.

Marketing and product standardization/adaptation

At Ford, the marketing functions are run autonomously. But the back office functions such as product development are centrally managed out of the headquarters. Each brand is limited to core vehicle models. Customers have to switch brands if they opt for another product type. Therefore, the main barriers to global products in the automotive industry are consumer tastes.

Ford has a regional focus for its product line and not a global one. Facing a heterogeneous market in Europe, Ford emphasized the core characteristics of each brand. As an example, the PAG automobiles are defined as luxurious. The Jaguar focused on luxurious sedans, convertibles and grand-touring coupes. Volvo, a brand known in Europe for safety at high speeds, had family wagons and sedans. Land Rover concentrated on the adventure of driving SUVs and country-tracking jeeps. Aston Martin is known for its luxury, high-performance sports car.

So one of the big challenges for Ford of Europe is to judge between all the competing demands of the market. And by the time you add all the demands of our markets you have an infinitive colour palette. And if you think about features, this becomes even more dramatic, so this is one of the big challenges of the business. (Ian Slater, Vice President for Public Relations, Ford of Europe)

Ford of Europe and PAG have separate marketing management functions. Each operation manages its own brands, even at the subsidiary levels. The European regional headquarters sets the directions in terms of marketing communications. It is managed centrally. In Ford of Europe, there is a Central European Marketing and Sales organization that serves as a coordinating body. The Ford of Europe marketing teams are in constant communication with the national companies. "For example, if we have a major product launch, the communications criteria that we use at Ford of Britain are first developed centrally and then adapted by us to be used locally," said Tim Holmes, Executive Director, Ford UK.

A toolbox is developed at the regional headquarters of Ford of Europe or PAG for the national sales companies to utilize. The brand promotional campaign is one example. Having one common TV shoot for the Mondeo saves resources and costs. The national organizations make use of this toolbox and adapt the TV commercial for their country by transposing the text or translating the language.

Nike headquarters develops a global strategy. The company also established product teams called "product engines" to further penetrate the different levels of the organization for various marketing functions. The product engine consists of persons with different skills who are globally dispersed. For example, the footwear is primarily centrally managed out of the United States. Nike has a global and regional product engine for sports apparel and sports footwear categories. Such product engines are essential in managing and updating the product design and looking for changes in consumer trends in Europe.

> The European market is so different, what is popular in Italy is popular may not be as popular in the Germany. The consumers are different. The business structure is different. The Americans wear the sports shoes all the time. In Italy it is fashion and style. In Germany, the sports shoes are worn for its performance value or as a fashion trend. Spain is like Italy and England is like America. (Hubertus Hoyt, General Manager, Nike Germany)

As mentioned above, Nike's European regional headquarters has three development centres. These entities are the source for new product ideas or technical designs for the European collection. Information such as consumer preferences or findings is channelled up the matrix structure back to headquarters in Oregon. Ideas generated by the European product engines are then discussed at the headquarters product engine group. Thus, footwear products are developed globally and adapted directly at the local country level. The country subsidiaries do not develop products per se. They can only suggest changes or variations to the product.

> The creative units get out. They don´t just sit here [headquarters] in isolation; they spend time in the market, listening, adapting, creating. And we use a similar process to get this product as a prototype out into markets and learn and see if we are on track or not. We believe this particular facility can be anywhere in the world right now but we believe that it's stronger if it's in one place as opposed to having it scattered all over. We find that if it's scattered all over, the product integrity is at risk. (Mr Peter Ruppe, Vice President for Global Equipment, Nike Oregon)

The European regional headquarters of Nike disseminates the marketing messages and how to best communicate. It makes sure that the country operations are on track in terms of imaging and storytelling.

In Pfizer there is a tendency towards centralizing general marketing policies and activities. Pfizer Europe manages the regional marketing strategies through the development of tactical operations and the formation of brand clusters. The country managers are responsible for the sales, marketing and execution of these programs.

There are brand teams or brand clusters for the key products, which are located in London, Paris and Karlsruhe.

> We are now building European brand teams and from here, marketing activities will be clustered for the different strategic products. We have 30 core products which can be marketed in the countries or are the most important products. The marketing function is partially centralized at the regional headquarters like the brand management and planning. There are localized marketing activities too which is the responsibility of the subsidiary. (Mr Penk, Country Manager, Pfizer Austria)

The brand teams normally follow the clinical trends and such clusters look into the long-term issues for the potential product. Every clinical study has to be approved by headquarters for patient safety and security reasons. The results of the study are carefully reviewed at headquarters. Labelling and packaging of the medicine are developed by the brand teams. The brand team is responsible for the general marketing framework for the new product such as medical events like congresses, meetings, doctors who will be invited and others. The brand team then distributes the budget for the development of the brand, promotion and further medical education.

The national organizations handle the operative marketing functions within the allocated resources. The subsidiary can organize medical meetings, invest in clinical studies as approved by R&D headquarters or decide on promotional materials for the local market. Sales are managed only by the subsidiary. Customer management and targeting potential customers are key functions for the national organization.

Distribution is direct, and there is a strict control of the distribution channel. Patient safety should be safeguarded from counterfeit drugs and grey imports. Recently, direct-to-pharmacy distribution was launched in the United Kingdom. The wholesaler is bypassed. This allows Pfizer to better understand how each pharmacy functions in terms of inventory, purchases and sales trends through an electronic booking system.

Management challenges

Relationship between global headquarters, regional headquarters and local subsidiaries

Ford Motor Company sets a global strategy in terms of operating guidelines for volume, target, financial targets and others. The regional headquarters CBG in the form of Ford of Europe and PAG determines what Ford's strategy for Europe will be. The European organization then determines what the product strategy is, the product development and sets the direction for product pricing as compared to the competition. The subsidiaries, as national sales companies, then customize the regional strategy to the local strategy. The primary role of the subsidiaries is to capture market share in their respective markets. Feedback from the subsidiaries is also expected by the European regional organizations.

One of the biggest challenges Ford Motors faces is balancing corporate needs versus regional needs versus local market needs. Headquarters may not always be aligned with the market needs. As one senior regional executive explains:

> What big global companies must do is to get objectives aligned... That is one of the biggest challenges, you always want to know what is the strategy. Headquarters tells us a strategy and the regional offices always feel there is some golden strategy. But you know that lot of times headquarters does not know what the hell they are doing either.

One of management's challenges is to align the priorities. What could be a priority to Ford Motors headquarters may not always be a priority for Ford of Europe or PAG. Management is challenged to help people understand that priorities are different. The solution is a management team that is qualified to do the job and have had experience by being close those local markets.

Because Europe is a mature, established market, Ford Motors headquarters and the European regional headquarters know that Ford has to be close to the local European markets. Ford has to be where there is "traction and growth." Therefore, it is a challenge for the smaller markets like Austria to be heard. How does the regional office maintain a balance of attention and resources for the larger and smaller subsidiaries?

First, the focus of Ford of Europe and PAG is primarily Europe. Thus, the identification of Ford of Europe and the national sales organization under its management is towards the region rather than to a Ford Motors global corporate identity.

Second, the European regional headquarters of Ford of Europe and PAG play a more strategic role while the national sales organizations are more tactical in their operations. The subsidiaries have the ability to react autonomously and make their own decisions. As a senior manager from the Ford Britain subsidiary says: "And when we need the back up from Ford of Europe, to be honest, it is pretty much there."

Third, one of the strengths of the European organization (Ford of Europe and PAG) is its structure. As a stand-alone entity, profitability is managed on the regional level and the responsibility of the national sales organization falls under the auspices of the respective regional headquarters. The national sales organizations have a direct line to the decision makers in the regional headquarters. The national sales organization in each country reports to a regional vice president at Ford of Europe or PAG. A senior executive said:

> We are set up to make sure that business units are more or less self-financing. Increasingly, we are trying to ensure that each business unit has a financial discipline so that we set the right targets in the business plan and that we can fund their future development programs.

Attention is given to the local subsidiary that voices its needs most strongly.

> You know our resources are limited compared to the demands of the markets, so we have to decide what the priorities are. If the countries are coming with clever ideas of how to improve their position versus competition, the regional headquarters has to listen to these repeating requests to be able to decide. I suppose the strengths and capabilities of the local management team will represent their needs at the regional headquarters. (Ian Slater, Vice President for Public Relations, Ford of Europe)

Therefore, conflicts between and among subsidiaries in Ford of Europe and PAG offices hardly exist. Each one is autonomous in its operations.

> I mean it is obvious that everyone wants to deliver or over-deliver the numbers, but... it is not like competing with different brands in the market. They are still colleagues, I would call it a natural competition of delivering... because that is why Ford has those brands, because they are an extension of opportunities and not direct competitors. (Hans Schep, Marketing Manager, Ford Netherlands)

Where Ford is region-oriented and fragmented in its European country operations, Nike is more centralized despite its complex organizational structure. Nike is also more US-oriented but maintains a dynamic drive through its corporate culture. Growth and innovation are the key elements that result in a flexible "team centric esprit de corps" and a collaborative management.

Having an open friendly culture minimizes the potential for conflict. There is, however, room for tension between Nike headquarters and its country operations.

> The tension is, you know, pretty natural, right? The further you get from being on the ground of a given country, the more the people in the country feel like you don't listen you don't get it. You know you don't understand our uniqueness...somewhere between that tension you have to build trust and get things to move through in the way that it is effective for the markets." (Mr Peter Ruppe, Vice President for Global Equipment, Nike Oregon)

The regional grouping structure and its location is another source of tension. Although locating the European headquarters in the Netherlands means it is closer to the markets, it also implies that the region is potentially not well represented at the Nike headquarters in Oregon. The Asia Pacific regional headquarters even has its own building at headquarters.

Management's challenge is how best to reduce such tensions. Part of Nike's corporate philosophy is being on the ground close to the consumers. The European consumer is more conservative and not easily influenced by global trends. Thus, the timing is critical for the launching of new styles and products. This is best observed when the regional headquarters are closer to the subsidiaries. How then does Nike headquarters address this issue?

> We try to make sure that we have people here [at headquarters] in different parts of the business that, on a full-time basis, represent European interest. So, we have people in the different divisions such as product creation in particular. Their job is to walk in and make sure decisions being made here consider the concerns of Europe. (Mr Peter Ruppe, Vice President for Global Equipment, Nike Oregon)

Despite Nike's complex matrix structure, management believes in communication within a team-oriented informal environment. This will minimize and prevent potential conflicts and tension.

> So the way we do it is in partnership. So the frustration is that it is never clear often on decision rights. The company operates very horizontally

and operates by collaborative spirit. What we are probably trying to solve is to get the right people on the problem, as a team address it and come with their solution. We actually mix the talent of the people that live in the country, live in the region, live in HQ to come to a solution. (Mr Peter Ruppe, Vice President for Global Equipment, Nike Oregon)

In this scenario, accountability for the decision stays at the headquarters level.

Pfizer primarily operates in one main division, human pharmaceuticals, and does not need to manage complex internal tensions among and within headquarters, the European headquarters and the national subsidiaries. Management's challenge is how best to maintain a coordinated system for its large, mature, formal business structure while encouraging creativity, flexibility and responsiveness at the ground level (subsidiaries). The European regional headquarters, therefore, focuses on more than an information exchange. It becomes a "promoter" and "pusher" of sorts, and it is important to be within physical reach of discussions and policy negotiations at headquarters.

Within Pfizer, the main tensions are primarily operational. The key factor relates to the impact of the regional headquarters on corporate strategy. Another issue is resource allocation. How much resources will be allocated to the European region? Having a presence at the headquarters is important. Pfizer's regional European management realizes that its ability to influence and to position the businesses brings value added for the region and for the national subsidiaries as a whole.

I see the value added in that we challenge the country subsidiaries in issues such as their budgets and their strategies, if there is more they can do. We surely have value added when we share best practices, when we are consistent in every area we do where we set benchmarks and compare the countries/markets with each other, like Brazil and South Africa and determine what we could bring the other. The leadership and the human resource development play a large role, too. When I do the annual business review, I also do a talent review in the countries and we see which managers/staff in the countries are outstanding and how we can develop their careers within the country or abroad. (Dr Fibig, Senior Vice President, Powers Business Unit and formerly Vice President for Latin America, Pfizer New York)

The main strategy of Pfizer has led to globalizing and integrating back office functions like finance, human resources and information management. The primary function of Pfizer New York has been to coordinate the US and international operations across the centralized business functions such as R&D, manufacturing and the commercial organization. The respective sites are run independently and do not interact directly with each other, for example, R&D to manufacturing.

Pfizer has had a presence in Europe for many years. Its business operations are extensive and well entrenched into the national markets. As such, it has a broad scale and a mature corporate life cycle. This implies that it has a structure and a culture that allows the country manager to function with autonomy within the guidelines agreed upon. In addition, some processes are so well established that the presence of a senior regional management is not necessary.

> We have very strong departments in Patent, in Regulatory, that do not need my direct supervision. I don't even see them. They are operational, their process is very well defined, it's optimized, it works very well and is part of the global process. So they do not need my direct intervention. But if you are just expanding internationally, you do need to be very close to the Patent management. (Dr Fibig, Senior Vice President, Powers Business Unit and formerly Vice President for Latin America, Pfizer New York)

The country managers within Pfizer have a dual role. First, they are responsible for managing the operations of their respective countries. Second, they participate in European initiative under their sponsorship. For example, two country managers are responsible for developing the oncology group. They visit other countries in the European region to formulate the strategy and prioritize resources. As Mr Penk, Country Manager for Pfizer Austria, describes:

> I was previously the coordinator for Oncology for Central and Southern Europe. And this was not yet a formal structure. I was in a Task Force where we had to share information, understand the technical issues involved and formulate a regional strategy for Oncology. The clinical studies in a CSE country would be small. So a regional based initiative made sense.

Twenty years ago, the country managers in Europe were responsible for their own operations. Each country had its own support systems and back office. They reported directly to the European headquarters on all matters. This is fast changing within Pfizer, where national talents within a subsidiary are pulled together into informal teams.

> If you look at the whole development, we're moving away from the kingdom-type country operations and country managers to more corporate-integrated country management styles. Many of the functions

are gone, because these are centralized, like back office finance, like some of the marketing concepts which come directly from headquarters New York. So, the country manager today is no longer the single point of decision making in the country because he or she is matrixed in other structures. (Dr Fibig, Senior Vice President, Powers Business Unit and formerly Vice President for Latin America, Pfizer New York)

So one way is by creating this matrix of geography and growth drivers that forces the countries to work as teams. (Pedro Lichtinger, Area President for Europe, Pfizer New York)

Pfizer Europe has also created a "mentoring" program. The country managers of more mature and developed markets such as Austria serve as mentors to the smaller and less mature markets such as Croatia and Bosnia.

In the Oncology brand team, we import key talents or persons who have the know-how to share and transfer their skills to other countries whose markets should be developed. I am the mentor for Croatia, Slovenia and Bosnia, even if I am not in the CEE country grouping. But the mentor program makes sense because you are responsible to take care and build up the knowledge within these countries. You are like a part time consultant for the European region and for Pfizer. (Mr Penk, Country Manager, Pfizer Austria)

The smaller and mid-sized European countries receive more management attention through the formation of subregional groupings. These are the higher margin markets that have more opportunities and the potential to serve as excellent test grounds for new medicines. Risk is contained and the parameters are less costly. As one senior executive would say, it is important to "listen because these markets will be the ones who can come up with the opportunities and solutions rather than the bigger mature markets."

As mentioned above, Pfizer's European regional headquarters in New York has functional support teams that cater only to the European countries. This matrix structure supposedly facilitates better interaction between the various countries, including the smaller markets like the CEE countries. The support teams not only support the marketing and general business functions of the commercial organization, but also identify how best to transfer research or manufacturing activities in each country at the regional headquarters level. Legal is another critical issue that is handled at the regional headquarters. Each country in Europe has different legal regulations in terms of drug approval, price setting and other areas. The support team at regional headquarters then makes sure there is no overlap of problems and brings critical issues to the attention of the area president and vice presidents for Europe.

Span of control

We observed that all three US multinationals manage their regional and national operations primarily through central corporate planning. This is then followed by operating budgets in each of the functions like marketing, production and sales. The European regional headquarters is responsible for controlling the performance of the local subsidiaries through the financial reports and market share data. The country managers have the autonomy to decide and the flexibility to run their respective local business within the confines of the agreed budget. Revised budgets and reviews are undertaken periodically during the operating year of the three US multinationals.

In Ford, a business plan is developed and presented to a corporate headquarters in Michigan. Once the business plan has been approved by regional headquarters and corporate headquarters, it is deployed into the functional areas. Budgets are then formed by the individual functional areas and agreed with both corporate headquarters and the regional headquarters. Adjustments are made from time to time.

The subsidiaries also have an operational structure that is based on a four-year budget. For example, the Netherlands office has a rolling three-year plan from which strategic priorities are derived, such as production numbers, sale volumes and others. A three-month marketing plan is then developed from this three-year plan. The plan is fine-tuned on a monthly or weekly basis. In addition, there is a weekly operating session with all the managers that drive the businesses in the country.

Nike headquarters establishes a five-year business plan to complement its long-term strategy of growth and innovation. An annual budget is set at headquarters that is divided among the geographic regional headquarters. Then the regional headquarters in the Netherlands determines the budget for the EMEA regional group. The larger subsidiaries and the subregional groups provide "bottom-up" input to ensure that the budget of the regional headquarters is achievable. Each subsidiary then develops its own marketing and sales plan.

Similar to the other two US multinationals, Pfizer has a comprehensive budgetary planning process. Pfizer New York sets a five-year plan in place, which the European regional headquarters then disseminates to the country heads. Each country manager then develops an annual budget called the Operating Plan Period. Budgetary planning is a bottom-up process with several feedback loops on regional and headquarters levels, in which the main role of corporate headquarters is to ensure worldwide consistency, challenge the regions and finally decide on resource allocations together with the regional heads.

Tensions and conflict can arise in the negotiation phase of the budgetary process. When Pfizer Europe questions the value of the budget for the larger markets like France and Italy, then the country managers can directly settle issues with the Area President for Europe. It is, however, difficult for the smaller markets like Austria and even more strenuous for the CEE countries like Poland. The discussion goes through layers of management before it is directly heard by the regional head. The information transfer and the value of the selected issues get muddled through the layers and result in differing degrees of impact.

Within Pfizer, country managers have a broad base of autonomy and decision-making power. Their decisions are mostly related to the local operations within their respective countries. But the agreed budgets and the centralized financial division helps Pfizer's Area President for Europe better observe the country operations.

> I have a wonderful dashboard where I have all the important ratios and numbers at my finger tip. This is updated once a month and compares the countries. This helps the finance division. (Dr Fibig, Senior Vice President, Powers Business Unit and formerly Vice President for Latin America, Pfizer New York)

Communication

Communication is the most important issue for a global organization such as the three US multinationals. Each company has its own style of maintaining information flow and sharing best practices.

Despite its formal organizational structure, Ford maintains communication within its headquarters, regional headquarters and subsidiaries through electronic means and face-to-face meetings. There is a direct contact and fast exchange of information between Warley or Cologne regional headquarters with Deerborn. Sometimes it is on a daily basis on specific company issues.

There are monthly operational meetings within Ford of Europe such as in marketing. In these meetings, the subsidiaries share best practices, set benchmarks for the region and inform the regional headquarters of coming changes in the national sales strategy. On a monthly basis, there is an audio communication with their respective European regional headquarters. The managing directors of the national sales organizations meet about five or six times a year.

Nike has a flat system of communication through the matrix and meeting flows to make sure that people do not have "blinders on."[8]

The matrix product engines report their results monthly to the Finance chief and to the Managing Director of the subregional headquarters. There are quarterly business reviews and year-end reviews. There are monthly and weekly updates between headquarters and regional headquarters.

> What are things that Nike emphasizes a lot is communication, we are very team centric. Large in terms how we like to operate so communication becomes very important as well. So we are making sure that everybody here is the same or whatever within the geography or every leader

part of the geography is getting the same message in terms of what business is strong what is weak, where the challenges are you know. (Mr Peter Ruppe, Vice President for Global Equipment, Nike Oregon)

At the regional headquarters level, the general manager for Europe has a corporate strategy meeting four times a year. Within the European region, there are bi-annual quarterly business reviews over the telephone or video-conferencing. The country managers attend face-to-face meetings for quarterly business reviews twice a year. The functional groups meet at similar intervals. Marketing meets with the global marketing group. The product engines also provide consistent communication across the functional and regional areas.

Pfizer has an audio conference and video conferencing facility. The company created a regional council integrating regional meeting management. Regional functional managers have contact twice a week with the country functional managers. The country managers have weekly phone calls with the Area President for Europe or with the vice president for the subregional group. There are also subregional and regional meetings that take place once in a while to foster functional exchange.

Conclusion

To conclude, the three US multinationals utilize different approaches in establishing and managing their European operations. The regional headquarters structure is dependent on the life cycle of a company and the markets it chooses to operate in. We observed that the US multinationals seem more hierarchical. But informal teams in the form of product task groups support and strengthen the information sharing and communication within the headquarters, regional headquarters and the local country operations.

The autonomous style of Ford resulted in a fragmented regional headquarters structure. Each subsidiary is a national sales organization and operates on its own. The brand-oriented regional headquarters for Ford of Europe and the PAG further reinforces this autonomy. Although Ford Motors has strong brand equity, its European base is separate and fragmented. Management at the regional headquarters level and the national subsidiaries do not identify with the global company, but remain loyal to the region. As such, conflicts seldom arise among the subsidiaries and the separate operating regional businesses in Europe. The challenge of Ford Motors headquarters is to determine if this formal structure will continue to support its corporate goals in the near future.

Nike and Pfizer are different from Ford. Both have a centralized base in terms of key business functions or geographic groupings. The regional headquarters structure is a combination of single market and subregional headquarters. The two companies want to be close to the market in Europe to create a local embeddedness in the respective countries. Both created informal teams to provide stimuli to the local subsidiaries, to establish fluid communication within the different layers of headquarters to subsidiaries and to be responsive to market changes or regulatory pressure. Nike's success drivers for the complex matrix corporate structure are the collaborative leadership, the open and outward-looking culture and the entrepreneurial esprit de corps. Pfizer is still on the verge of integrating its resources and corporate structure after many years of mergers in the 1990s. As such, Pfizer's approach in establishing its European regional headquarters close to global headquarters assures the proper communication links among its subregional headquarters and subsidiaries.

7
Japanese Companies in Europe: Going West

Having discussed some of the key challenges and solutions from the vantage points of the United States going to Europe, we are now taking the perspective of the Japanese companies going west. Specifically, we are presenting a cross-sectional analysis covering the automobile, pharmaceutical and sports footwear and apparel industries. Our primary objective is to determine if there are similarities or differences in the corporate structure, the regional headquarters groupings as well as functional competences in three Japanese multinational firms operating in Europe. Further, we attempt to identify what challenges these Japanese multinationals face in finding solutions to resolve conflicts or problems. Finally, we focus on some external drivers that affect the regional strategy formation. The companies reviewed for this project are Honda Motors, Astellas and Asics.

Organizational structure

Global corporate strategy affects corporate structure

> In Japanese companies it is quite different and I could not answer you how this works.
>
> Senior European Manager of a Japanese company

We observed that all three Japanese MNCs defined their corporate strategy while maintaining their unique national culture. Despite attempts to instigate a western form of organization, there seems to be an underlying need to maintain strong control within the upper levels of management. There is evidence, however, that the companies prefer to have Japanese nationals as heads of the regional headquarters and at headquarters in Japan. Competitive pressure within the respective industries requires the three companies to restructure their corporate organization constantly. The matrix structure combined with a subregional and the combined single market cum subregional approach seems to be the best form by which the regional headquarters maintain their control over the subsidiaries. These also facilitate the flexibility for the companies to respond to heterogeneous European market dynamics. As Mr Matsuda, President of Honda Nordic says, *"Europe is a mosaic."*

Honda Motors Inc., headquartered in Tokyo, is the world's largest motorcycle producer and a major automobile manufacturer. Global sales amounted to approximately US$119.8 million (€90 million) in 2008 with a net income of US$3.3 million (€2.49 million). Honda's core business segments are motorcycles, automobiles, financial services and power products and related businesses. The motorcycle segment, comprising 13 per cent of total net sales, is primarily focused in the Asian region. On the other hand, the automobile segment is the major source of revenue income for Honda with a 79.1 per cent portion.

North America is the largest market for Honda in the automobile segment followed by Asia, Japan and Europe. The automobile manufacturing centres are located in Japan, Canada, Thailand, United Kingdom and United States. The car models range from passenger cars, multi-wagons, mini-vehicles and sports utility vehicles (SUVs). The major car brands are Accord, Civic, Acura and Legend while the Odyssey, Fit, Jazz, CR-V and Ridgeline are the multi-van brands.[1]

Honda's founding principles of "Respect for the Individual" and "The Three Joys" are its success drivers. The cultural belief of "harmony with nature" coupled with the resourcefulness of the Japanese resulted in Honda's strengths. Technological innovation is the basis for the top quality products of Honda. The company is highly regarded for the engineering of highly efficient combustion engines and fuel-efficient low-level CO_2 emission technology.

Honda initially faced several years of difficulty in breaking into the European market. In the mid-1990s, the Honda head office in Tokyo decided to find a solution to this issue. Honda, therefore, developed a regional strategy for major geographic groups as a response to its challenge to "find a balance between the global integration and local responsiveness."[2] During the initial phase of Honda's entry into the European market, the whole continent was considered as one common market. It was a challenge for the senior Japanese management to understand the heterogeneity of Europe. Satoshi Aoki, Executive Vice President and Representative Director, Honda Japan stated:

> We have studied a lot about Hanse and the medieval ancient distribution alongside the Rhine River as well as the commercial history after Mediterranean Sea.... Hanse is quite an interesting way of studying the distribution of goods and of managing the regional management. There is a very good hint there to see and to recognize the needs of the market at from a different perspective.

Globally today, Honda has a matrix organization with the different geographic regional headquarters interlinked with a product and/or a functional business unit (see Figure 7.1).

In most cases, the geographic area for which the regional headquarters is responsible is further subdivided into areas or country groupings based on proximity and cultural similarities (hereafter referred to as "subregional offices"). Thus, Honda's regional headquarter structure in Europe can be classified as a subregional approach.

Honda Motors Europe Ltd., the European regional headquarters, is located in London, United Kingdom. The group is further subdivided into the subregional headquarters Honda Motors North, based in Frankfurt, Germany, and Honda Motors South, located in Paris, France. There is also a subregional headquarters in Sweden, and all other subsidiaries report directly to Honda Motors London. Honda Motors North consists of the Benelux countries, Netherlands, Germany and Austria. Honda Motors South consists of France, Spain and Italy. Honda Nordic, based in Mälmo, is responsible for

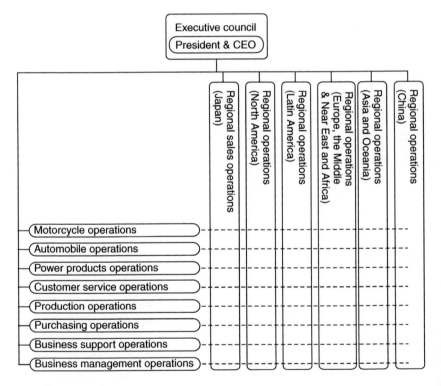

Figure 7.1   Global matrix structure of Honda
Source: 2008 Honda Annual Report.

the Scandinavian countries, Estonia, Lithuania and Latvia. Subsidiaries such as in Portugal are controlled directly by regional headquarters in London. Central European "gempos" are independent – like Honda Czech, Honda Poland, Honda Hungary and Honda Slovakia. "We call it 'gempos' meaning local companies," says Mr Yokohama, President, Honda Czech Republic. The latter grouping was established because these are large markets with distinct languages and buying behaviour.[3]

Each regional headquarters has its own geographic strategic plan as defined from the head office in Tokyo. This is then relayed to the sub-regional headquarters, the local subsidiaries and branches. Each country subsidiary is then responsible for adapting the strategy to its local market conditions such as in dealer relationships, marketing and sales approaches and to a certain degree product adaptation.

Honda Motors London is responsible for some marketing, product development and adaptation, pricing strategy, public relations, as well as financial and administrative tasks like logistics, budget variance analysis and internal reporting. Moreover, it is in charge of maintaining an overview of the European dealer network, which is critical in obtaining market feedback. The subregional headquarters are responsible for sales administration, marketing activities, information technology, service and warranty, accounting and human resources.

The challenge for Honda is how best to understand the demands of the local market and reacting in a timely manner. The country subsidiaries such as Honda Czech Republic are important initiators for sourcing information through the dealer network. "A good thing about Honda is that they empower local operations. The head office people will not say too much about what local operations should do" (Mr Yokohama, President Honda Czech Republic).

Because technical innovation is an important part of Honda's operations, the research and development divisions are organized along geographic groupings as subsidiaries. Each regional headquarters, therefore, interacts closely with its R&D entities with regards to product development.

According to a UK-based Honda manager, London was chosen as the home office for the European regional headquarters based on market and historical reasons. First, the United Kingdom is historically Honda's largest market. Second, Honda has been doing business in the United Kingdom for a long time and, thus, has the existing infrastructure such as the manufacturing plant in Swindon.

Asics, a global sporting goods company, is headquartered in Kobe. Its core business is the manufacture and sale of "performance-driven" athletic shoes, technical active sports apparel and equipment. These are primarily sold under two basic brands: Asics for the athletic shoes, sports apparel and accessories and Onitsuka Tiger for the sport fashion label for retro shoes of the 40s, 50s, 60s and 70s.

With its head office based in Japan, Asics identifies three key regions worldwide: Japan, Europe and the United States. About half of global sales in 2006 were made in Japan, followed by 30 per cent in Europe and roughly 20 per cent in the United States.

Realizing the importance of the highly competitive global sports and apparel market, Asics faced the challenge of repositioning its products and its brand in 2004. It developed a five-year management plan, the Asics Challenge Plan, which aims to "transform the corporation to a global enterprise with emphasis on three domains, namely: athletic sports, sports style, and health/comfort.[4] Its consolidated net sales are targeted to reach ¥300 billion (€2.26 billion) by 2011 with one-third sourced from overseas operations. The global initiative is to focus on final retail sales rather than distributor sales. Asics views technology and research and development as critical factors in augmenting its brand awareness in the industry as a whole.

Asics then organized its regions based on geographic groupings and cultural similarities (see Figure 7.2). The global headquarters in Kobe is responsible for the larger domestic Japanese market. The three regional headquarters are Europe, the Americas and Oceania.

Asics Europe, the regional headquarters, is located in the Netherlands. Its regional structure follows the mix of single market and subregional approach as described in Chapter 3 above. There are 18 European subsidiaries and offices as shown in Figure 7.3. The Middle East, Africa or South Africa and similar emerging markets are directly managed by Asics Europe.[5] Asics Italy will serve as the subregional headquarters for Bulgaria, Croatia and Romania till 2010.[6] In October 2005, the Austrian subsidiary was established to handle the expansion of Asics into Eastern European markets such as Slovenia, Hungary, the Czech Republic and Slovakia. Similarly, Asics Spain was established in 2005, and it is possible it will serve as the subregional headquarters for Portugal.

The regional functions of Asics Europe are organized in a matrix system of functions interfaced with the different product domains of apparel, equipment and footwear (see Figure 7.4). The functions as defined in the matrix

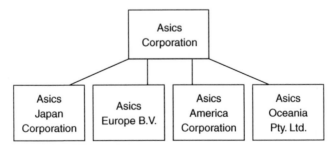

Figure 7.2   Global corporate structure of Asics

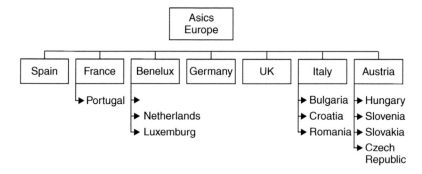

Figure 7.3   Asics Europe regional structure

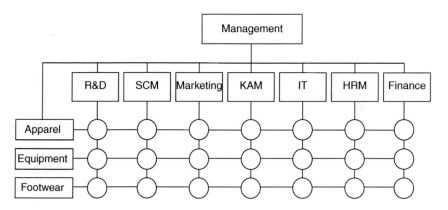

Figure 7.4   Matrix structure of Asics

are research and development, supply chain management, marketing, key account management, information technology, finance and human resources. Asics Europe as a regional headquarters serves as a "facilitator" between the product domains and the functional groups.[7]

In order to streamline its segregated business operations and become more resourceful, Asics underwent a centralization process in 2006 by consolidating administrative and supporting functions. Selective tasks of functional areas like marketing and finance were gradually consolidated at Asics Europe. The objective of this European Centralization process was to free up the local subsidiaries from redundant administrative functions and concentrate on marketing and sales functions.

Asics Europe has a free hand, that is, independence to operate. The head office in Japan does not have direct control or influence on the European regional operations except over matters referred back by the functional regional managers. Once the budget for Asics Europe has been set and agreed with head office, then Asics Europe acts autonomously.

Unlike Honda, the European regional headquarters for Asics is located in the Netherlands. Asics Europe was previously located in Germany, but the office was eventually relocated due to the advantageous business and labour environment in the Netherlands. These benefits are an acceptable corporate tax system, transportation logistics with the Rotterdam shipping yard and the international airport, less restrictive labour law requirements, the personnel pool is fluent in English as compared to Germany and, finally, most competitors have located their European headquarters here.

Astellas Pharma, headquartered in Tokyo, is one of Japan's largest pharmaceutical companies. Its global product portfolio focuses on the areas of transplantation, urology, cardiology, dermatology, immunology and infectious diseases. The European core products are concentrated in the areas of transplantation, urology and dermatology.

Astellas Pharma was formed by a defensive merger of two Japanese companies, Yamanouchi and Fujisawa, in an attempt to survive the competitive global race in the pharmaceutical industry. Since then, the company's objective is to be a "global company" in its core product areas. In 2007, Astellas consolidated sales stood at ¥973 billion (€1.33 billion) of which Japan contributes 52 per cent, followed by the United State (20 per cent), Europe (25.1 per cent) and Asia (2.9 per cent).

Competitive advantage in the pharmaceutical industry is based primarily on the product. The product components are basically the same worldwide. What differs is the written indication or the dosage instructions. Each country in Europe has its own Drug Approval Authority, and each national authority has its own requirements about what should be written in the indication. Patents are, therefore, critical for Astellas to remain an industry leader in Japan or overseas.

Astellas Pharma's corporate message "Leading Light for Life" was developed at headquarters in Tokyo following the merger. This vision implies the delivery of "hope and elation to all who wish for a healthy life, a life supported by state-of-the-art science, technology and insight."[8] In 2006, Astellas Pharma, with its objective to be a global player in the pharmaceutical industry, faced the challenge of unifying the operations of two well-positioned companies in Japan and abroad. How did Astellas Pharma undertake this task – especially for the European market?

First, Astellas developed a new corporate culture. Mr Ohtani from the Internal Auditing of Astellas Europe says, "It's not the kind of top-down culture but we would like to create a more bottom-up culture." The core principles are then customized to the European environment.

We would create a very generic concept which would be applicable in each country. And after having that generic message, each manager or senior management would transfer it not in the language but in the culture of that country. (Mr Ohtani, Internal Auditing of Astellas Europe)

Second, Astellas Pharma identified the key markets for its global products. The corporate structure was then divided primarily into three geographic areas: Japan as headquarters and two regional headquarters in the United States (Astellas North America) and Europe (Astellas Europe). Astellas Europe, currently located in London, was divided by market size and by managerial factors. Market size is defined by the sales volume in the larger countries. The smaller markets are grouped in order to allow them a better presence at the regional level.

There are 18 local subsidiaries under the Astellas Europe (see Figure 7.5). The five largest markets, namely, Germany, United Kingdom, Italy, France and Spain have a country general manager located in London. The high growth potential of emerging markets such as Poland, the Czech Republic and Slovakia deserves recognition and is grouped into a specific region. A regional director will be in charge of the marketing issues in those countries. Similarly, the established but smaller markets like Switzerland, Austria, Portugal and others are grouped as one region with one regional director. In addition, Africa is considered as part of Europe. There is only one subsidiary

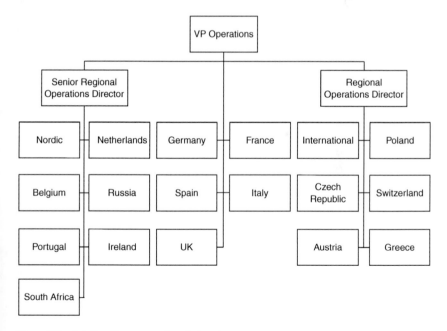

Figure 7.5   Astellas Europe regional structure
Source: Astellas Annual Report.

in South Africa, and this is grouped under the International subsidiary. All the regional directors are located or have offices in London.

We can classify Astellas Europe's regional structure as a mix of single market and subregional approach.

Astellas Europe is responsible primarily for overseeing marketing and sales. The administrative and information management functions combined with controlling are also centralized here. The local subsidiaries control the direct contact with customers through its marketing and sales effort. Human Resources are, however, localized to each country. The HR managers report to a Human Resources senior vice president in Astellas Europe through a matrix organization. However, R&D and manufacturing are directly controlled by Astellas Pharma headquarters in Japan.

Similar to Honda and Asics, Astellas Pharma utilizes a matrix structure to allow the local subsidiary functional managers to interact directly with the regional functional managers in Astellas Europe (see Figure 7.6). These national functional managers have a dual reporting line to the regional managers as well as to the country manager.

The board members of Astellas Europe include two executives from Astellas Pharma Japan as well as senior executives from the development, finance and corporate group. There will be one other board member from Astellas Europe or a subsidiary.

Prior to the merger, Yamanouchi had its regional headquarters in Leiderdorp, the Netherlands, and Fujisawa had its regional headquarters in Munich, Germany. Post merger, Astellas Europe established the European

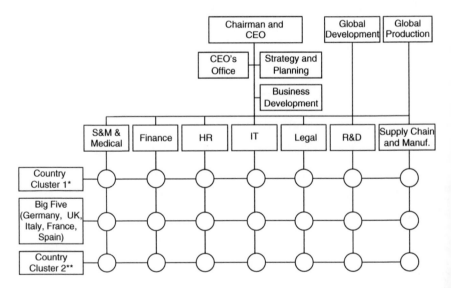

Figure 7.6   Matrix structure of Astellas Europe

regional centre in London. Essentially, London was selected because it is the seat for the European Authority for Drug Development (EADD), which approves the new products, maintains the high quality standards of the products and regulates the industry in the region. Another reason is that Astellas Pharma Japan realized that talent could be readily sourced in England, and it was easier to speak in English than German or Dutch.

In summary, the global corporate structure of the three Japanese MNCs defines their respective regional headquarters approaches for their European operations. The Japanese national culture combined with external factors such as industry regulations and the diversity of consumer preferences in Europe affect the corporate regional structures. In their need to be responsive, a matrix structure grouped by product domain and/or functional business units is then interfaced with the regional headquarters.

Value activities within and across the region

Research and development

How do the three Japanese MNCs maintain their direct control over R&D and obtain feedback directly from the consumers? That is the challenge that Honda, Asics and Astellas Pharma face today.

We observed that the research and development for Honda, Asics and Astellas is centralized at headquarters in Japan. The basic technology for new products is discovered within the "controlled" environment in Tokyo or Kobe. Thus, the main creative discoveries and new scientific and technical developments in terms of processes, materials and mixtures are normally centralized in Japan. During the research phase, initial feedback from the regional groups and subsidiaries is important for the final product. Product adaptation is undertaken closer to the local markets at the regional or country level. The local subsidiaries and/or branches in Europe are responsible for the customizing the product in terms of style, colour, packaging and physical design. An exception would be the automobile development in Honda USA's R&D centre.

As mentioned, Honda's research and development division is divided into separate subsidiaries to provide technicians the liberty to pursue their scientific and creative engineering designs. The process of research for a new model is about three to four years. The base production technological "discovery" is normally initiated in Japan and/or the United States. Product-related development is carried out at the R&D subsidiaries in Japan, the United States and Germany. "The core research and development for major foundations of a car, platform like engines and transmissions, these are done in Japan. Adaptations to a major degree are done locally" (Simon Sumita, Director, PR Division Honda Europe).

This is then discussed with the respective regional headquarters and sub-regional offices.

Direct contact with the local supplier network is important during the product development phase for the maintenance of product quality and costs.

> In the U.K., because the R&D centres are situated at the same premises as our factory, the main function is to transfer or to nurture the local parts manufacturers and teach what we require in terms of quality, in terms of consistency in quality and having R&D help as they can go out to suppliers, talk to the engineers directly and that helps us to get better parts and better consistency and better delivery and that makes better cars for the factory. So these maybe help increase and maintain the locally delivered parts. In our R&D centre in Germany, they're into design. In addition to car design, they also do some adaptive engineering things like engines and drive train components. But in Europe we are still not capable of designing cars from scratch like they do in the US. ... We still have room to grow in terms of capability in R&D in Europe. (Simon Sumita, Director, PR Division, Honda Europe)

The research and development for Asics is centralized in Japan. R&D comprises about 1 to 2 per cent of global sales. Product development for materials, product functions and technical processes for athletic shoes, which normally takes between nine to twelve months, is managed out of Japan. The product development for apparel and accessories is located at the regional headquarters in Europe. In 2006, there was an attempt to centralize all R&D functions for all products in Kobe.

New products for footwear are developed in Kobe. The initial concept is normally presented to the subsidiaries that have the highest sales potential for a specific product category. Feedback from the local subsidiaries regarding product attributes for the local target segment and regional characteristics influence the final design and function of the new product. Discussions are held at regular product meetings among the R&D team and the local managers. Product samples are designed in Kobe and the features such as fitting, flexibility, cushioning and gripping are evaluated and compared with competitors. Product testing is undertaken regionally. Feedback is then given back to the R&D central in Kobe through the regional R&D and marketing managers. Product design is finalized in Asics headquarters; but the product adaptation, such as physical features and colour preferences, are handled at the regional level.

In order to maintain its competitive advantage, patent procurement for its know-how on material and technical design processes are part of Asics R&D strategy.

Research and development for Astellas Pharma is also centralized in Japan. The gestation period for research of pharmaceutical medicines takes about ten years or more. The development phase is more medium term oriented, taking about five years. Research and clinical trials are two different businesses. Licensing can help expand the global product portfolio of Astellas.

Research activities are now concentrated in the central laboratories in Japan. Development activities primarily in the form of clinical trials are decentralized and located in Japan, the US and Europe. And right now, most of our products or projects are starting the first human trials here in Europe. This is based upon a European global unified protocol. (Mr Ohtani, Internal Auditing, Astellas Europe)

The development centres for Astellas Europe are located in Munich and the Netherlands.

Astellas Pharma organized a global R&D committee that focuses on the development of products. Regular meetings are held between the committee and Astellas Europe in London. If a project arises in the European R&D centre, and it is discussed as part of the agenda of the global development committee, then Astellas Europe could ask Astellas Pharma Japan for financial support for the regional marketing program. In the event there are very locally oriented projects (such as in the subsidiaries), then it is possible to use the resources of R&D centres in Europe. These would primarily be development projects.

In addition, Astellas is involved in a network research system.

We have tons of research collaborations with institutions or other companies all over the world. So, right now, maybe hundred of the research collaborations are ongoing within our research group. So of course research work is controlled by headquarters and those kinds of insights or new findings are shared among the regional areas. (Senior Marketing Manager, Astellas Europe)

The cross-Atlantic relationship between the United States and Europe is important for Astellas Pharma in the testing phase. It is easier for the company to be considered as one chemical entity and as one group than to start and pass human trial studies as separate units in the United States or Europe rather than only in Japan. This facilitates access to a wider spectrum of individuals for testing purposes as well as shortens the amount of time to complete the testing phase.

The licensing of products is handled at both the corporate headquarters and regional headquarters levels. Astellas Europe has a business development group. Identifying the opportunity could originate from the head office in Tokyo and "sometimes a local subsidiary finds a good candidate to license for the global markets," according to Mr Sakurai of the Corporate Development group of Astellas Pharma Japan.

In terms of product development, the centres are located in Munich and the Netherlands with a direct reporting line to the global R&D function at Astellas Pharma Japan. Astellas Europe also supports the administrative needs for the R&D centre in the Netherlands.

Sourcing/procurement

Sourcing of raw materials among the three Japanese MNCs differs due to the difference in the product mechanics and industry infrastructure. Honda has a decentralized system while Astellas has a global sourcing system. Asics, on the other hand, has the option to source globally but benefits from cost-efficient suppliers concentrated in the Far East. Each company had to identify its own suppliers depending on the requirements of the production as well as the location of such suppliers. In the case of Honda, the localized suppliers are partners in developing its car models and in maintaining the quality as well as the consistency in the performance of its cars. Athletic footwear as produced by Asics is highly technical and, thus, quality control of the supplier is critical. The quality of raw material is an even stronger factor for Astellas because its products deal with human life.

In Honda, more than 70 per cent of a car's component parts are out-sourced. The choice of a supplier is contingent on the car component part's quality and cost level. A local R&D presence in the same location as the factory is essential. In the United Kingdom, Honda has both an R&D subsidiary and a production facility. This is essential because the R&D technician can communicate directly with the supplier. The supplier becomes part of the team to find a solution to the defective part.

> Cars with wrong parts or defective parts just cannot be done because that results in a delay in output. The relationship is always better when things are closer. And that's why we have R&D supporting the Swindon plant (U.K.), because if something is wrong, they can take the blue print and the engineers from the factory can go to the supplier and say, "Can you fix that, how can we fix this problem?" This communication is imperative in creating quality, constant quality for our company. (Simon Sumita, Director PR Division, Honda Europe)

Most of Asics's production is outsourced to manufacturing facilities located in China, Vietnam, Korea and Taiwan for cost reasons. Product fabrication is developed in more than 1,000 production plants worldwide. Asics delivers the final material to the manufacturing facilities in order to protect its technical know-how.

Most of the products are then shipped from the Far East to Rotterdam. The goods are then sent via third party distribution companies or forwarded to Neuss, Germany, which is the central European Distribution Centre. Other industry specialists regard Asics as "one of the best suppliers in terms of customer service and quick deliveries in Germany" in terms of this distribution centre.

Astellas Pharma's sourcing for top-quality substances is undertaken on a global basis. In 2006, Astellas wanted to centralize procurement of items as much as possible. This, however, is not simple to establish due to the broad spectrum of vendors and the regulatory standard set by the pharmaceutical authorities in each region such as Europe. Furthermore, Mr Ohtani, Internal Auditing, Astellas Europe, explains, "It's not a matter of nationality of the vendors. It's a matter of the quality of the matter."

Production

The production for the three Japanese companies tends to be decentralized. It was important for Honda to have manufacturing facilities in different regions due to the heterogeneous demands of car drivers in Europe. The closer the production plant is to the customer, the easier it is to customize car models. Similarly, Astellas has decentralized production because the European market has different types of medicinal needs as compared to Japan and the United States.

The manufacturing facilities of Honda are located primarily in Japan, Canada, Thailand, United Kingdom and the United States. Although the major car parts are sourced in-house, a large portion of the car components is outsourced.

> The suppliers, the engineers, the technology development team and the production team work together to come up with the best solution ... typical model cycle is 4–5 years, we probably work with the suppliers for about 7 years. So 3 to 4 years before the model is launched they know exactly what they need to design and to produce. We know what we can expect and if that component part is close to our target. (Mr Sumita, Director of PR Division, Honda Europe)

As mentioned, Asics normally produces its high-performance sports footwear in factories in the Far East.

At Astellas, production is centralized and controlled at the European regional headquarters. There is a vice president for production and a branch office in the Netherlands. The firm has six plants in Europe, and each plant has a separate responsibility. In Ireland, there are three different plants. The Dublin plant produces a chemical compound material for the final products manufactured in the Netherlands factory.

Marketing and product standardization/adaptation

The heterogeneous market infrastructure in Europe affects the product portfolio of the three Japanese MNCs. In most cases, the basic product such as the car, the footwear and the core compound remains the same globally. What differs are the product attributes. The challenge for the companies is how best to bring its respective products to the local markets and at the same time be responsive to the differences in each of those markets. Each company has tried to address this issue by decentralizing marketing and sales. The subsidiaries or branches are given the "free hand" to develop their own advertising campaigns. In general, headquarters in Japan provides a global corporate design such as a logo, corporate product colours or slogan. In the case of Asics, there did not seem to be sufficient marketing competence initially at head office. The regional marketing manager at the European regional headquarters had to develop marketing guidelines for the European subsidiaries and even specific concepts such as the "shop-in-shop" program. Eventually the head office in Japan did respond to this problem and organized a global marketing team to develop and create a global marketing strategy. It is interesting to note, too, how the transfer of knowledge from European regional headquarters motivated the head office in Japan to resolve this problem.

Marketing in Honda is largely decentralized and is the responsibility of the subsidiaries and/or branches. The subregional headquarters and Honda Europe merely oversee the subsidiaries and handle some marketing tasks. Pricing is controlled at the regional headquarters level. There is, however, a global marketing concept and key messages originated from the head office in Tokyo. "The colours are specified and dealer signs are specified, but the way of advertisement itself, the design or style of advertisement can be varied by each operation" (Satoshi Aoki, Deputy General Manager, Honda Japan).

Because the regulatory environment within the countries in Europe is similar, product variation within the region is primarily market driven. The customer demand for cars in the European market is highly diversified. The cars are technically the same but the product features differ as shown in the model lineup.

> The market preferences are totally different between our Nordic group and the southern part of Europe. Even in our group of 7 countries, you can find something in common and also something not common. That is why it is not easy to find a common product. The preference for the car body colour itself and even the snow fall is totally different. In the Nordic region we do mind a lot about the performance of the car. (Mr Matsuda, President, Honda Nordic)

Another example is the preference of the subregion Honda Motors North for "top laid" cars where price is not an issue. Customers in the subregion Honda Motors South demand more economical and cheaper cars.

The dealership network is critical for the profitability of Honda's European operation.

> We want our dealers to improve their image, their presentation, the quality of business. As a manufacturer we have to bring in a good quality

products to enhance this overall image of a Japanese premium brand. (Mr Yokohama, President, Honda Czech Republic)

Honda Europe and the subregional headquarters will not say too much about what the local national subsidiaries should do. The local subsidiaries are responsible for creating programs to motivate their respective dealers and how to manage the local competition through advertising or through pricing strategy.

So the product is pan-European. But the place, the dealers – the dealer development is one of the most important businesses in our operations. Without strong dealers, you will never be strong. ... When you think that one of the core important businesses in sales and marketing is how to have good quality dealers, then one of the answers is that you have to make good decisions at local country level to improve dealer operations. (Mr Yohoyama, President, Honda Czech Republic)

In 2005, a global marketing team was established by Asics Japan to develop a corporate marketing strategy. The head office also handles the local marketing function for Japan as a whole. A global branding strategy was developed by Strawberryfrog[9] in 2006 and launched in 2007. The new logo presents "a brand with a faster, modern feel" and a corporate slogan "sound mind, sound body."[10] The marketing strategy also focuses on the "Made in Japan" concept.

The current global marketing structure is a response to the needs voiced from the European regional operations. In 2005, there was only one person in the whole firm who had more than ten years' marketing experience.

The regional marketing team developed the marketing corporate guidelines for the region. It was inevitable that Asics Japan had to set up a long-term solution and anchor its marketing competence in Kobe.

In addition, global campaigns are created and launched concurrently with each new season collection in a market. Local advertising agencies then revise specific promotions for the local market as defined by the global brand guidelines developed by Strawberryfrog.

Asics is a product-focused company. Brand awareness for Asics products is high in Japan but not in Europe and the United States. Asics Europe is responsible for overseeing that the Asics brand image is strengthened throughout the region.

Asics Europe plays a critical role in product adaptation. It gathers the feedback from the subsidiaries, which are inputs for the customization of the footwear product for the markets; for example, the German sport market is functional and performance oriented. Thus, high-performance products and the technical process is an important consideration for the running footwear. The Italian and French markets, on the other hand, are more oriented towards fashion and lifestyle, resulting in products that are style or design oriented. The difference in demand results in different sports shoe models for the north and the south.

Sponsoring is an important marketing tool for Asics. Mr Onitsuka, the founder of Asics, built the company through sponsorship. To date, Asics sponsors several events such as the Olympics, the New York Marathon and smaller local community events.

We observed that Astellas's products are more standardized compare to Honda and Asics. The pharmaceutical industry is highly regulated and requires full compliance with the requirements of the national regulatory authorities or by the European Agency for the Evaluation of Medicinal Products (EMEA). New medicinal products go through a rigid review process prior to market launch. The pharmaceuticals are evaluated in three criteria of quality, security/safety and efficacy. The review includes an intensive look at the R&D procedure even before human trials are allowed. Risk factor ratios during the testing phase are evaluated, and the drug's success factors are weighed against such risks. Therefore, the marketing for pharmaceutical products is tied to the success of Astellas to obtain approval from the proper regulatory authorities.

Astellas has a global marketing department located in Tokyo headquarters. The department is responsible for creating a global brand concept and a global principal marketing strategy. For example, attendance at a major medical conference is coordinated company wide and attendance is open to all essential persons.

Licensing products from other pharmaceutical companies is "maybe 20 per cent to 30 per cent of our development projects" as described by Mr Sakurai, manager, Corporate Development of Astellas Japan. The licensing of products is handled at both the headquarters and regional headquarter levels. Astellas Europe has a business development group. Sometimes a local subsidiary finds a good candidate to license for the global markets and vice versa. Information originates from the relationship and network of individuals.

> So, sometimes, those opportunities come from the subsidiary side. And sometimes our top management may have some good relationship with other companies. They may initiate such discussion and give it to the licensing group to proceed with those processes. And of course literature search is another source and another source is the congress or those scientific meetings. (Mr Sakurai, Manager Corporate Development, Astellas Japan)

Astellas global products have a unified brand concept and brand image. A joint team is organized between the United States, Japan and Europe for one brand for a global symposium or exhibition. There is direct contact between the head office in Japan and the regional headquarters in the United States and Europe that prevents discrepancy on the product brand image or the marketing concept in general.

Co-branding of products is also common in the pharmaceutical industry. A co-promotional deal can be with one category like antibiotics that deals directly with one company like Pfizer USA.

Each country or authority requires a specific type of packaging and information pamphlet. "For instance the US final product has a US oriented packaging and package inside that is not applicable to the European countries and vice versa" (Mr Ohtani, Internal Auditing Astellas Europe).

Management challenges

Relationship between headquarters, regional headquarters and local subsidiaries

Honda Japan's guiding corporate principles define the corporate strategy and ultimately the pan-regional strategy for Europe. The CEO at Honda Europe has complete autonomy. "Right now our structure is such that we have enough authority. All 6 regional headquarters worldwide, such as Honda Europe, are given sub autonomy" (Mr Sumita, Director for PR, Honda Europe).

The role of Honda Europe is to develop the regional strategies. These are so-called high-level strategies, such as increasing market share, achieving customer satisfaction or reducing global warming. "Then based on those regional strategies each subsidiary is responsible to develop their own local strategy which is in line with the total European strategy" (Mr Matsuda, President, Honda Nordic).

The autonomy of Honda Europe and subregional headquarters is curtailed by the agreed budget. The annual budget is broken down into monthly plans and provides sales targets that should be reached. Should there be a change in operating activity that requires more investment, a revised budget is negotiated in midyear or sometime in July.

Subregional headquarters have an administrative and supporting role. "We have a very clear definition of the role and responsibility between Honda Europe and our office here at Honda Nordic" (Mr Matsuda, President Honda Nordic).

Honda's subregional headquarters managers claim that all subsidiaries are treated equally by Honda Europe. Duplication in certain administrative and functional tasks exists within the hierarchy.

As mentioned, subregional headquarters have the flexibility to resolve intercountry issues such as overspending.

Sometimes certain markets are overspent and certain markets are under spent. As long as our total region is ok on the line, we can say ok. ... We can enjoy a very flexible and speedy discussion among ourselves without mentioning the issue to Honda Europe in London. (Mr Matsuda, President, Honda Nordic)

Subregional headquarters do not have a direct contact with Honda Japan. All issues are directed to Honda Europe. Subsidiaries within a subregional headquarters do contact each other in specific cases.

In Asics, final decisions/rulings for the strategic issues are normally decided by the board of directors. The European board consists of a group of managing directors who are part of the daily operations of the regional business as well as the CFO and COO in Japan. The former managing director of Asics Europe also sits in the board of Asics Japan as the global marketing person and as the director for overseas business.

To get top head office management support on regional issues, it is essential to identify the right persons within the Asics Japan corporate structure who have the power to execute decisions.

Even people with top positions in a Japanese company do not automatically execute this power on a daily basis. They are very sensitive and cautious to avoid any conflict. That is how you are trained under Japanese management. You should always avoid asking clear recommendations to a Japanese superior in a group environment because they will never speak out. They will seldom choose a position in front of a large group. One to one they can be quite clear. They would prefer someone like me to state the idea or decision to the group and they would like to see what the group reaction will be. It is after listening and observing that they, the top manager, will take a position. (Senior Sales Executive, Asics Europe)

Conflicts arising between regional markets such as knockouts and pricing differences are referred back to head office. As a senior marketing executive says: "Most of the time we go to headquarters in Japan and ask them can you please tell the US to control the inventory."

Asics Europe is responsible for managing the European operations. Regional functional managers have direct contact with the functional managers at Asics Japan. Top management in Asics Japan is primarily focused on the domestic Japanese market, which produces 50 per cent of corporate sales. As such, Asics Europe senior managers have a high level of independence in running its regional business operations. "There are not always Japanese that look over our shoulder to question what we do or want to challenge it" (Senior Sales Executive, Asics Europe).

In selective functional areas, the responsibilities for the European-based regional functional managers are not clearly outlined, resulting in conflicts with the national functional managers in the subsidiaries.

In the event there is a need to interact with other subsidiaries, local subsidiaries are instructed to communicate only via Asics Europe. Direct contact with other subsidiaries is discouraged.

Astellas Japan's general corporate strategy is normally filtered down to the regional headquarters in general policies and further fragmented into country policies. Take an example of the marketing policy.

> We should create a common marketing concept of each product. After creating a brand image or a brand concept, those concepts should be translated into each country's language or each country's business area or each country's Medicare system, etc. Therefore after finishing the branding of one product, that product should be handed from the regional European headquarter to subsidiary marketers. And those marketers would start to develop the customized business strategy for targeting the national audience or network while maximizing profit. (Mr Ohtani, Internal Auditing. Astellas Europe)

Similar to Honda and Asics, Astellas Europe commits to a budget and agrees to contribute to the global profitability. "Under the budget we are enjoying the full autonomy, but if we are obliged to use more money than the agreed budget, we should invite the approval from the Tokyo headquarters" (Mr Ohtani, Internal Auditing, Astellas Europe).

This is no difference between the relationship between Astellas Europe and the local subsidiaries. Local country managers are required to commit each year to Astellas Europe's profit objective. This happens at the beginning of each financial period. The national budget amount is then reported to Astellas Europe, and this information is further consolidated in the global corporate budget.

In Astellas Europe, standardizing policies or processes is difficult to implement at the subsidiary level for various reasons. Each country manager is, therefore, allowed the flexibility and the independence to adapt policies in his country for as long he reaches the agreed committed target/budget. "If a German subsidiary would like to incorporate an incentive scheme it would be alright if that incentive scheme would contribute to the committing bottom line" (Mr Ohtani, Internal Auditing, Astellas Europe).

In other words, the country manager in each subsidiary can manage the local subsidiary, and the means by which he achieves the budget is up to him. The local country manager's success in achieving such budget commitments is a result of his so-called management autonomy and lack of conflict or tension with Astellas Europe.

Span of control

The three companies maintain their own flair and Japanese style of management. In some cases, this results in conflicts among the European regional headquarters, subregional headquarters, the local subsidiaries and branches of the companies.

Honda's top management prefers to maintain a tightly knit Japanese culture at the head office. Despite Honda's global presence, control is maintained in several facets of its operating business such as in the origination and development of engineering and technical ideas. Furthermore, senior management positions at both Tokyo headquarters and regional head positions are Japanese. The company prefers to maintain its national culture at the highest echelon of the firm for better communication and strategic decision-making.

> [In Honda] there is totally no motivation for the local ... If you want to learn about product marketing, you start working with Honda for two years and then go some other place. They say Honda is a training school for the business. (Satoshi Aoki, Deputy General Manager, Honda Japan)

Non-Japanese persons will have to work hard to break the glass ceiling of homogeneity maintained within the executive positions of the company.

Asics's headquarters executives and the regional heads are Japanese. The CEO of Asics Europe normally has a tour of three to four years, and then he is repatriated back to Japan. There are a total of approximately 60 persons at the regional office, most of whom are Europeans or local Dutch. With its objective to be a "global company" post merger, Asics management is open minded and flexible to consider having heterogeneous a mixture of Japanese and local senior executives in the future.

Currently, Astellas senior management positions at headquarters and the regional headquarters, such as the CEO and the finance director, are held primarily by Japanese. However, the "creative" positions, which require basic knowledge of the local countries, are non-Japanese. Mr Sakurai, a manager for Corporate Planning at Astellas Japan says, "Of course at staff level, we have non-Japanese but not in management." The senior managers in Astellas Europe in London are mostly Japanese. There are several non-Japanese persons at both the senior and middle management levels. The subsidiaries' senior positions are normally headed by a local national.

When a local country manager, say a French or Italian, visits the regional offices in London, he may be confronted primarily by Japanese senior executives. It may seem that local subsidiary country managers face a "glass ceiling" at the both the regional and head office level. This, however, is not corporate policy of Astellas Japan.

> Our top management policy is the best person for best position. Who cares about nationality? Let's say one French manager will be so successful and we think that he is the best person for the European regional headquarters ... we may recommend him to be in that position. And sooner

or later we will change the current management at each regional head-quarters position to be localized. (Senior Manager, Corporate Planning, Astellas Japan)

Decision making

Leadership and the decision-making process in the West are normally straightforward, direct and immediate. This does not work in a typical Japanese company, which prefers a nonconfrontational, consensus style of decision making. The consensus style is a democratic group decision where all managers partake in the decision process. It is time consuming because it requires the approval or implicit "signature" of everyone involved in the project, product or region. The final decision is always a "compromise of ideas."

> Our leadership is to listen to the European managers and make a compromise by taking a lot of time. And that compromise sometimes loses its original initiative and its idea, although it is understood by all of them...you listen to your staffs' opinion quite a lot. (Satoshi Aoki, Deputy Manager, Honda Japan)

Under the Japanese management style, leadership means taking into account the opinion of the group and then taking the responsibility for the compromised decision. The final decision is then a form of commitment that the leader, in this case the CEO or the managing director of the regional headquarters, takes as his own. If the plan or process fails, then he has to go. This is sometimes referred to as "hara-kiri." A public apology is made by the Japanese leader and then a resignation is expected.

Most of the conflicts for local country managers arise due to the misunderstanding of the Japanese style of responsibility, commitment to the company values and the consensus decision-making process.

Communication and language

We observed that communication in terms of personal contact (face to face, written or verbal) is an important ingredient for relaying messages for the three Japanese MNCs. It is one way by which headquarters can gather information regarding the performance of its regional headquarters and, subsequently, the subsidiaries or branches.

Although regular meetings are aimed at sharing knowledge and best practices, the level of importance given to such meetings differs considerably.

Honda encourages meetings among the functional areas.

> In order to make sure that each subsidiary is in line with the corporate goal, etc., each function has a periodical meeting. We don't know

how often we have this kind of meeting, it depends on the situation. (Mr Matsuda, President, Honda Nordic)

The subregional headquarters have regular monthly meetings to discuss the strategic goals for Europe. In these meetings, there are general budget discussions followed by a variance analysis six months later. Adjustments to the budgetary needs of each subregional headquarters are then made. Otherwise, the subregional headquarters has no contact with its corresponding counterpart in Honda Motors North or Honda Motors South.

Meetings between Honda Europe and the subregional headquarters occur regularly.

In Asics, product management meetings are held twice a year for three days. There are standardized meetings for marketing managers from the largest subsidiaries in February, April, July and October. In Europe, there are sales meetings every six months. Financial budgeting and planning meetings are also held about twice a year.

Four times a year I share a European Key Account meeting. So every 3 months we come together and we discuss a range of topics to exchange information such as what is going on ... just to exchange the knowledge and to get regular information on key accounts which does not automatically come out of financial reporting lines. At the same time we share best practices and how key accounts can be better managed at the regional level. The meeting creates a better group feeling. (Senior Sales Executive, Asics Europe)

As Astellas Japan completes its integration process post merger, communication plays a key role in preventing conflicts and tension that may arise between the local country managers and Astellas Europe. Continuous communication and explicit communication is seen as a critical step in this phase of the merger.

Therefore the way of the communication is to have the number of face-to-face meetings in the current changing situation. The regional management teams are touring around in the European countries frequently and they are visiting the subsidiaries, getting to know the personnel and discussing the responsibility between the regional headquarters and the general managers. (Senior Marketing Manager, Astellas Europe)

The regional heads come together once a month to Astellas Japan or meet in London. There are also periodic board meetings to learn what is currently happening in the market and what the decisions are. In addition, periodic meetings are held by functional groups in Japan. As one example, the licensing group of Astellas Europe had the global licensing meeting for three days in Japan. The Human Resources and Finance groups have the same type of meetings.

Outside the Japanese head office, English is the official business language for all three companies. Most company documents are in English, but head office documents are primarily in Japanese. The Japanese executives assigned as heads at the regional headquarters realize that Europe is multi-lingual. This challenge is a big task for these Japanese executives because often they find themselves reporting back to headquarters in Japanese. They themselves are aware that each language, in this case English and Japanese, has its own idiosyncrasies in meaning and implications that are not directly translatable in certain business situations. Below are issues highlighted by senior managers with regards to language.

> [In Honda] top management positions are normally held by the Japanese executives in Europe and the USA. The most important decisions are made in the head office Japan, information sharing wise. This is the difference in the role of responsibility in Japanese management and in local management because especially in Europe for us (Japanese) it is almost impossible to have the full capability of the local languages. (Mr Matsuda, President, Honda Nordic)

When a report needs to be issued, one can be written in Japanese and the other in English. "Both have a slightly different meaning in the way of expression. That's how the conflict starts in day-to-day operations" (Satoshi Aoki, Deputy General Manager, Honda Japan).

A regional manager for marketing at Asics explained another type of language barrier.

> What can be a problem is, because we naturally have many meetings is the phenomenon of 20 people in one room; of which ten are Japanese. Five understand English fluently. When the other five do not speak English and the Europeans do not speak Japanese communication is difficult. (Senior Marketing Executive, Asics Europe)

In Astellas, the strategic plan is developed first in Japanese. All communication is in Katakana and then later translated and transmitted to the global network in English.

> So after compiling this midterm plan,... be one big midterm plan, Mr. Sakurai is going to interpret the English version, to all over the world. And we don't care about the discussion either Japanese or English, but of course the majority of the management is Japanese, it's easy for us to discuss in Japanese. (Mr Hatanaka, Director Corporate Planning, Astellas Japan)

Communication conflicts arise resulting from the multitiered translation. Some Japanese expressions cannot be translated or transposed into its real meaning. English-speaking experts are often hired to translate ideas or issues exactly as intended. But there is always a slight difference in the understanding and interpretation by some local managers who are not as fluent in English themselves.

Conclusion

For companies going west from their country of origin in Japan, we observed that there is value added for the three Japanese MNCs when a regional headquarters was established in well-chosen sites in Europe. All three MNCs aimed to be global players in their respective industries and, therefore, faced the challenge to create a business structure that would address their needs. Honda Motors developed a subregional approach for its regional headquarters in an attempt to have an equilibrium between its global integration and local responsiveness. Asics established a regional corporate structure using a combination of the single market and subregional approach driven by cost efficiency and market similarity. Astellas Pharma is a product of a merger that had resources and management in place. Its challenge was to find a regional corporate structure that would maximize the utilization of existing resources and redefine economies of scale. Astellas Pharma created a regional structure using single market and subregional approach due to market size and managerial factors.

We further observed that problems and conflicts could arise between the head office in Japan and the regional headquarters. Misunderstandings about the global strategy may occur due to the idiosyncrasies and misinterpretation of the Japanese style of management and culture. Honda Motors, Asics and Astellas Pharma still prefer to maintain tight control over their regional headquarters and their subsidiaries in Europe.

Part III

Selected Cases – the Best in Class

8
Learning from the Pharmaceutical Industry
Astellas – the European Challenge[*]

In 2007, Dr Bina Montemayor, senior partner of a large multinational consulting company stared absentmindedly at the display of her new notebook. She had just received an e-mail from Astellas's European Vice President for corporate strategy, Mr Tadashi Yukino, asking her to prepare some notes for the annual board meeting at Astellas's European headquarters in London. The e-mail explained that the board was especially interested in Dr Montemayor's assessment of Astellas's current European strategy and matrix management system, which had been newly introduced by Astellas' European Vice President and his team two years ago. Contrary to early enthusiasm, results of Astellas's regional strategy and design were disappointing: flat sales coupled with accelerated pressures from both local and international competitors raised questions about Astellas's strategic focus. Many analysts questioned whether it made sense for Astellas to pursue a regional integration strategy in a highly fragmented region such as Europe, which was clearly dominated by individual country markets such as Germany or France. The strategic problems were aggravated by organizational concerns: the double reporting system of Astellas's newly introduced matrix increased coordination efforts and was sagging employee motivation tremendously. The pressure was felt at all levels. As a result, Mr Yukino wrote, the board had to decide whether or not to put an end to Astellas's current strategy and design. However, before turning around Astellas's strategic and organizational plans, the board wanted to discuss Astellas's new strategic way in an open plenum discussion at the next board meeting in a few weeks.

---

[*] This case was written by Bodo B. Schlegelmilch and Björn Ambos, WU Vienna, Institute for International Marketing and Management. It is intended to be used as the basis for class discussion rather than to illustrate the effective or ineffective handling of administrative situations. The case was made possible by the cooperation of Astellas. The identities of the individuals mentioned in this case study have been disguised.

Recognizing Dr Montemayor's expertise and experience, the board wanted her to provide an evaluation of Astellas's European strategy and organization, including concrete proposals for possible changes.

Leaning back in her chair, Dr Montemayor wondered what she should reply. Why did they ask her? She already alerted some of Astellas's senior management to the potential dangers of Astellas's new management system and strategy. In her mind, there was no doubt that Astellas needed a regional strategy to strengthen its position in Europe. However, there was more than one way to skin a cat.

Background: Astellas – seeing synergy

When Yamanouchi, Japan's third largest pharmaceutical company, announced its plan to take over its rival Fujisawa Pharmaceutical to form Astellas Pharma in 2005, the world's big pharma companies were not exactly shaking with fear. Although Astellas was expected to become Japan's second-biggest drugmaker behind Takeda Chemical, it would just rank 15th internationally, with annual sales barely a seventh of those of Pfizer. Yet the merger showed that Japanese firms were increasingly being forced into defensive moves to bolster their international standing and expansion strategy. Hatsuo Aoki, chairman of Astellas Japan, stated that the principal factor behind the merger had been to fend off predators and enhance the new corporation's international competitiveness:

> In a sense our merger was defensive, but at the same time it was offensive. Astellas doesn't want to become the Japanese branch office of a multinational company – we want to be the global office of a global operation.

Like many advanced economies, Japan had been facing a crunch in its health-care spending since the early 1990s. The life expectancy of Japanese men and women had been the highest in the world for a decade and was continuing to rise, helped by good diets, a healthy lifestyle and an insurance-financed health-care system. By 2009, the average Japanese life expectancy was expected to approach 82 years, which compared favourably with developed-country peers like Germany, France and the United States. But as life expectancy had risen steadily, so too had health-care costs.[1] The striking demography had taken a financial toll, and rising health-care costs continued to put further pressure on the country's already creaking public finances, forcing Japan's government to act.[2]

In August 2002, Japan's Ministry of Health, Labor and Welfare initiated a series of reforms by articulating a new vision for the industry. No change could be achieved overnight, he acknowledged. But in order to contain spiralling health-care costs while at the same time creating an environment that would nurture productivity and innovation within domestic pharmaceutical manufacturers, several matters had to be addressed. One of them was the introduction of a government-mandated patient co-payment system that would reduce health-care spending among the increasingly aging Japanese population. The introduced reform aimed at discouraging the Japanese fondness for pill-popping and put pressure on pharma companies and doctors to hold down the price of drugs. As listing requirements had kept out most foreign competitors, domestic pharma firms had been able to extend their monopoly relations with the doctors and hospitals that prescribed their drugs. As a result, the Japanese had become some of the world's biggest pill-poppers, and cheap generics accounted for just 12 per cent of the market – compared with around 50 per cent in most other developed markets. Thanks to the co-payment system, drug prices fell by 6.3 per cent on average in 2002 and then again by a similar amount in 2004, pushing the industry into a slump.[3]

Nearly simultaneously, Japan's government began actively promoting international competition by opening the economy to foreign drug companies, not at least by harmonizing drug approval regulations with Europe and the US. It is clear, wrote the Ministry of Health, in a report titled "To Reinforce the Global Competitiveness of the Pharmaceutical Industry, Mainstay of the 'Century of Life' that:

> In contrast to the U.S., U.K., Switzerland and France, Japan has a multitude of pharmaceutical firms of a similar medium size. For Japanese companies to emulate their U.S. counterparts in using their home-based activities as a platform for overseas expansion an appropriate corporate size is called for.

The result was a nasty shock for Japanese pharma companies. Accustomed to sheltering behind protectionist barriers, most of them had ignored international expansion in the past. Traditionally, the cosy Japanese market allowed domestic companies to depend mainly on their home market to derive revenue growth and use license deals with foreign companies to gain access to new drugs. This changed rapidly under the new health-care system. Many Japanese pharma companies were dwarfed by some of the new foreign competitors moving into Japan, such as Pfizer, Merck and Roche of Switzerland (see Table 8.1).[4]

This all had been enough to frighten Japanese pharma firms out of their traditional rivalries into some overdue mergers, and one of them was Astellas. Astellas Pharma Inc. (Astellas) was established on 1 April 2005 through the historic merger of Yamanouchi and Fujisawa Pharmaceutical, Japan's third and fifth largest pharmaceutical companies.[5] Founded in 1894 in Osaka, Japan, Fujisawa had been one of the largest and oldest pharmaceutical manufacturers in Japan with strong international presence in the

Table 8.1   Japan pharmaceuticals market share per cent, 2005

2005 Ranking Japan	Company	Country	Global rank
1	Takeda	Japan	15
2	Pfizer	USA	1
3	Sankyo	Japan	26
4	Roche	Switzerland	9
5	Otsuka	Japan	24
6	Novartis	Switzerland	5
7	Daiichi	Japan	36
8	Eisai	Japan	20
9	Yamanouchi	Japan	33
10	Merck & Co	USA	3

Source: IMS MIDAS, 2006.

US pharma market – generating almost 20 per cent of its annual sales in the United States. Founded nearly 30 years later, Yamanouchi Pharmaceutical ranked third in Japan and had, like Fujisawa, developed a strong international business network, especially in Europe and Asia. Because of the two companies' complementary product ranges, regional concentrations and capabilities, logic of the merger had been acclaimed by both investors and pharmaceutical industry analysts. The merger was considered to be a positive step in the right direction for the two companies, and it was even expected to act as a kind of catalyst for further consolidations within the Japanese pharmaceutical industry.[6]

Although a new Japanese giant had been created, Astellas's freshly appointed CEO, Dr Takenaka, was well aware that two things would be especially important to secure the young company's success: As a scientist who had been deeply involved in R&D before he had been appointed president of former Yamanouchi Pharmaceutical, he firmly believed that a pharma company's success was directly related to its R&D pipeline and investment on the one hand and its global presence on the other. This conviction, he stressed in a later interview, was a major driver that pushed him when he had to decide for the merger between former Yamanouchi and Fujisawa. His central goal, he noted in a later interview, had been to create a research-driven pharmaceutical company with a promising R&D budget and a strong international standing that could easily catch up with global competitors such as Pfizer, Takeda, and Roche. He called it "the merger to win in global competition."

An internal company memo summarized the expected synergies as follows:

• Complementary R&D pipeline and product portfolio
• Reinforcement of sales and marketing capabilities in Japan
• Expansion of global presence

○ Acceleration of US market penetration
○ Enforcement of European operations
• Improvement of profitability by sales and cost synergy reform of corporate culture (creativity from bureaucracy)

The European pharmaceutical industry

Traditionally, the global pharmaceutical industry was characterized by rapid growth, high profits and structural stability (see Table 8.2). In 2005, global pharmaceutical sales reached USD565.9 billion with an annual growth rate of 6.9 per cent, which was slightly lower than the year before. North America accounted for 47 per cent of the total, while the European Union, which had similar demographics to the United States, accounted for 30 per cent, resembling an increase of 7.1 per cent over the previous year. Sales in Latin America grew an exceptional 18.5 per cent to USD24 billion, while Asia Pacific (outside of Japan) and Africa grew 11 per cent to USD46.4 billion. Japan, the world's third largest market, which had historically posted slower growth rates, performed strongly in 2005, growing 6.8 per cent to USD60.3 billion, its highest year-over-year growth since 1991 (see Table 8.3).[7]

Table 8.2 Global pharmaceutical sales and market growth

	Total pharmaceutical market sales (USD billion)	Growth over previous year (%)
1998	298	7
1999	331	11
2000	356	11
2001	390	13
2002	427	9
2003	497	10
2004	559	8
2005	602	7

Source: IMS Health, 2006.

Table 8.3 Global pharmaceutical markets, 2005

World market	Sales 2005 ($bn)	% of global sales	% annual growth
North America	265.7	47.0	5.2
Europe	169.5	30	7.1
Japan	60.3	10.7	6.8
Asia, Africa and Australia	46.4	8.2	11.0
Latin America	24.0	4.2	18.5

Source: IMS MIDAS.

For pharma companies, Europe presented a difficult but attractive market. Ranked second in the world at nearly USD169.5 billion, Europe appeared to be rife with opportunity to many pharmaceutical companies (see Table 8.3). The expansion of the European Union was expected to boost total revenues significantly over the coming years and offered exciting opportunities for pharmaceutical companies. Expanding into new territories and taking advantage of high-growth emerging markets were two of the most obvious advantages among many others.[8] However, despite its attractiveness in terms of market value, Europe's economic structure presented a major paradox and challenge for global pharma companies. Although the European Union operated as a single market without trade barriers between its member states, by the turn of the century, global pharma firms still faced an amalgam of independent government-run health-care systems. Although the European Union had vested the European Agency for the Evaluation of Medicinal Products (EMEA) with its central headquarters in London, United Kingdom, foreign companies still faced major hurdles compounded by 27 national authorities operating at 29 sites in 23 languages.[9] In contrast to the United States and Japan, the pharma industry in Europe was highly fragmented and characterized by national governments and heterogeneous markets.[10]

Leading pharmaceutical markets

Historically, the top pharmaceutical markets by value in Europe had been Germany, France, the United Kingdom and Italy (see Table 8.4). According to external industry analysts, this balance was also likely to remain unchanged in the near future, although the introduction of ceiling prices for more than 100 major drugs in Germany and other similar cost-containment pressures in Italy, France and the United Kingdom were expected to significantly influence the profitability of the local markets.[11] However, for the six-year period spanning 2000 to 2005, France and the United Kingdom especially had enjoyed strong rates of growth, driving the regional market's value significantly up. Taken together, Europe's key markets had accounted for almost 70 per cent of the region's total market value. France generated 19.9 per cent of the region's total market value, Germany accounted for 19.4 per cent, Italy for 15.2 per cent and the United Kingdom for 13.4 per cent. However, whereas the performance of the leading pharmaceutical markets was forecasted to deteriorate with growth rates between 1 per cent (Germany) and 4.7 per cent (United Kingdom) within the next three to five years, the emerging markets in the CEE were expected to grow even faster, at an average annual growth rate of nearly 9 per cent. Specifically, the pharmaceutical market in the CEE was dominated by four countries – Poland, Hungary, the Czech Republic and Russia.[12]

Competitive situation

The pharma industry was certainly a highly global and fragmented industry. However, due to large-scale mergers and acquisitions between pharmaceutical

Table 8.4   Pharmaceutical sales and growth rates of selected countries, 2005

Country	Total sales 2006	CAGR* 2002–2006
Austria	2,312	n.a.
Belgium	3,539	6.5%
Czech Republic	1,163	7.9%
Denmark	1,410	6.9%
Finland	1,689	n.a.
France	22,760	6%
Germany	21,551	1.4%
Hungary	1,556	7.9%
Ireland	1,306	n.a.
Italy	15,195	2.4%
Netherlands	3,579	5.4%
Norway	1,223	3.2%
Poland	2,939	7%
Portugal	2,879	n.a.
Russia	n.a.	16.8%
Spain	10,671	6.9%
Sweden	2,608	3.3%
Switzerland	2,624	n.a.
United Kingdom	16,110	5.8%

Note: *CAGR = Compound annual growth rate.
Source: Datamonitor (2006).

companies over the last 10 to 15 years, the concentration of the industry was clearly increasing.[13] While the top ten companies accounted for one-fourth of sales in 1988, they covered about one-third of the market in 1996. In 2005, the combined market share of the ten leading pharmaceutical companies amounted to 47 per cent. Looking at the market shares of the top ten pharma firms revealed a similar picture. In 1994, market leader Merck & Company had a market share of only 4 per cent. In 2005, Pfizer's market share was 8.4 per cent. In Europe, Pfizer ranked first with a market share of nearly 10 per cent, followed by Sanofi-Aventis (8.8 per cent), and GlaxoSmithKline (6.3 per cent). The remaining 75 per cent were split among a number of small- to medium-sized pharma firms (see Figure 8.1).[14]

According to external industry analysts, consolidation was inevitable in an industry as fragmented and price sensitive as pharmaceuticals. Virtually all of the top ten companies (see Table 8.5) had been involved in major horizontal mergers and acquisitions over the past years.[15] Market leader Pfizer mainly owed its global leading position to two acquisitions: Warner-Lambert and Pharmacia. The hostile takeover of Warner-Lambert for USD87 billion occurred in 2000. Warner-Lambert developed and manufactured the best-selling prescription drug Lipitor, which significantly boosted Pfizer's

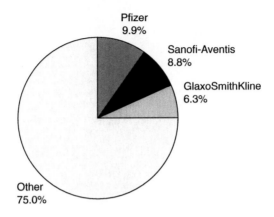

Pfizer
9.9%

Sanofi-Aventis
8.8%

GlaxoSmithKline
6.3%

Other
75.0%

Figure 8.1 Europe's pharmaceutical market share, 2005
Source: Datamonitor (2006).

Table 8.5 Sales ranking worldwide, 2005

Rank	Company	Country	Sales 2005 (Billion US$)	Growth rate (%)	Market share (%)
1	Pfizer	USA	47.7	−7	8.4
2	GlaxoSmithKline	UK	34.9	5	6.2
3	Sanofi-Aventis	France	30.5	8	5.4
4	Novartis	Switzerland	28.7	11	5.1
5	Johnson & Johnson	USA	25.4	0	4.5
6	AstraZeneca	UK	24.2	9	4.3
7	Merck & Co	USA	23.6	−3	4.2
8	Roche	Switzerland	19.9	17	3.5
9	Abbott	USA	15.7	9	2.8
10	Bristol-Myers Squibb	USA	14.8	−6	2.6
	Top 10		*265.4*		*46.9*

Source: IMS Health.

market share. That takeover was followed by the acquisition of Pharmacia for USD58 billion in 2003. Pharmacia itself had been created through mergers of Pharmacia with Upjohn and Monsanto/Searle.[16] GlaxoSmithKline was established in 2000 through the merger between GlaxoWellcome (a merger between Glaxo and Wellcome) and SmithKline Beecham (a merger between SmithKline and Beecham) with a deal value of USD76 billion.[17] Sanofi-Aventis incorporated a large number of different companies: Aventis was created in 1999 through the merger of Hoechst Marion Roussel with Rhône-Poulenc. In 1999 as well, Sanofi merged with Synthélabo, both from France, to form Sanofi-Synthélabo. In 2004, Sanofi-Synthélabo acquired

Aventis for about €52.4 billion.[18] Novartis was established in 1996 through the merger of Ciba-Geigy and Sandoz, two Swiss companies. The merger of Swedish Astra and British Zeneca led to the formation of AstraZeneca in 1999.[19] Roche expanded its pharmaceutical business with the acquisition of a majority interest in the US biotechnology company Genentech and the takeover of Syntex, a pharmaceutical manufacturer, during the 1990s. Later, in 2001, Roche acquired the majority of Japanese Chugai. Also in 2001, Abbott purchased Knoll, the pharmaceutical division of BASF, for USD6.9 billion, while Bristol-Myers Squibb acquired DuPont Pharmaceuticals for USD7.8 billion.[20]

Political pressures: The European pricing game

Although the European Union had repeatedly tried to extend its reach by coordinating efforts to "harmonize" pricing and reimbursement across the European Union, these steps had produced few, if any, positive results. National governments jealously guarded their rights to deal nationally with the financial implications of drug pricing and reimbursement. In their view, the pricing issue especially was too important to be "left to Brussels."[21] The resulting fragmentation of the EU pharmaceutical market, however, created an unsolved paradox between the existence of national price controls and the free movement of goods across borders, which was a principle of the European single market. Due to direct and indirect national price controls, prices for the same product often differed considerably from country to country (see Table 8.6). In combination with the free movement of goods inside the European Union, this frequently resulted in lucrative parallel trade between EU member states.[22] Price differentials were exploited by buying pharmaceuticals in low-price countries, such as Spain, Greece or Portugal, and selling them in high-price countries like the United Kingdom or Germany. For products launched in Europe in 2000, the average price band spanned from 30 per cent above to 30 per cent below the average EU price. Although the average price gap had somewhat narrowed since then, price differentials for individual products were still large enough for parallel trade to remain a profitable business.[23] According to an estimate, parallel trade in the European Union cost the pharmaceutical industry about €3.5 billion in lost profits every year.[24]

External reference pricing. Germany (1989) and the Netherlands (1991) were the first countries that adopted a system of "external referencing" or "cross national referencing" pricing. By 2006, however, most European countries had turned to a system of reference pricing (see Table 8.7). A product launched in the Netherlands was priced according to an average level of its official price in France, Germany, the United Kingdom and Belgium. The price of any drug in Greece was determined by comparing its price in all EU member countries and then taking the minimum price. In Austria, the EU

Table 8.6   Price level of pharmaceuticals, 2005

Country	Relative price level of pharmaceuticals* 2005
Austria	107
Belgium	106
Cyprus	102
Czech Republic	71
Denmark	121
Estonia	79
Finland	111
France	91
Germany	128
Greece	73
Hungary	74
Ireland	119
Italy	118
Latvia	79
Lithuania	70
Malta	106
Netherlands	109
Norway	120
Poland	68
Portugal	94
Slovakia	71
Slovenia	86
Spain	77
Sweden	95
Switzerland	187
United Kingdom	93

Note: *EU25 = 100.
Source: EUROSTAT, 2005.

average price was used to determine price levels and in the Czech Republic the lowest price of any drug in Greece, Poland, Spain and France was used as its maximum price. Until 1998, Italy had limited its comparator countries to Spain, France, Germany, and the United Kingdom, but changed to include all EU countries over concerns that the previous scheme would violate the EU rule of free movement of goods. And, although Ireland compared drug prices of a selected number of EU countries, it specifically identified the UK wholesale price as a point of comparison. In some countries, these comparisons were only used as one factor in price determination, whereas in other countries price comparisons were the main factor in determining a drug's price, as in Greece. However, it was important to bear in mind that the final drug price was not set in stone. On the average prices were recalculated

Table 8.7 Selected reference countries and basis of calculation, 2005

Country	Reference countries	Basis of calculation
Austria	Average Price in Europe	Average Price in Europe
Belgium	Ex-manufacturers' prices in France, Germany, the Netherlands and Luxembourg	Average
Cyprus	n.a.	n.a.
Denmark	Average European ex-manufacturers' prices excluding Greece, Portugal, Spain and Luxembourg, but including Liechtenstein	Average
Germany	n.a.	n.a.
Greece	Lowest Price in Europe	Lowest Price in Europe
Ireland	Denmark, France, Germany, Netherlands and United Kingdom	Average
Italy*	All EU countries (excluding Luxembourg and Denmark)	Average
Netherlands	Belgium, France, Germany and United Kingdom	Average
Luxembourg	n.a.	n.a.
Portugal	France, Spain and Italy	Minimum price of identical products in France, Spain and Italy
Sweden	Denmark, Netherlands, Germany, Switzerland, Norway, Finland and United States	Price is lower than in Denmark, the Netherlands, Germany, Switzerland and similar to the price in Norway and Finland
Slovakia	n.a.	n.a.
Slovenia	Italy, France and Germany	85% of the average of most products 96% of the average for innovative products
Czech Republic	Greece, Spain, France and Poland	Lowest
Norway	Sweden, Denmark, Finland, United Kingdom, Ireland, France, Germany, Netherlands, Belgium and Austria	Average of the two lowest

Note: *Used for pricing "old" products only.
Source: Adapted from Pannagel (2006).

every six months to control for price changes and late launches in the reference countries.[25]

Profit regulations.   Some European countries followed a system of profit regulation whereby the government determined the maximum profit that a pharmaceutical company could achieve. In the United Kingdom, where prices were not regulated directly, pharmaceutical companies were indirectly controlled through the Pharmaceutical Price Regulation Scheme (PPRS), which restricted the amount of profits that drug manufacturers were allowed to make. The United Kingdom allowed a maximum profit margin of 21 per cent, whereas Spain restricted it to 18 per cent. The maximum profit range was, however, negotiable if the company was able to prove that its profits would be less than 75 per cent of its target returns. In countries such as France and Finland, a drug's price was negotiated and agreed upon by the national government and the respective pharma company. If a product exceeded the revenue forecasts presented to the national government as part of its pricing negotiations, prices were reduced even further. A problem associated with lengthy pricing and reimbursement negotiations was the considerable delay in market launch. In some countries, the price and the portion that the state would reimburse were determined in separate processes, which further postponed market introduction, resulting in high levels of lost sales for pharmaceutical companies. Some companies even gave a swift market entry priority over securing premium prices.[26]

Competition from generics

When a popular drug came off patent, it typically faced fierce competition from generics. The launch of generic copies forced companies to heavily discount the price of their branded drugs. Generics were regularly priced at a 30 to 90 per cent discount compared to the branded drug prior to patent expiration. Generally, branded products lost between 15 and 30 per cent of their market share after the first generic version reached the market, and then between 75 and 90 per cent on subsequent generic launches. If one generic drug was launched for each branded product coming off patent, then the pharmaceutical (innovator) market lost between USD2.1 billion and USD4.2 billion, and if two or more generic copies were launched, the market dropped between USD10.5 billion and USD12.6 billion per year (see Figure 8.2).[27]

In addition, generic substitution had become a central policy in the drive for health-care cost containment across European countries. Where generic substitution was allowed, a doctor prescribed a specific product, and the pharmacist was either free or was obliged to substitute it with a less-expensive generic product (see Table 8.8). By accepting generic substitution and actively promoting it as a national price control mechanism, the generic market literally exploded over the last couple of years and was expected

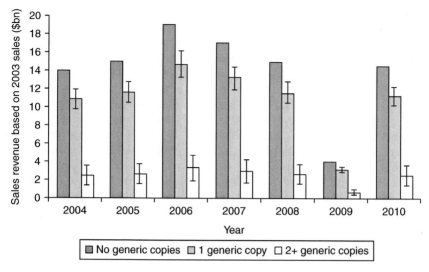

Figure 8.2 Total value of drugs going off patent per year and impact on revenues of generic copies, 2004–2010

Source: Hamilton (2005).

Table 8.8 Generic substitution in European countries, 2005

Country	Substitution allowed	Actively promoted
Austria	n.a.	n.a.
Belgium	No	–
Czech Republic	Yes	Yes
Denmark	Yes	–
Finland	Yes	Yes
France	Yes	Yes
Germany	Yes	Yes
Greece	No	–
Italy	Yes	Yes
Ireland	Yes	Yes
Netherlands	Yes	–
Portugal	Yes	–
Spain	Yes	–
Sweden	Yes	Yes
United Kingdom	Yes	–

Source: Seget (2006).

to further grow in the future. By the end of 2006, countries were generally clustered into three groups according to their generic market share:[28]

• Less than 10 per cent market share by value: Austria, Belgium, Finland, France, Ireland, Italy, Portugal and Spain

- Between 10 and 40 per cent market share by value: Denmark, Estonia, Netherlands, Slovakia, Slovenia, Sweden, Turkey and United Kingdom
- Greater than 40 per cent market share by value: Croatia, Czech Republic, Germany, Latvia, Lithuania, Hungary and Poland

Market differences

The pharmaceutical industry was often cited as the standard example of a global industry in terms of product standardization and consumer homogeneity. In practice, there was, however, a surprising degree of heterogeneity, especially across European countries (see Table 8.9). To a large part, this heterogeneity was reflected in the demand for a different product mix across countries. For example, the dosage forms of drugs used to differ considerably between markets. In France, drugs were frequently administered as suppositories, a form, for instance, considerably less common in the United Kingdom. Similarly, the quantity of drugs prescribed in the United Kingdom tended to be less than that in Germany and Austria where the fear of litigation caused doctors to be wary of under-medication.

Astellas – A new strategy for Europe

Astellas's earliest activities in Europe dated back to the 1980s when Fujisawa and Yamanouchi first entered the European region. Like most Japanese companies, both firms started their foreign operations by establishing an international sales office in London from where they further expanded their operations throughout Europe in a, for Japanese firms, typical step-by-step approach.

Table 8.9 Similarities between countries in terms of offered pharmaceutical products in per cent, 2005

Country/ Country	ATS	BEL	DNK	FIN	DEU	IRL	ITA	LUX	NDL	SPA	SWE	UK
ATS	100	59	49	51	81	51	60	63	57	53	48	54
BEL	72	100	55	54	79	60	67	82	66	61	52	60
DEN	81	73	100	75	84	67	69	76	76	65	73	71
FIN	78	67	70	100	79	61	68	71	69	60	70	67
DEU	68	54	43	44	100	47	54	59	50	49	42	49
IRL	65	63	53	52	72	100	58	64	59	55	50	66
ITL	62	56	43	45	66	46	100	58	50	54	42	50
LUX	71	75	52	52	79	56	63	100	60	58	49	57
NDL	80	76	65	63	84	65	69	75	100	63	61	69
SPA	69	65	51	51	75	55	68	66	58	100	48	59
SEW	79	71	71	76	83	65	69	73	72	62	100	70
UK	68	62	55	55	73	65	62	64	62	58	53	100

Source: EURO-MED-STAT.

Fujisawa and Yamanouchi in Europe

At the time of the merger, Fujisawa had a European headquarters in Munich, Germany, and 8 wholly owned subsidiaries in the United Kingdom, France, Italy, Spain, Sweden, Germany, Austria and Switzerland (see Figure 8.3). Fujisawa accessed the CEE countries as well as Ireland, Portugal, Norway, Finland, Denmark and the Netherlands via distributors. Fujisawa's European headquarters was responsible for the development and marketing of the company's pharmaceuticals throughout Europe. It had a largely coordinating and integrating function and was very hands-off, granting a large amount of autonomy to its local subsidiaries. Fujisawa's subsidiaries were encouraged to act entrepreneurially and to manage their operations as individual companies. To reduce organizational complexity and to profit from market similarities within Europe, Fujisawa had developed a "subregional" or "lead country structure" across its European operations. Its German market subsidiary, which was legally separated from Fujisawa's European headquarters, was responsible for Austria and Switzerland; Sweden was Fujisawa's Nordic hub being responsible for Denmark, Finland and Norway; Fujisawa Spain managed the company's operations in Portugal; and Fujisawa's distributor in Belgium oversaw the company's operations in Luxembourg and the Netherlands.

Within its network of European operations, Germany was the company's strongest market followed by the United Kingdom, Spain and France (see Appendix).

Like Fujisawa, Yamanouchi had fully integrated pharmaceutical operations in Europe including R&D, manufacturing and marketing. In 1986, Yamanouchi established its first overseas production base for bulk drug substances in Ireland. Five years later, in 1991, the company acquired the pharmaceutical division of Royal Gist Brocades, a Dutch-based multinational, and established its European headquarters in Leiderdorp, the Netherlands.

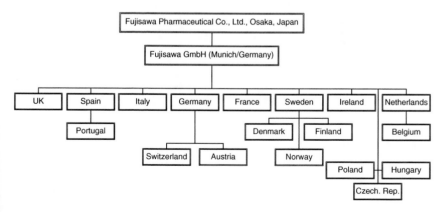

Figure 8.3 Fujisawa's European structure

Yamanouchi had a stronger competitive standing in Europe than Fujisawa. Its European operations included sales bases in 13 countries with two R&D operations – one in Meppel, the Netherlands, and one in Oxford, England. In addition, Yamanouchi had two manufacturing facilities in Ireland and Italy. In addition to its European headquarters being in the Netherlands, Yamanouchi had wholly owned subsidiaries in Belgium, the Netherlands, Germany, Switzerland, France, Italy, Spain, Portugal, Greece, Sweden, Czech Republic, Poland and Russia.

In contrast to Fujisawa, Yamanouchi did not pursue a clear subregional strategy in Europe. With the exception of the Netherlands, which was responsible for the company's operations in Belgium, and Sweden, which handled Yamanouchi's distributorships in the Nordic countries, all other countries reported directly to Yamanouchi's European headquarters in the Netherlands (see Figure 8.4). Yamanouchi's European headquarters served mainly as a legal, tax-accounting and public-relations entity. A country manager once described the role of Yamanouchi's European headquarters as follows: "The EHQ acts as an advocate for the region and as a mentor and supporter for us the national units in the region." As in the case of Fujisawa, Yamanouchi's subsidiaries enjoyed a large degree of autonomy, which was considered to be of utmost importance in a region as fragmented as Europe.

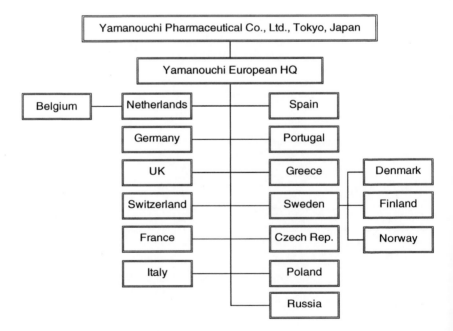

Figure 8.4   Yamanouchi's European structure

Astellas Europe – Preparing for the future

Through the integration of Yamanouchi's and Fujisawa's European operations in 2005, Astellas Europe had 18 marketing and sales subsidiaries, 6 manufacturing plants and 2 R&D sites in Europe. The merger had enabled Astellas to increase its market coverage in Europe and external analysts expected that it would significantly strengthen its competitive position in the market. All in all, Astellas Europe employed over 3000 people across sales, marketing, R&D and manufacturing. Besides being responsible for its European operations, Astellas Europe was also responsible for the distribution of Astellas's products in the Middle East, Africa, and Latin America.

European headquarters. Shortly after the merger had been completed, Astellas announced the establishment of its European headquarters in London. In a press release, the European headquarters' objectives were defined as the centralization of key management functions at the European headquarters level, consolidation of European business activities, expansion of existing European operations, and the re-enforcement of subsidiary management across European countries. Specifically, Astellas's European headquarters saw its role as identifying synergies and pursuing a consistent policy across the region, which entailed the direct control of subsidiaries' activities and strategies within the region. Although it was not surprising that Astellas would set up a European headquarters to manage its European operations, the location choice was surprising. Because Yamanouchi had its former European headquarters in Leiderdorp and Fujisawa's European headquarters was located in Munich, Germany, there was a common belief among Astellas's management staff that the Astellas European headquarters would be located either in Munich or Leiderdorp. Whereas Yamanouchi's European headquarters was a rather small regional office, Fujisawa's European headquarters in Munich had fully equipped management functions, and its management team had gained years of experience with regional management issues. Because of this, external analysts of the company suggested that Munich would be the ideal location for Astellas's European headquarters. In addition, many other global pharmaceutical companies had their European headquarters in Munich. When Astellas Japan announced that Astellas's European headquarters would be located in London, many of Fujisawa's and Yamanouchi's former European management staff refused to move to the United Kingdom and left the company. Partly because of this, Astellas's new European management team was composed of Japanese managers who had limited or no prior business experience in Europe.

Regional integration strategy. Former Yamanouchi's and Fujisawa's national responsiveness strategies were questioned by Astellas's new European management team. The prime argument was that, in a business environment characterized by open markets, regional integration and global competition, autonomous subsidiaries with national identities were not well suited to achieve synergies and meet international competition. Within former Yamanouchi and Fujisawa, the core building blocks of each company's strategy were independent, largely self-sufficient and highly entrepreneurial operations. Country managers had sometimes been described as the "kings of their countries" because they were fully responsible for the market strategy in their responsible country. The establishment of Astellas's European headquarters in London and the subsequent introduction of Astellas's regional integration strategy in 2005 symbolized a significant power shift between Astellas's subsidiaries and its European headquarters. Led by the pursuit of regional integration, the new structure removed considerable autonomy from the local subsidiaries. Although it was argued that Astellas would preserve the autonomy and responsiveness of its local units, subsidiaries' responsibilities were often downgraded to tailoring the company's regionally developed programs to local markets and using their knowledge of local consumers to increase profit margins.

Clustering of country markets.   Driven by the goal of regional integration and functional strength, Astellas Europe took a somewhat different approach to clustering its country markets. Unlike Fujisawa's lead country structure that divided Europe into subregions of similar countries in terms of language and market similarities, while giving the strongest market within the region the strategic lead and responsibility for the subregion, Astellas Europe divided its operations into two subregions of small countries and five stand-alone countries that reported directly to a regional manager at the European headquarters level. The first subregion comprised the Nordic countries (that is, Denmark, Sweden, Norway and Finland), Belgium, Portugal, the Netherlands, Russia, South Africa and Ireland. Astellas's second subregion included Austria, Switzerland, the Czech Republic, Poland, Greece and International, which in turn comprised the Middle East, Africa and Latin America. All countries reported to a regional operation manager represented at Astellas's European headquarters in London. Germany, Italy, France, Spain and the United Kingdom – Europe's biggest pharma markets – constituted the big five and reported directly to the region's vice president of operations (see Figure 8.5). In Europe, only Pfizer followed a similar approach. Most other pharma firms opted for a lead country structure to benefit from market similarities and reduced complexity. However, whereas Astellas's new clustering approach was resisted and heavily criticized by Europe's key markets that, as in the case of Fujisawa Germany, saw their strategic influence substantially reduced, the new approach was most warmly welcomed by many of Astellas's small country markets, which felt that they gained a greater voice within Astellas Europe.

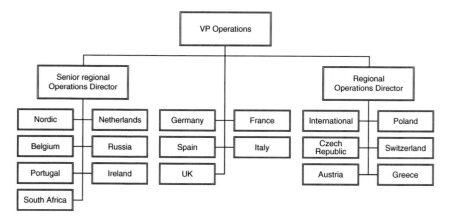

Figure 8.5 Astellas's country markets

Advent of matrix management. Whereas the role of former Yamanouchi's and Fujisawa's European headquarters had largely been hands-off and driven by their local units, Astellas Europe took a more proactive, hierarchical approach. Due to its strong commitment to Astellas corporate headquarters in Tokyo, and the consequent large concentration of power at the regional level, the Astellas European headquarters was soon considered as the "enforcer and controller" among Astellas local units. In order to achieve an optimal balance between its regional integration strategy and its local units' flexibility, Astellas Europe introduced a matrix reporting structure whereby functional managers reported directly to their country leadership and also had a dotted-line relationship to Astellas functional heads in London (see Figure 8.6). However, although the new matrix design was supposed to equalize power between the individual country markets and functions, many country managers did not understand any longer how they fit into the picture, feeling subordinated to Astellas's functional leadership. Astellas's strong regionally coordinated functions were introduced to produce extraordinary competitive advantage, but by the end of 2006, they appeared to create gridlock. Opponents of the matrix management system were convinced that the matrix had never been symmetrical. Though functional managers nominally had straight-line reporting to their country manager and only dotted-line reporting through functional management, the function retained a high degree of de-facto control because it determined career paths and promotion plans for employees. In addition, most strategic issues fell under the responsibility of Astellas's functional heads in London. By the end of 2006, ultimately each function had developed its own strategic agenda, which largely revolved around maximizing its own

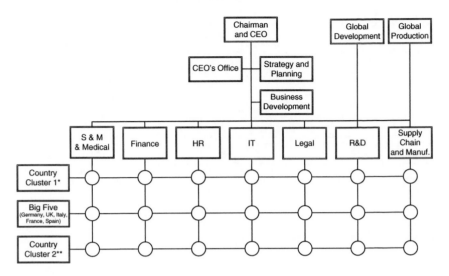

Figure 8.6   Astellas matrix structure

Notes: *Cluster 1: Nordic, Belgium, Portugal, South Africa, Netherlands, Russia and Ireland;
**Cluster 2: International, Czech Republic, Austria, Poland, Switzerland and Greece.

power within the company rather than cooperating with other functions and businesses to win in the marketplace. Management by functional conflict did not serve, as initially expected, as an effective system of checks and balances but eventually led to poor strategic alignment and demotivation among employees. Many country managers saw their early criticism confirmed that Astellas's regional matrix had never fully resolved the tension between regional functional and national responsiveness country management. Because Astellas's country managers still had the sole responsibility for financial results, they expected that it was up to them to ultimately decide whether or not to launch certain strategic initiatives provided by Astellas's European headquarters in their country. However, in the new organizational model, the power lay in the Astellas European headquarters, and, thus, in the functions. The power shift was especially criticized by Astellas's big five – Germany, France, Italy, United Kingdom and Spain – which saw their decision rights and autonomy substantially reduced. As in the case of Astellas's pursued clustering approach, Astellas's small country markets, however, acknowledged the increased professionalism at Astellas European headquarters through the introduced matrix and welcomed the new management approach despite its complexity.

Rethinking Astellas European structure

Shortly after the merger had been accomplished, Astellas's freshly appointed European vice president stated that Astellas's success would be based on its intelligent combination of local subsidiary autonomy on the one hand and international innovation leverage on the other. The challenge, he acknowledged, would be to manage the conflicting demands of integration and responsiveness by implementing a regional strategy and organizational design that would fully resolve the tension of the two conflicting demands. However, nearly two years after Astellas Europe had been established, it seemed that Astellas had not been able to manage the conflicting forces. Early results had been disappointing: flat sales coupled with negative core earnings had forced Astellas to sell two of its manufacturing units and to close down its R&D lab in Munich to realize positive sales growth. The matrix, which was originally introduced to increase Astellas regional flexibility, resulted in rigidity and inflexibility due to its complexity. To make matters worse, many of former Yamanouchi's and Fujisawa's key managers had left the company, because they "couldn't identify themselves with Astellas new management style." Yet, at the beginning of 2007, few doubted that Astellas's management had to act quickly. But there was little agreement on what had to be done first.

Preparing for the meeting

As Dr Montemayors's secretary entered her office to tell her that she was going home because it was already 7 p.m., she found Mrs Montemayor eagerly walking up and down in her office. She had read Mr Yukino's mail again and again. She knew that the proponents of Astellas's European strategy argued that it was far too early to judge it. However, the implementation of Astellas's regional strategy and the integration of the two companies' operations had proven far more difficult than originally expected. Thus, the common argument, especially under Astellas's European top management team, was that organizational change needed time – time that Astellas did not have. So, Dr Montemayor thought – would the strategy ultimately prove to be successful? No – definitely not, she was absolutely sure about that. Some major changes had to be made to secure Astellas's competitive advantage. But what exactly was Astellas's Achilles heel? Was it the pursued regional strategy? Was it the matrix management system? Would another country clustering approach be more efficient? And, even more important, which issues had so far been overlooked by Astellas's European management team, but were important to increase Astellas's performance in the region? She sat down and began to prepare her presentation.

Appendix

A8.1   Fujisawa's European sales, 2004

Country	Sales per country, 2004 (€ million)*
Germany	123.0
UK	53.4
Spain	47.8
France	46.4
Italy	23.0
Austria	19.3
Netherlands	13.2
Belgium and Luxemburg	12.0
Ireland	10.5
Sweden	10.1
Switzerland	6.1
Portugal	6.0
Poland	5.2
Denmark	3.4
Norway	2.9
Finland	2.8
Hungary*	2.8
Czech Republic*	2.8
Slovakia*	0.1

Note: *Distributor sales.
Source: Company data.

A8.2   Yamanouchi's European sales, 2004

Country	Sales per country, 2004 (EUR million)*
Germany	73.5
United Kingdom	46.0
Spain	44.6
France	57.9
Italy	65.1
Austria	–
Netherlands	24.4
Belgium and Luxemburg	13.6
Ireland	–
Switzerland	n.a.
Portugal	11.8
Poland	31
Czech Republic*	8.6
Russia	26.5
Scandinavia (Sweden, Denmark, Norway and Finland)	25

Note: *Distributor sales.
Source: Company data.

A8.3   Astellas European sales, 2006

Country	Sales per country, 2006 (EUR million)*
Germany	235,440.2
Spain	133,494.7
France	122,317.6
Italy	109,377.2
UK	114,721.5
International	79,890.4
Nordic (Sweden, Denmark, Norway and Finland)	50,338.9
Poland	44,234.2
Russia	52,862.6
Netherlands	37,652.5
Belgium	33,159.6
Portugal	22,456.8
Austria	20,227.5
Ireland	19,911.8
Czech	21,557.5
Greece	14,519.1
Switzerland	7,784.4
South Africa	4,861.3
Hungary	11,375.1
Others	−1391.0

Note: *Distributor sales.
Source: Company data.

Opportunity Development and Centrality: The Case of Boehringer Ingelheim*

Introduction to Boehringer Ingelheim

The company was founded by Albert Boehringer in Ingelheim, Germany. In 1885, he founded a chemical factory producing acids for several products such as soft drinks and baking powder. A decade later, Boehringer Ingelheim became a pioneer in producing biotech products when it discovered the use of certain bacteria for the production of lactic acids. The new technology fuelled growth and financed the company's early ventures into the emerging pharmaceutical industry at the beginning of the twentieth century.

After the world wars, new drugs laid the basis for Boehringer's strengths in respiratory, cardiovascular and gastrointestinal diseases. These programs should bring forth several highly innovative new drugs throughout the next decades. Also, shortly after the Second World War, international expansion started into the neighbouring European countries and quickly spread into Latin America and Japan in 1961. The world's biggest pharmaceutical market, the United States, was not entered until the early 1970s. Boehringer's international expansion profited from high growth rates and low competition in the developing pharmaceutical industry during these years.

The company has remained privately owned and has followed a strategy of long-term, organic growth driven by innovation and a network of strategic partnerships. This was especially visible in the early 1990s, when the group faced low profits and a weak pipeline of new drugs. However, instead of following the new fad of engaging heavily in mergers and acquisitions, the owner families stuck to their principles and invested in "value through

---

* This case was written by Phillip C. Nell, assistant professor at Copenhagen Business School, under the direction of Bodo B. Schlegelmilch and Björn Ambos, WU Vienna, Institute for International Marketing and Management. It is intended to be used as the basis for class discussion rather than to illustrate the effective or ineffective handling of administrative situations. The case was made possible by the co-operation of Boehringer Ingelheim.

innovation."[29] Boehringer concentrated its efforts on stable organic growth based on high research productivity. This research was, to a large extent, based on a strong network of strategic alliances and partnerships with academia and technology-driven firms for research on the one hand, and many of its biggest pharmaceutical industry competitors for co-marketing on the other. The strategy has proven very successful, as Boehringer has tripled its global market share to around 2 per cent within a decade, outgrowing the market every year since 1999.

In 2007, Boehringer Ingelheim reported sales of €11.0 billion, selling products in almost 150 countries worldwide. Operating with two main divisions, the company has almost 150 affiliates in 47 countries worldwide and employs roughly 40,000 people. Its human pharmaceuticals division dominates with 96 per cent of total net sales, supplemented by animal health, contributing the remaining 4 per cent. Human pharmaceuticals is further divided into three divisions, Prescription Medicine (PM) including a smaller generics business in the United States, Consumer Health Care (CHC) and its chemical and biotech manufacturing franchise, Industrial Customer. Despite this diversification, Boehringer's key focus is research-driven prescription medicines. In terms of worldwide market share, Boehringer ranks among the top ten companies worldwide in animal health and consumer health care, while its human pharmaceuticals business usually places in the top 15.

Overall organizational logic and the need for regional structures

During the early years of internationalization, most of the pharmaceutical markets were still relatively young and underdeveloped. In these highly dynamic, developing markets, Boehringer's country managers were given substantial autonomy, and the company's operations were strongly decentralized. Regional divisions did not exist, and Boehringer's principle was to focus on the larger markets and to ignore the smaller ones.

International expansion continued, but the industry dynamics changed substantially as the pharmaceutical markets became more mature and governments started using strategies to limit public health care expenditures. A new management structure with a board of managing directors was introduced, and subsidiary reporting lines became tighter and degrees of freedom smaller. Many functions, such as R&D, business development, manufacturing or also strategic marketing, were gradually centralized and moved to Ingelheim, the location of the corporate headquarters. Although this streamlined the operations, the continued expansion led to increased complexity and information overflow at corporate headquarters, which had to deal directly with almost 50 local operations. Furthermore, the pharmaceutical markets differed substantially between the different regions or even within regions because national health-care systems are organized differently. For instance, drugs for which costs are reimbursed to the patients by public health care in Germany might not be reimbursed in other countries. Of course, this has a strong influence on demand in the countries and increases the need to be locally responsive, especially in the area of marketing and sales.

In the early 1990s, Boehringer decided to define three broad marketing and sales regions along the triad markets, each headed by a regional director (area director). Furthermore, with these triads, some fully fledged regional headquarters were installed. Based on the original logic of focusing on large markets, the regional headquarters were introduced by giving large established subsidiaries the responsibility for smaller markets in the same region. For example, Japan became the regional headquarters for Southeast Asia, and Argentina received responsibility for a number of smaller Spanish-speaking countries such as Paraguay and Bolivia. The regional headquarters structure still exists today and is complemented by some large and important countries reporting directly to the corporate headquarters (and the area director) while not being regional centres themselves. For example, Germany, France and Italy neither have a regional role nor do they report to a regional headquarters. Instead, they report directly to the corporate headquarters similar to Brazil in South America, or the United States in North America. Hence, all regional management centres are by definition centres for a group of smaller countries and markets.

Regarding the different functions, however, some upstream functions clearly remained at the responsibility of the corporate headquarters, and they experienced no decentralization towards the regions. Driven by scale economies and globally standardized products, the company has maintained strong centralization of manufacturing and R&D. The importance especially of R&D, both to Boehringer and to the pharmaceutical industry as a whole, is illustrated by the representation of the function in Boehringer's four-person board of managing directors.

The global management of production allows Boehringer to use its international manufacturing facilities to offer contract manufacturing of fine chemicals, specializing in the production of advanced intermediates and the development and synthesis of active pharmaceutical ingredients. Besides diversifying its revenues base, it optimizes the use of manufacturing capacity and saves costs. For example, the group just recently expanded its facilities in Mexico, previously used for the local market only, to become the country's first Food and Drug Administration (FDA) approved contract manufacturer exporting to the United States and Canada.

In contrast, the worldwide structure for regulatory affairs, marketing and sales is much more decentralized where the regional offices take on a much greater role. Boehringer is faced with strong pressures for regionalization or localization in these downstream functions. Regulatory affairs and sales in pharmaceuticals probably face the most intense pressures for national responsiveness of all industries, because the health-care systems are very different in almost every country, and governments have resisted moves for harmonization. For example, national laws for pharmaceutical advertising are very diverse, allowing substantial advertising (e.g., in the United States) or forbidding advertising almost completely (e.g., in Germany). Furthermore, the overall drug procurement and distribution system can vary substantially between the markets regarding wholesaler structures or the actual influence of the final buying decision. In fact, some countries demand that general practitioners prescribe the active substances and not the branded product. In such a situation, a lot of influence on the purchasing decision is moved towards the pharmacies, which are in turn required to favour low-cost products that contain the active substance.

On the other hand, marketing is somewhat more open to regional and global integration. Most importantly, the increasing substantial R&D costs in combination with decreasing effective patent protection for new drugs require a quick and worldwide exploitation of a newly found substance. This calls for a global marketing strategy. Furthermore, the pharmaceutical markets are very strongly regulated, and it is of utmost importance to maintain a clear and globally harmonized communication approach with regard to side effects and effectiveness issues of all products in the portfolio. Hence, there is a strong need to coordinate these activities on a global basis. In the following sections, there will be a detailed description of Boehringer's CEE region with a focus on Marketing and Sales.

Boehringer Ingelheim's RHQ for Central Eastern Europe (CEE)

Today, the Americas contribute 50 per cent, followed by the home region Europe with 33 per cent and Asia/Australasia/Africa with 17 per cent to total revenues. However, the growth dynamics are highly different between stagnating Western (European) markets and fast-growing Eastern Europe.

In Western Europe, the market for prescription drugs has become very difficult and competitive. Faced with rising health-care costs, governments have turned to pharmaceuticals in an effort to limit public spending. The mechanism of "price referencing,"[30] as well as direct price cuts, has become common practice, putting increasing pressure on pharmaceutical companies. This decreases the possibility for price discrimination. Hence, the Western European markets have become rather unattractive, especially in terms of growth. Although Boehringer has managed to counter some of these pressures particularly by launching new, innovative drugs, the main contributor to European growth is CEE (see Table 8.10).

Across CEE, markets have been growing quickly, but at the same time, volatility and risk are a lot higher. The region as a whole has experienced double-digit growth rates for years, reaching more than 25 per cent growth

Table 8.10   Boehringer Ingelheim CEE turnover (in millions of euros) and size (in number of employees)

Turnover within CEE in Mio. EUR

	2003	2004	2005	2006	2007
Turnover Austria PM	50.9	56	58.5	57.4	55.3
Turnover Austria CHC	10.9	11.4	11.5	11.5	10.8
Turnover CEE PM	59.5	74.6	136.3	175	215.3
Turnover CEE CHC	28.2	32	58.2	72	78.3
Sum PM	110.4	130.6	194.8	232.4	270.6
Sum CHC	39.1	43.4	69.7	83.5	89.1
Sum Total	149.5	174	264.5	315.9	359.7
Employees CEE excl. Austria			1704	1991	2193

in prescription medicines in the last few years. While pharmaceutical market growth in Western countries is mainly driven by innovations, high growth rates in emerging markets can be attributed to economic growth and rising treatment rates. Many CEE markets are also important contributors to the consumer health-care division. As public reimbursement rates of research-based drugs are often very low, over-the-counter (OTC) drugs are of major importance in their health-care systems. Russia and Poland, for example, are core markets for Boehringer Consumer Health Care.

Another important difference between most of the CEE countries and the other Western European countries is the maturity of the markets. As mentioned above, this refers to growth potentials. However, the markets are also qualitatively different. In fact, due to the CEE countries' limited financial resources, they are not able to invest in health care as much as in Western countries. Certain new, innovative and hence expensive drugs that are launched in North America and Western Europe do not get launched in CEE simultaneously. Instead, CEE country market launches often lag some years until the market conditions are ready for a new drug. On the other hand, some relatively cheap drugs that have long stopped being sold in the Western markets (because there are better-performing successors that cause fewer side effects and/or achieve higher levels of effectiveness) are still marketed in CEE country markets. For example, in the treatment of hypertension, older drug classes such as angiotensin-converting enzyme (ACE) inhibitors, beta-blockers and diuretics are still very popular due to their cost-efficiency, whereas newer calcium channel blockers and angiotensin receptor blockers are only adopted slowly. Diseases for which generics are not available are often undertreated due to the low access to innovative therapies.

These differences were one of the reasons why the CEE region was clustered together and reports into a regional headquarters. Located in Austria, Boehringer's CEE regional headquarters is responsible for 28 CEE countries for which it has full profit and loss responsibility. All other European countries report directly to corporate headquarters in Ingelheim, that is, to the Corporate Area Director Europe.

In short, there is a twofold regional structure at Boehringer Ingelheim. First, on the corporate level, the area directors basically represent the whole area on top-level boards and committees and taking care that the regional voice is heard at the corporate level (against divisions and functions). The region at this level is defined by the triad markets. Second, on the regional level, regional headquarters provide two-way windows of information and communication flow between local and corporate levels. The country markets belonging to these regional headquarters on this level are grouped based on similarity and size considerations. The regional headquarters coexist with large countries that report directly to the corporate headquarters (see Figure 8.7).

One particularity in CEE that differs from other Boehringer regional management systems is the fact that Austria – the location of the regional headquarters – is not part of the region itself but managed independently (see organizational chart). This breaks the Boehringer internal principle of allocating regional responsibility to lead countries (such as Argentina in Spanish-speaking South America) and is mainly due to historical reasons. Before the fall of the Berlin Wall, the very limited business to CEE and especially to Eastern Germany was not managed via Germany. Instead, Boehringer Ingelheim recognized that organizing this business from the independent country of Austria had political advantages. Subsequently,

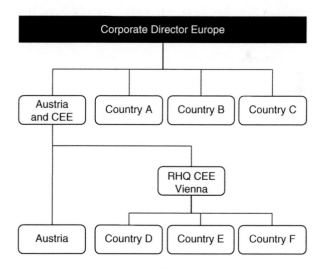

Figure 8.7 European regional structure of Boehringer Ingelheim

Austria grew into the role of being the host for the CEE regional operations, although the market characteristics of Austria are rather similar to other Western European countries. However, although it is recognized that this is not necessarily a structure that would have been created again, there is much consent that the double structure does not hurt either. Instead, the strong East-West bridging position of Austria is referred to in virtually every industry sector. Public discussion of CEE topics in newspapers, TV and business is very profound in Austria as compared to any other Western European country. Therefore, it is widely acknowledged within Boehringer Ingelheim that the regional headquarters' level of understanding of political, cultural and economic developments in CEE is very high compared to headquarters staff. For instance, the political revolution in Ukraine in 2004 and 2005 created substantial discussion and uncertainty at the corporate level. Yet the regional headquarters put forward a different interpretation of the changes and of the business prospects – a counterpoint that turned out to be a good forecast for Boehringer's activities in Ukraine.

Advantages and issues connected to regional marketing operations

The regional headquarters of Boehringer in Vienna is in principle responsible for both main divisions within CEE, PM and CHC. However, for the above-mentioned reasons, Boehringer has defined global core products for which a global strategy and a global marketing plan are developed. It is normally demanded that regional and local management focus strongly on marketing and selling these products. To this end, the role of the regional headquarters CEE is the adaptation of the global strategy and the successful and efficient implementation in CEE.

For products that are limited to the region, the CEE regional headquarters clearly has a stronger role in strategy development and formulation. This is the reason why the marketing function has strong resources at the regional headquarters (see Figure 8.8). In both divisions (PM and CHC) a number of product group managers are installed at the regional level who are mainly responsible for the turnover in the whole region. This responsibility is shared with the product group marketing managers in the single country operations.

However, the strong marketing and sales organization is accompanied by the overall profit and loss responsibility of the regional headquarters for the region and the country heads for the individual countries. This is illustrated in Figure 8.8. The large circle represents the overall profit and loss (turnover and costs) responsibility of the regional headquarters, which is replicated in each country organization (smaller circle within the regional headquarters circle). The marketing organization within the regional headquarters (small circle on the turnover side of the regional headquarters circle) has a strong focus on pushing turnover, especially with regard to the globally defined core products and based on globally developed marketing and sales

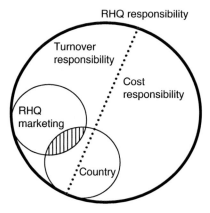

Figure 8.8 Opposing interests between the functional and the geographical organization of Boehringer Ingelheim CEE

strategies. Hence, there is only partial congruence of goals with the individual country organizations. This has certain implications that will be described in the following section.

Key advantages of the regional marketing organization

One key task of the regional headquarters marketing managers is the recognition and development of turnover opportunities with regard to the different product groups. That is why all marketing managers are, in principle, product group managers having exactly defined corresponding product (group) managers at the level of the subsidiaries. As mentioned above, this key task is in opposition to the quest for financial performance optimization of the country manager.

To some extent, the activity of opportunity perception and development is happening purely within the regional headquarters. Regional marketing managers supervise the performance in the CEE countries. They engage in creating region-wide business intelligence by conducting benchmark studies and comparing individual country approaches with each other. For example, a product group manager compiles business data about sales of the product group in all countries and compares the countries to each other but also to data gathered from other European countries outside the region. The manager also initiates marketing research activities on the regional level in case outside data is needed and for which the regional level has a certain budget. Moreover, regional marketing managers frequently take note of best practices in some countries that lead to above-average effectiveness. All these activities create insights and knowledge on the regional level, which is then regularly shared with local marketing. The latter is done either through the standard daily contact between regional and local product group marketing – or through larger meetings covering all product groups. The primary aims of these insight-generating activities at the regional level are two-fold. First, one aim is to challenge local marketing plans constantly from the perspective of turnover maximization, which is in line with global and/or regional strategy. Second, in view of the many small, less-mature countries in CEE, it allows for achieving common quality standards and in professionalizing the marketing activities in the region.

Besides the constant value-adding "challenging function" on the regional level, the regional headquarters can acknowledge and support opportunities identified on the level of the subsidiaries, for example, in the CEE country Poland, the national health-care system modified regulation for a group of products. The products became reimbursable for insured patients while before, patients had to pay for the drugs on their own. This status change for certain drugs is not an unusual process. The health-care regulation is constantly evolving. Older products get replaced by newer, more effective products, generics are being allowed to the detriment of the original branded products, and sometimes already approved and reimbursed drugs are delisted due to unforeseen side effects or new evidence regarding their (in-) effectiveness. Usually, the listing of products as reimbursable boosts demand and therefore offers large growth opportunities. However, demand does not develop automatically but is triggered to a large extent through the active presentation and explanation of drugs at the level of the prescribing institutions, that is, general practitioners and hospitals.

Early recognition of such developments within the health-care system is key because such a marketing and sales process is very resource consuming. In the CEE region (like in every other region), large numbers of sales force employees are constantly visiting general practitioners and hospitals to elucidate the prescribers about the available drugs. Such huge investments can often only be covered by products that are reimbursable. This cannot be organized overnight and – more importantly – for a subsidiary, a rapid increase of sales and marketing resources (e.g., sales force personnel) can quickly exceed the local budget. Hence, the effective management of this process requires the involvement of higher levels in the organization. In the case of Poland, the local subsidiary informed the regional headquarters quickly about a potential listing of a Boehringer product in the reimbursement status. Together with regional marketing, a business plan was developed and it was agreed upon to invest in the opportunity. Regional marketing brought in its experience in quantifying the estimated demand effect and the required sales force. For such events, the regional headquarters has its own regional budget in addition to the local budgets as agreed in a bottom-up process with Ingelheim.

Another key advantage from the perspective of corporate and regional headquarters is the increased level of control and coordination. The increasing regional marketing resources put more attention on the rather smaller countries than before the corporate headquarters. Procedures are reviewed and guidelines set up, the implementation of global strategies is constantly surveyed, and requests for adapting global marketing strategies are put under more scrutiny. In sum, the level of decision-making autonomy and freedom for smaller markets was higher when they reported to corporate headquarters. Two subsidiaries within CEE – Poland and Czech Republic – experienced this effect twice in recent years because they changed status due to several reasons. They went from a subsidiary reporting to the regional headquarters CEE to a subsidiary reporting to corporate headquarters (like the large European countries), and then back to the regional headquarters CEE. Both countries reported that substantial autonomy was gained when they were transferred to the corporate level even though the geographic distance is by and large equal between the subsidiary and corporate head office or regional headquarters.

Key issues of the regional marketing organization

The above-mentioned structure of dual reporting lines creates ambiguity, especially on the level of the marketing managers within the country organizations. Every subsidiary marketing manager has to report to the Marketing CEE (the product group managers) but also to the head of the subsidiary. However, the head of the subsidiary has a clear profit-and-loss focus whereas the Marketing Manager CEE is focused on turnover instead of profit.

Although this setup helps to focus neither too narrowly on aggressive sales growth (agenda of marketing) nor too narrowly on short-term financial performance (agenda of country heads), and it helps to bring key corporate marketing strategy elements into local decision-making via the "interface" of the regional headquarters, this structure creates some level of dissatisfaction among local marketing managers. A Boehringer internal study conducted in 2006, which involved all CEE countries as well as the regional headquarters, revealed increased dissatisfaction with the regional headquarters' interface role when the local marketing managers perceived high levels of ambiguity. Figure 8.9 illustrates this relationship. Such a lack of convenient and easy decision-making processes (from the perspective of local marketing) leads to some frustration and complaints about lack of trust on the regional level.

The effect on motivation is also reflected in another survey question. As an example, Figure 8.10 illustrates the perceptions of subsidiary managers and regional headquarters managers. Subsidiary marketing managers (here, managers of the CHC division) reported relatively high evaluations of direct communication with the corporate headquarters mainly based on expectations that this would improve internal information flows and decision-making, local employee motivation and local autonomy. Regional headquarters managers had much lower expectations, except for the issue autonomy and flexibility. Here, both the regional headquarters and the

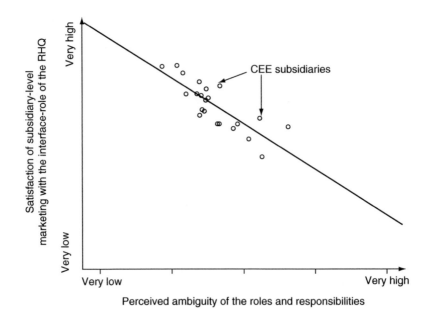

Figure 8.9 Ambiguity of roles and responsibilities – results from a Boehringer internal survey

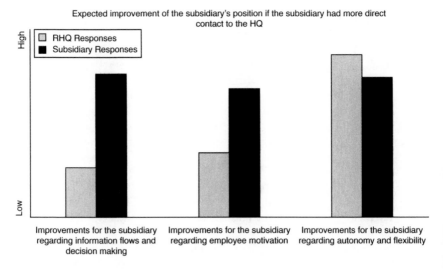

Figure 8.10   Issues of information flow and control between global and local levels – results from a survey

subsidiary managers recognize the control function of the regional head-quarters. In sum, it seems as if subsidiary managers have motives to circum-vent the regional headquarters.

Similarly, corporate head office managers are sometimes motivated to bypass the regional level and to contact local subsidiaries directly. This might occur because headquarters managers do not know the relevant con-tact persons at the regional level, or they expect an increased speed of infor-mation dissemination when the regional interface is not interfering.

How Boehringer overcomes issues while keeping the strengths of the marketing organization

Boehringer Ingelheim is very successful in managing these tensions. One of the key initiatives of the regional headquarters was a formalized written agreement with the corporate head office about the role of the regional head-quarters. The agreement states six basic principles that contain information about profit and loss responsibility but also the relationship between cor-porate, regional and local levels. Figure 8.11 lists the six principles, which apply not only to the marketing organization but also to the regional head-quarters as a whole.

In sum, the principles help the regional headquarters in maintaining cen-trality in every process that involves corporate and local organizational levels, that is, it confirms the regional headquarters role as the primary interface.[3] This applies to turnover as well as profit goals and makes clear that all sub-sidiary upward communication as well as headquarters downward commu-nication has to be channelled first to the regional headquarters. Principles 2 and 5 also describe the effect of the regional headquarters and imply the

---

1. The head office as has delegated to the regional headquarters the business responsibility as well as the responsibility for the functions (HR, Medicine, Finance,...) for the region

2. Regional headquarters is considered by the head office like one business

3. One top and one bottom line goal is agreed upon (turnover and profit) for the whole region for PM and CHC

4. The regional headquarters agrees with each country specific division objectives (PM and CHC)

5. The delegation of business responsibility to the regional headquarters reduces work load and complexity at the head office

6. Regional headquarters management conducts the performance review with each country head

---

Figure 8.11 Six basic principles agreed upon with RCV and corporate headquarters

message that cost savings at the corporate level due to reduced complexity and workload will not be achieved if direct communication exists between the corporate and the local country level. Although these principles seem straightforward and they are not extremely sophisticated, they have proven helpful in delivering a basis for discussions around roles and responsibilities. For example, discussions in marketing have produced the insight that there is one exception to the general rule that the regional headquarters occupies an interface position. Highly sensitive issues related to new knowledge regarding drug side effects and effectiveness can be disseminated from global to local directly because speed of dissemination is very important. In such a situation, from the perspective of the regional headquarters, the principles are a formalized document that helps to maintain the influence of regional headquarters vis-à-vis the corporate headquarters but also vis-à-vis the local subsidiaries.

Boehringer Ingelheim also considers the managerial and satisfaction issues rising from the matrix organization. The regional headquarters CEE has been granted a substantial budget for integrating and socializing subsidiary operations. Multi-day regional meeting are held twice or even thrice a year involving all product group managers on the local and regional level as well as the country heads of all subsidiary countries. These meetings contain, for example, moderated workshops in which specific issues are discussed in mixed groups. For example, typical workshops are centred on issues of communication and best practice transfer, and on explaining the logic and advantages of the ambiguous marketing roles on the level of the subsidiaries. Another element of these processes is the involvement of external workshop moderators and additional insight into the internal situation, for example, through surveys. In sum, these meetings help to increase transparency about the organizational choices – a method that has proven to be an important first step in solving tensions and conflicting goals.

Conclusion

Regional management at Boehringer Ingelheim is an additional management level that challenges the autonomy of subsidiaries and relieves the corporate headquarters of certain tasks. The regional headquarters has copied the matrix setup on the top of the organization and has institutionalized conflicting interests mainly between regional marketing focusing on turnover optimization, the business divisions focusing on divisional performance and the geographical organization (the country heads) focusing on country performance. The regional headquarters continuously supports and professionalizes the country operations and challenges the business and marketing plans. One important input into the latter is a strong regional knowledge base built through benchmarking and market research activities. Boehringer engages in several activities to smooth the processes between the corporate, regional and local levels. A very important element is thereby a formalization of six principles that describe the differentiation of roles and responsibilities between the levels.

9
Learning from the Automotive Industry

Ford Motor Company*

Introduction

It was Thursday, 8 p.m., and Peter Burger was still in the office going through his presentation for the next day's meeting. It was two weeks ago that he received an urgent telephone call from his boss to meet in his office immediately.

Mr Burger started working with Ford of Europe in 2006, the year when Ford reported one of the worst losses in the company's history. Being part of the corporate strategy team in Europe and working as assistant to the head of this team, Mr Burger soon found himself in the middle of a restructuring process called the "Way Forward Initiative." The initiative was started by Bill Ford and would be continued by the new CEO, Alan Mulally, who succeeded Bill Ford in September 2006. The aim was to restructure the operations of Ford Motors and bring the company back into making profit. Ford began going through a troubled phase in 2000. Especially in the US market, Ford was facing a tremendous downward trend. For decades, Ford concentrated its effort on selling SUVs and pickups and built its reputation on manufacturing big trucks and selling big cars with big engines. It left the growing segments of manufacturing small- and medium-sized cars to its foreign competitors. As a result of the increase in the oil prices, the demand for small- and medium-sized cars was increasing. Ford somehow missed that trend. Although Ford had made changes to the product portfolio recently, it would take time to shift the image in consumers' minds. In addition, bad news on the company's financial performance had not helped Ford's reputation.

---

* This case was written by Ursula Haas-Kotzegger under the direction of Bodo B. Schlegelmilch and Björn Ambos, WU Vienna, Institute for International Marketing and Management. It is intended to be used as the basis for class discussion rather than to illustrate the effective or ineffective handling of administrative situations. The case was made possible by the co-operation of Ford Motors and the text setting of the case is 2008.

Together with his boss, Mr Burger was assigned to prepare a presentation for the Board of Ford of Europe. Given the current economic situation and its impact on the automotive industry, the board meeting was planned to discuss the position of Ford of Europe within the organization and its future strategy. The board meeting was scheduled for Friday morning. Reflecting on the next day's meeting made Mr Burger shiver, he knew that the presentation and their recommendations would be of major importance to the European Board. So he started going through the facts and figures once again to make sure that he presented a realistic picture of the current situation of Ford of Europe and provided steps regarding the strategic directions for the future.

Company background

Since its establishment in 1903, Ford has successfully developed its position in the global automotive industry, ranking among the top of the world's biggest car manufacturer. It manufactures and distributes automobiles in more than 200 markets across five continents. Ford primarily operates in the United States and Europe with 95 plants worldwide. It is headquartered in Dearborn, Michigan, and employed 246,000 people as of December 2007.

The company recorded revenues of USD172,455 million through December of fiscal year 2007, an increase of 7.7 per cent over 2006. The operating profit of the company was USD5,631 million in fiscal year 2007, as compared to an operating loss of USD8,190 million in 2006. The net loss was USD2,723 million in 2007, compared to a net loss of USD12,613 million in 2006.[1] Ford is divided into two businesses: the automotive division and the financial services division.

Automotive division

In the automotive business, Ford produces a variety of vehicles, among them cars for the small, medium, large and premium segment as well as trucks, buses, vans and SUVs. The company's automotive vehicle brands include Ford, Jaguar, Lincoln, Mazda, Mercury and Volvo. It also owns a 33.4 per cent controlling stake in Mazda. Following the consumer trend towards smaller and more economical cars, Ford has increased its business in this segment.

The automotive business is organized into five segments: Ford North America, Ford South America, Ford Europe, Premier Automotive Group (PAG) and Ford Asia Pacific and Africa and Mazda. In addition to manufacturing and selling cars and trucks, Ford also provides a variety of after-sales services and products through its dealer network.

Financial services division

The financial services division, Ford Motor Credit Company, was established in 1923 as a wholly owned subsidiary of Ford. It provides automotive financing for Ford, Lincoln, Mercury and Volvo dealers and customers. Ford Motor Credit was established so Ford Motor Company dealers could provide competitive financing services to both individuals and businesses. The key financial services include retail financing, wholesale financing and third-party claim management services.

The revenues of the two divisions in fiscal year 2007 were split as follows: automotive, 89.5 per cent, and financial services, 10.5 per cent.[2]

History

Ford Motor Company was established in 1903 by Henry Ford and 11 business associates. At that time, the United States was home to 87 other car companies. Before Ford, cars were luxury items, very expensive and only affordable by the wealthy. Ford's genius was to recognize that with the right technology, cars could be made available to the public at an affordable price. He focused on making the process more efficient and as a result produced more cars and charged lower prices. Within a short time, Ford became an innovative company and one of the most successful car producers in the United States.

After 20 years of experimentations, the company launched its first model "T," also known as "Tin Lizzie," in 1908. It was a powerful car with a possible speed of 45 mph. It could run 25 miles on a gallon of gasoline. It carried a 20-horsepower, side-valve four-cylinder engine and two-speed planetary transmission on a 100-inch wheelbase.

But some of Ford's greatest innovations were not in cars themselves but in the manufacturing process. In 1914, Ford introduced a moving conveyor belt at the Highland Park plant, which led to a dramatic increase in production. As a result, in 1914, Ford produced 308,162 cars, more than all other automakers combined, thus making Ford the inventor of mass production.

In 1917, he took the first step toward an all-in-one manufacturing complex, where the processing of raw materials, parts and final automobiles could happen efficiently in a single place. Also in 1917, the company began producing trucks and tractors.

In 1919, after a conflict between Henry Ford and the stockholders, several investors left and the company became wholly owned by the Ford family.

In 1922, Ford bought Lincoln Motor Company, named after Abraham Lincoln, for USD8 million. Lincoln became the first "outsider" to join the Ford family of vehicle brands and initiated the company's entrance into the luxury market.

In the mid-1950s, Ford went public. In the same decade, Ford introduced the legendary Ford Thunderbird at Detroit's first auto show after the Second World War. The two-seated sports car became a legend that grew with each generation during the next five decades. Thunderbird went through several design changes with coupes, sedans, convertibles, hardtops, and mid-sized and large-sized configurations. It went on hiatus after the 1997 model year, but returned in 2001 as a retro-styled roadster.

The global expansion of Ford was intensified in 1960s when the company established Ford Europe in 1967. The North American Automotive Operations group was established in 1971, consolidating the operations in the United States, Canada and Mexico. Throughout the 1970s and 1980s the expansion continued, with further moves into Europe and Asia.

In 1987, Ford helped to form the Park Ridge Corporation in order to acquire the Hertz car rental business. Seven years later, Ford increased its stake in Hertz to 100 per cent. During the 1990s, as a result of the growing US economy and the low fuel prices, Ford succeeded in selling a large number of vehicles in the home market. Also in the 1990s, the company acquired Jaguar and Land Rover.

Ford's presence in China and Thailand was further extended during 2002 und 2003. In 2004, Ford signed a deal with the Chinese government to secure rights to land in Nanjing, where the company plans to build a second Ford plant in China. In 2005, Ford took full control of its operations in India with the purchase of a nearly 16 per cent stake from its partner, Mahindra & Mahindra Ltd. Ford Motor had set up its Indian subsidiary in Madras in 1995 as a 50–50 joint venture with Mahindra.

Then, in the 2000s, Ford experienced a downwards trend in its performance. The slowing economy, an increase in fuel prices as well as its product mix – the focus on fuel-intensive passenger cars – led to a decrease in sales.

Also in 2000, Ford was facing a major loss of reputation. Firestone tires that were fitted to all Ford Explorer vehicles were tipping and causing accidents. Bridgestone/Firestone recalled more than 6.5 million tires after more than 200 rollover deaths occurred in Ford Explorers. The tires exploded while the vehicle was moving; as a result the SUVs lost control. Ford recalled another 13 million tires in 2001. As a consequence, Firestone/Bridgestone dumped Ford as a customer and accused the company of using Firestone/Bridgestone as a scapegoat to deflect attention from the Ford Explorer. Ford's cost for the product recalls added up to USD2 billion. After federal investigators concluded that the tire defects were the main cause of the rollovers, Firestone/Bridgestone decided in 2005 to pay Ford USD240 million to help cover the costs of the recalls. However, as a consequence of the recalls, the reputation and credibility of Ford sank and the public lost confidence in the company.[3] In addition, major product recalls on Mazda in 2004 and Ford pickup trucks and SUVs in 2005 contributed to the negative trend the company was facing.

Markets

Global operations

Ford Motor Company has organized its automotive business activities into five segments: Ford North America, Ford South America, Ford Europe, Premier

Automotive Group (PAG) and Ford Asia Pacific and Africa and Mazda. Ford is therefore divided into geographical regions on the one hand and separates its Ford brands from luxury brands on the other hand. Whereas Ford Europe sells Ford brand vehicles and related service parts in Europe, Turkey and Russia, PAG – also located in Europe – sells its luxury brands (Volvo, Jaguar and Land Rover) throughout the whole world.

Table 9.1 illustrates the global market share of automobiles; Ford Motor Company is currently ranked in fourth position.

During the fiscal year 2007, the automotive division of Ford recorded revenues of USD154,379 million, an increase of 7.8 per cent vs. 2006. North America, the largest geographic market, reached USD93,063 million (+0.5 per cent vs. 2006) and accounted for 54 per cent of total revenues in 2007. In comparison, Europe accounted for 34.8 per cent of total revenues in 2007. Revenues in Europe increased by 19.9 per cent and reached USD60,044 in 2007. Other regions accounted for 11.2 per cent of total revenues in 2007. Revenues reached USD19,348 million, an increase of 11.5 per cent over 2006[4] (see Figure 9.1).

Table 9.2 provides an overview of Ford's core and affiliates brands, the retail vehicle sales per brand and the presence in the various regions. Whereas the Ford brand is sold in every region, Lincoln and Mercury are purely North American brands and almost unknown outside North America. Volvo and Land Rover have a strong presence in Europe, whereas the focus of Mazda lies in the region of Asia Pacific.

North America

Ford North America represents the most important geographical region within the company, accounting for more than 50 per cent of total revenues. The North America business includes the United States, Canada and Mexico.

Although Ford is among the key players in the US automobile industry, it has been losing market share during the past five years. Ford's overall market share in the United States has declined from 20.5 per cent in 2003

Table 9.1   Global market share, 2008

Company % Share, by Value, 2008	
Toyota Motor Corporation	12.80%
General Motors Corporation	8.90%
Daimler AG	8.10%
Ford Motor Company	7.80%
Other	62.40%
Total	100.0%

Source: Datamonitor, Global Automobiles, 2009, p. 13.

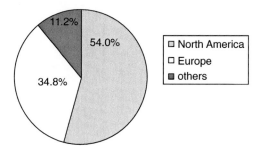

Figure 9.1 Ford's revenues by geography in 2007
Source: Datamonitor, Ford Motor Company, November 2008, p. 18.

to 14.7 per cent in 2008. This downward trend was primarily a result of increased competition, an industry shift away from Ford's traditionally strong segments (for example SUVs and pickups) and the discontinuation of a number of company's vehicle lines over the last couple of years.[5]

Figure 9.2 illustrates the market share within the US market in 2008. The US market is dominated by the "Big Three" national manufacturers, General Motors, Ford and Chrysler, which account for approximately 48 per cent of the market. The Big Three are heavily challenged by Japanese producers, which already account for more than 30 per cent of the US market.

Compared to 2005, when Ford was ranked number two with 18.2 per cent market share, Ford lost one rank in 2008. Toyota increased its market share over the last few years from 13.0 per cent in 2005 to 16.4 per cent in 2008 and overtook Ford, which is now ranked number three (14.7 per cent in 2008). GM is market leader with 22.1 per cent in 2008.[6]

Europe

Europe has always been of major importance to the automotive industry. The region is the world's largest vehicle producer: one-third of the 50 million cars produced globally are manufactured in the European Union.[7]

Ford broke into the new market quite soon after the company was established. In 1903, the first car model was imported to Britain. In the following year, the Central Motor Car Company of London was set up as Ford's overseas sales organization. In 1925, Ford Motor Company AG in Berlin was established. Ford Europe as a separate regional business was established in 1986. "It was Henry Ford II who was very interested in Europe, and he ensured the leadership at the top of the company to develop a European organization" (Ian Slater, Vice President, Public Relations, Ford Europe).

Since then, Ford Europe has built a solid position in Europe. It is the second largest geographical region for Ford and accounts for 34.8 per cent of

Table 9.2 Automotive core and affiliate brands

	Ford	Lincoln	Mercury	Jaguar	Volvo	Land Rover	Mazda
Dealers and markets**	10,963 dealers 111 markets	1,466 dealers 31 markets	1,916 dealers 20 markets	869 Dealers 93 markets	2,369 Dealers 105 markets	1,397 dealers 175 markets	5,899 dealers 133 markets
Retail vehicle sales and sales mix	5,298,471 **Sales mix:** 46% N. America 35% Europe 9% Asia Pacific 8% S. America 2% Rest-of-world	143,886 **Sales mix:** 99% N. America 1% Rest-of-world	177,896 **Sales mix:** 96% N. America 4% Rest-of-world	60,485 **Sales mix:** 59% Europe 27% N. America 9% Asia Pacific 5% Rest-of-world	458,323 **Sales mix:** 57% Europe 26% N. America 9% Rest-of-world 8% Asia Pacific	226,395 **Sales mix:** 60% Europe 23% N. America 8% Rest-of-world 7% Asia Pacific 2% S. America	1,335,148*** Sales mix 36% Asia Pacific 30% N. America 24% Europe 6% Rest-of-world 4% S. America

Source: Ford Motor Company/2007 Annual Report, p. 129.

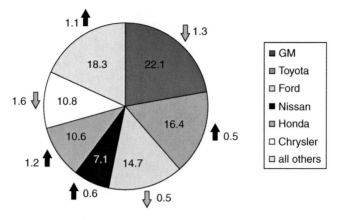

Figure 9.2   Competitive situation in the US automobile market, 2008[8]

total revenues in 2007. In addition to Ford Europe, the Premier Automotive Group (PAG), which comprises the luxury brands (Jaguar, Volvo and Land Rover), is located in Europe, selling its vehicles throughout the world.

The European car market is extremely competitive. For the past ten years, the six top car manufacturers – Ford, General Motors, Volkswagen AG, PSA Group, Renault Group and Fiat SpA – have accounted for more than 70 per cent of the total market. The competition is expected to become more intense because Japanese and Korean manufacturers have increased their production capacity in Europe and offer vehicles at lower prices.

Table 9.3 illustrates the top ten brands in the European automotive industry as of March 2008. Volkswagen is Europe's top-selling brand, followed by Ford and Opel. As a result of the difficult economic climate in most European countries, every brand had to face decreasing sales in 2008 compared to 2007.

Table 9.4 illustrates the top ten models in March 2008 compared to the previous year. Ford Fiesta is ranked number two, just slightly behind Peugeot 207. The top ten models in Europe comprise small- and medium-sized cars, which is in line with the global trend to smaller and less fuel-intensive vehicles.

Organizational structure of Ford Motor Company

Ford Motor Company is headquartered in Dearborn, Michigan, and employed 246,000 people as of December 2007. Since September 2006, Alan Mulally holds the position of Ford's President and CEO. He succeeded William C. Ford, who now serves as Executive Chairman and Chairman of the Board. The board of directors is elected by and responsible to the shareholders.

Table 9.3   Top European car brands, March 2008 vs March 2007 (Top ten brands)

Brand	Mar 08	Mar 07	% Change Mar	Mar YtD 08	Mar YtD 07	% Change YtD
VW	152,92	175,562	−12.9	399,953	399,041	+0.2
FORD	151,709	169,59	−10.5	350,914	365,931	−4.1
OPEL/VAUXHALL	144,547	165,588	−12.7	334,152	364,911	−8.4
RENAULT	121,848	129,55	−5.9	306,657	311,981	−1.7
PEUGEOT	109,639	126,794	−13.5	293,014	300,249	−2.4
FIAT	98,411	104,687	−6.0	275,799	267,242	+3.2
CITROEN	87,122	101,404	−14.1	241,041	257,779	−6.5
TOYOTA	86,638	105,74	−18.1	224,471	253,316	−11.4
BMW	74,869	76,074	−1.6	175,908	163,847	+7.4
MERCEDES	74,086	81,783	−9.4	186,246	184,043	+1.2

Source: Jato Dynamics quoted in Finfacts Business News Centre, www.finfacts.ie/irishfinance news/article_1013319.shtml (accessed 3 March 2009).

Table 9.4   Top ten European models, March 2008 vs March 2007 (Top ten models)

Marke & Model	Mar 08	Mar 07	% Change Mar	Mar YtD 08	Mar YtD 07	% Change YtD
PEUGEOT 207	46,5	49,802	−6.6	123,15	115,444	+6.7
FORD FIESTA	45,666	49,821	−8.3	98,229	105,511	−6.9
VW GOLF	45,484	47,209	−3.7	123,555	102,633	+20.4
OPEL/VAUXHALL CORSA	45,459	50,345	−9.7	106,624	118,607	−10.1
FORD FOCUS	45,274	54,104	−16.3	106,502	118,832	−10.4
OPEL/ VAUXHALL ASTRA	43,794	51,492	−14.9	99,94	108,229	−7.7
RENAULT CLIO	39,123	46,264	−15.4	97,643	110,087	−11.3
FIAT PUNTO	32,89	47,125	−30.2	89,605	116,247	−22.9
BMW SERIES 3	29,397	37,219	−21.0	66,942	75,718	−11.6
VW POLO	29,356	32,133	−8.6	74,168	73,424	+1.0

Source: Jato Dynamics quoted in Finfacts Business News Centre, www.finfacts.ie/irishfinance news/article_1013319.shtml (accessed 3 March 2009).

Their duty is to monitor the performance of the CEO and senior management to guarantee shareholder interests are being served. The board of directors has established the following committees to assist its work: Audit, Compensation, Environmental and Public Policy, Finance and Nominating and Governance.

Strategic operations (for example, global manufacturing, global product development, human resources and labour affairs) and regional strategic operations (for example, the Americas, Europe, Asia Pacific and Africa and

Mazda) are managed by senior managers (executive vice presidents and group vice presidents).

Ford of Europe

Ford of Europe was set up in 1986. It is the largest overseas operation of Ford with about 70,000 employees and eight vehicle plants. Originally, the European headquarters was located in Britain, because Ford had already been there for several decades. In the 1990s, the headquarters was relocated to Germany. Several reasons led to this decision: first, in Britain, Ford had a very strong position for several decades and even though Ford is an American company, many British people tend to think of Ford as a British company. This was not true in Germany. Therefore, due to the importance of this market, Ford wanted to increase its presence in Germany. Second, Germany is well known for its quality, which is also true for the automotive industry. "We came to regard Germany increasingly as the real bellwether for quality in the automotive industry" (Ian Slater, Vice President, Public Relations, Ford Europe). The move was planned in order to further increase Ford's position as leader in quality. Third, Germany is known for its high environmental standards. With the relocation, Ford has taken advantage of the sensitivity within the German organization towards environmental issues. This was in line with the global trend in the automotive industry to show more environmental commitment.

The PAG, which includes luxury brands such as Jaguar, Volvo and Land Rover, is also located in Europe but does not belong to Ford of Europe. It is a separate consumer business group (CBG). PAG oversees the sales, marketing, communications, franchise development, parts, distribution and customer service efforts of these premier brands on a global basis. PAG is headquartered in the United Kingdom. Both Ford of Europe and PAG report into the same office in London.

> Which is interesting from an academic point of view, because you have a regional, what we call consumer business group, which is Ford of Europe reporting into this management structure, but also global business like Volvo, Jaguar, etc. reporting into the same unit, which in turn reports to the US. (Ian Slater, Vice President, Public Relations, Europe)

Ford of Europe sells cars under the brand Ford to 51 European countries. The major focus is on 19 main European countries, called the "EU 19." In addition, Ford of Europe also comprises Russia and Turkey, markets with high growth potential.

Tables 9.5 and 9.6 show the top five markets by volume and by market share for Ford of Europe (January – September 2008). The United Kingdom is leading in both categories accounting for more than 330,000 vehicle sales and a market share of 16.1 per cent January to September 2008. In terms of

Table 9.5 Top five markets, volume and market share

Top 5 markets by volume Jan–Sept 2008		Top 5 market share Jan–Sept 2008	
UK	335,804	UK	16.1
Germany	181,134	Turkey	14.6
Italy	147,345	Ireland	13.6
Russia	141,420	Hungary	11.6
France	106,080	Spain	9.5

Source: Ford Europe, November 2008, p. 7.

Table 9.6 Suppliers

OEM Supply base for NA vehicles	Chrysler (%)	Ford (%)	GM (%)	Asian OEMs (%)	European OEMs (%)
GM	56	51	100	58	37
Ford	64	100	70	65	46
Chrysler	100	54	66	59	44

Source: CSM Worldwide (www.csmauto.com).

volume, Germany is ranked in second position, whereas in terms of market share it is not among the top five. Germany's market share in the period of January to September 2008 was 7.7 per cent. Across the main 19 European countries, Ford had a market share of 9.3 per cent (September 2008). Throughout Europe, Ford's market share was 8.6 per cent in September 2008 (–0.7 per cent compared to 2007).[9]

The year 2008 was full of contrasts for Ford Europe. For the last few years, Ford was accused of not launching enough new models in Europe and offering an aging product line. In the first half of the year 2008, the company launched three models – the Fiesta small car, Kuga crossover and Ka minicar – as well as a refreshed version of the Focus. As a result, new-car sales of 1 million units were the division's highest ever. However, as a result of the economic crisis, sales dropped during the second half of 2008.

In addition, overcapacity has been an issue for the company for several years. Ford Europe was facing excess capacity of 15 per cent in 2008. The new vehicle sales for the EU 19 (the main markets in Europe) were forecasted for 18 million units in 2008. Due to the difficult economic situation, the market was down to 15 million units. Confronted with the falling demand, the company needed to adjust its capacity on a weekly basis.[10]

Structure within Ford of Europe

The role of the regional headquarters. With Europe as leading manufacturer of cars, one-third of the global production is done in Europe. Ford has recognized the importance of a strong presence in the market.

Further to that, the automotive industry is a highly regulated industry, with a trend towards even more regulations and governmental interferences. The European Union is further increasing the environmental standards within the car industry, for instance, setting directives on CO_2 emissions. Further to EU directives, car manufacturers are also confronted with different regulations on the local level. Due to the complexity within Europe – many countries and various regulations – it would be very difficult to manage it from far away. This is an additional reason for the presence of a strong regional headquarters in Europe.

Ford Europe, in its function as regional headquarters, is a highly autonomous business entity.

> We do everything in Europe. I mean this effectively – I mean it is not autarky, but is effectively an autonomous business entity. It is still very much a regional business – producing European cars for Europeans. (Ian Slater, Vice President PR, Ford Europe)

The company imports engines and components on a global basis and also exports to some degree. Ford Motor Company operates with regional product lines, selling different cars to different geographical regions. As a result, the product portfolio of Europe is different than that of North America. "We have a regionally consistent product line, but we don't have a globally consistent product line" (Mark Schirmer, Head of Public Relations, Asia and Africa).

In addition to production facilities in Europe, the company also established two R&D centres; one is located in Germany and one in the United Kingdom. These centres were separately built and existed parallel for many years. Instead of shutting down one and growing the other, Ford Europe's strategy was to maintain both R&D centres and specialize the role and responsibility of each. These helped to build the two strongest pillars of Ford of Europe: United Kingdom and Germany. "We try to keep a balance between the two centres and it works remarkable well" (Ian Slater, Vice President PR, Ford Europe). In its R&D process, the company also takes advantage of so-called shared technology, that is, a set of technologies that come together in different forms to make different vehicles. Ford considers shared technology as being a more sophisticated model and a further development compared to platforms.

> For example the new generation Focus had a lot of technologies in common with Volvo S40. But if you look at the two vehicles they have nothing in common. Whereas, a generation ago, in terms of the automotive industry, the Mondeo in Europe and the Contour in America were very similar-looking vehicles. (Ian Slater, Vice President, Public Relations, Ford Europe)

Further to R&D, marketing activities are carried out by Ford of Europe independently of the Ford Motor Company. The organizational setup also guarantees that the business units are more or less self-financing and therefore responsible for their own budgeting.

The role of the local markets.   Within Ford of Europe, the local markets, called national sales centres, are concerned with local sales, customer service and local public relations. Most of the European countries are handled through these national sales centres; they are 100 per cent subsidiaries of Ford Motor Company. In countries where Ford has no local presence third-party importers are applied. These operations are coordinated by an office in Budapest, responsible for export countries.

Manufacturing, purchasing and product development are done on a European level and belong to the responsibility of the European business group. The European headquarters also provides the countries with the long-term product strategy and gives directions in product pricing and guidelines for communication. All marketing communication on above-the-line levels, such as TV commercials, billboards and the Internet, is managed by the European headquarters,. "It is more or less a toolbox for the national sales companies to make use of – you know – everything is there" (Hans Schep, Marketing Manager, Ford Netherlands). The tactical work and the adaption of the European communication materials are carried out by the local teams.

In terms of reporting, local marketing managers report to the local managing directors. The local managing directors in return report to the vice president of marketing and sales of Ford of Europe, who is located in the United Kingdom. Although the regional headquarters is based in Cologne, Germany, some headquarters functions, such as marketing and sales, are located in the United Kingdom. This goes back to the time when the regional headquarters was located there.

The major focus of the local markets is on managing the dealer network. Over the years, support functions such as sales planning and finance have been locally reduced and centralized. The company bundled these functions in order to make use of synergies and achieve economies of scale.

Trends and challenges for the automobile industry

Not only had the global financial crisis left marks on the automobile industry, but also trends and changes such as increasing competition and stronger environmental regulations already have and will continue to challenge the automobile market. Especially the saturated markets such as Europe, in particular Western Europe, will face major impacts. It will be of great importance to Ford Europe on how it manages and responds to these challenges and how it adapts to the changing environment.

Bankruptcy of a major automobile manufacturer

The automotive crisis, as a result of the financial crisis, has come to a head, and even bankruptcy has become a major topic in the business press. According to CSM Worldwide, an automotive research firm, a bankruptcy filing by one of the Big Three – General Motors, Chrysler or Ford – would have an immediate impact on the financial health and stability of suppliers and every automaker operating in North America, including the Asian and European manufacturers, because they are mutually dependent on the same supply base.

As the following graphic shows, 46 per cent of Ford suppliers also supply European automakers, and 59 per cent of Ford's suppliers also supply Asian manufacturers.

Excess capacity

In 2007, the estimated automotive industry global production capacity for light vehicles of around 85.4 million units exceeded global production by about 16.8 million units. In North America and Europe, excess capacity was estimated as 17 per cent and 11 per cent, respectively. This trend is projected to continue over the next couple of years.[11]

Pricing pressure and Asian competition

The pressure on prices will stay at a high level due to excess capacity, new product developments and increase in competition from Japanese and Korean manufacturers. Asian manufacturers have increased their manufacturing capacity in Europe and US in recent years. This has already contributed and will further contribute to the pricing pressure in the markets.. For instance, the Korean carmaker Hyundai announced plans to double its European engine production capacity by 2012. Hyundai and the sister brand Kia need more locally produced engines to power cars made in their new Central European factories.[12]

Consumer spending trends in Western Europe

Sales of passenger cars and light commercial vehicles are predicted to further decrease in 2010 as credit remains tight and consumers avoid replacing their vehicles until absolutely necessary. CSM Worldwide projects that passenger car sales in Western Europe will fall by 12.4 per cent to 12.0 million units in 2009 compared to 2008.[13]

Growth potential in emerging markets

Because the market for light vehicles in Western Europe and the United States is saturated, the growth potential lies in the emerging markets such as India, China as well as Central and Eastern Europe. The importance of Eastern and Central Europe in the automotive sector has increased tremendously over the last few years. This is true for production as well as sales.

New member states (EU12) accounted for 15 per cent of EU motor vehicle production by the end of 2007. This represents an increase of 25.2 per cent in 2007. Although still small, the new member states are highly specialized road vehicle producers. Based on skilled workers, low labour costs and a high potential demand, the importance of EU12 is increasing continuously.

Whereas the new car registration in Western Europe is flat or even declining, the Figure is increasing in Eastern and Central Europe. In the new EU member states, where car density is still much lower and many households have been able to afford buying a new car only recently, a steady growth was recorded in 2007 (+13.9 per cent). Mainly the Baltic States, Bulgaria, Poland and Romania are contributing to the high growth rate in EU12.[14]

EU vehicle regulations

The automobile industry is one of the most regulated sectors within the European Union. Before a car can be sold in the EU market, it must comply with what is known as the Framework Directive for Whole Vehicle Type Approval. This framework directive consists of a long list of technical requirements for motor vehicles as well as for components and separate technical units from which vehicles are assembled. These requirements are set up for the following categories: environment, lighting and signalling, active safety, passive safety and others.[15]

Further directives of the European Union include increasingly stringent emission standards for passenger and light commercial vehicles for model years 2005 and thereafter (EURO 4). Manufacturers are responsible for the emissions performance of these vehicles for five years or 100,000 kilometres, depending on which occurs first. Even more stringent emission standards (EURO 5 and EURO 6) are planned for 2014–2015.[16]

The European Union is a party to the Kyoto Protocol of the United Nations Framework Convention on Climate Change, and therefore has agreed to reduce greenhouse gas emissions. As a result, for the automobile industry, the CO_2 legislation of the European Union says automakers will have to reduce CO_2 emissions from new cars to 130 grams per kilometre by 2012–2015, with an additional 10-gram reduction coming from "complementary measures," including a greater use of biofuels. Furthermore, 65 per cent of new cars will have to comply with the emission requirements in 2012, 75 per cent in 2013, 80 per cent in 2014 and 100 per cent in 2015. This regulation also includes car labelling and CO_2 information in advertising.[17]

To follow these directions will be challenging and costly for Ford of Europe and the automobile industry.

Ford's restructuring efforts

Ford was going through a troubled phase starting in 2000 onwards. Especially in the home market US, Ford was facing a tremendous downwards trend.

The rising healthcare costs for its aging workforce and the increase in fuel prices led to a downturn in profit. For decades, Ford concentrated its effort on selling SUV's and Pickups and left the growing segments of small and medium-sized car to its foreign competitors. As a result of the increase in oil price, the demand for small and medium-size cars was increasing. Nowadays, small cars have reached nearly 45 per cent of total industry sales globally.[18] Ford somehow missed the trend and started to face a decrease in sales, resulting in decreasing plant utilization and huge discount activities. The troubles reached a peak in 2006, when Ford Motors posted a loss of USD 12.7 billion for the fiscal year 2006, one of the worst losses in the company's history.[19]

In order to improve its operations, the company started the Way Forward Plan in 2006 to restructure the operations of Ford Motors and bring it back into profit. The initiative was started by Bill Ford and will be continued by the new CEO, Alan Mulally, who succeeded Bill Ford in September 2006. Prior to his position at Ford, Mulally served as Executive Vice President at the Boeing Company and as President and CEO of Boeing Commercial Airplane. He is known as a turnaround expert, which he successfully demonstrated at the airplanes division at Boeing.

The restructuring plan of Ford comprises four key priorities:

- Aggressively restructuring to operate profitably at the current demand and changing mix
- Accelerating development of new products customers want and value
- Financing the plan and improving the balance sheet
- Working together effectively as a global team

Alan Mulally described the plan in the company's annual report for 2007:

> To achieve profitable growth we need to take advantage of every potential economy of scale and best practice we can find. That means operating as a team around the world, with one plan and one goal. One team, one plan, one goal – one Ford.

As a first result of the restructuring process, the company recorded revenues of USD172,455 million during the fiscal year ending in December 2007, an increase of 7.7 per cent over 2006. So far the restructuring process has mainly affected the North American operations, where thousands of jobs had been shed since 2006. However, faced with ongoing sales decreases, Ford Europe announced that it also needs to return to profit as soon as possible.

Preparations for the European Board Meeting

After he had gone through the presentation again and again for several hours, Mr Burger became convinced that Ford of Europe would play a major role in the restructuring process and in bringing Ford back into the fast lane. He is certain he and his boss have developed reasonable answers to the following questions: What will be the effects of the company's restructuring plans on Ford of Europe? How can Ford meet the challenges resulting from the difficult state of the economy? How will Ford of Europe deal with future trends and challenges to its European operations? What role will Ford of Europe play in bringing the company back into profit?

It is already midnight when Mr Burger leaves the office to get some sleep before the next day's meeting. He feels that he is well prepared to meet tomorrow's challenges – just like Ford of Europe will meet its future challenges.

Appendix

A9.1   Consolidated statement of income

Ford Motor Company and Subsidiaries
For the Years Ended December 31, 2007, 2006, and 2005
(in millions, except per share amounts)

	2007	2006	2005
Sales and revenues			
Automotive sales	$ 154,379	$ 143,249	$ 153,413
Financial Services revenues	18,076	16,816	23,422
Total sales and revenues	172,455	160,065	176,835
Costs and expenses			
Automotive cost of sales	142,587	148,866	144,920
Selling, administrative and other expenses	21,169	19,148	24,588
Goodwill impairment	2,400	–	–
Interest expense	10,927	8,783	8,417
Financial Services provision for credit and insurance losses	668	241	483
Total costs and expenses	177,751	177,038	178,408
Automotive interest income and other non-operating income/(expense), net...	1,161	1,478	1,247
Automotive equity in net income/(loss) of affiliated companies	389	421	285
Gain on sale of The Hertz Corporation ("Hertz") (Note 20)	–	–	1,095
Income/(Loss) before Income taxes	(3,746)	(15,074)	1,054
Provision for/(Benefit from) income taxes (Note 19)	(1,294)	(2,655)	(855)
Income/(Loss) before minority interests	(2,452)	(12,419)	1,909
Minority Interests in net income/(loss) of subsidiaries	312	210	280
Income/(Loss) from continuing operations	(2,764)	(12,629)	1,629
Income/(Loss) from discontinued operations (Note 20)	41	16	62
Income/(Loss) before cumulative effects of changes in accounting principles	(2,723)	(12,613)	1,691
Cumulative effects of changes in accounting principles (Note 28)	–	–	(251)
Net income/(loss)	$ (2,723)	$ (12,613)	$ 1,440
Average number of shares of Common and Class B Stock outstanding	1,979	1,879	1,846
AMOUNTS PER SHARE OF COMMON AND CLASS B STOCK (Note 21)			
Basic income/(loss)			
Income/(Loss) from continuing operations	$ (1.40)	$ (6.73)	$ 0.88
Income/(Loss) from discontinued operations	0.02	0.01	0.04
Cumulative effects of changes in accounting principles	–	–	(0.14)
Net income/(loss)	$ (1.38)	$ (6.72)	$ 0.78
Diluted income/(loss)			
Income/(Loss) from continuing operations	$ (1.40)	$ (6.73)	$ 0.86
Income/(Loss) from discontinued operations	0.02	0.01	0.03
Cumulative effects of changes in accounting principles	–	–	(0.12)
Net income/(loss)	$ (1.38)	$ (6.72)	$ (0.77)
Cash dividends	$ –	$ 0.25	$ 0.40

Source: Ford Motor Company, 2007/Annual report, p. 54.

Sector statement of income

Ford Motor Company and Subsidiaries
For the Years Ended December 31, 2007, 2006, and 2005
(in millions, except per share amounts)

	2007	2006	2005
AUTOMOTIVE			
Sales	$ 154,379	$ 143,249	$ 153,413
Costs and expenses			
Cost of sales	142,587	148,866	144,920
Selling, administrative and other expenses	13,660	12,327	12,704
Goodwill impairment	2,400	–	–
Total costs and expenses	158,647	161,193	157,624
Operating income/(loss)	(4,268)	(17,944)	(4,211)
Interest expense	2,252	995	1,220
Interest income and other non-operating income/(expense), net	1,161	1,478	1,247
Equity in net income/(loss) of affiliated companies	389	421	285
Income/(Loss) before income taxes-Automotive	(4,970)	(17,040)	(3,899)
FINANCIAL SERVICES			
Revenues	18,076	16,816	23,422
Costs and expenses			
Interest expense	8,675	7,788	7,197
Depreciation	6,289	5,295	5,854
Operating and other expenses	1,220	1,526	6,030
Provision for credit and insurance losses	668	241	483
Total costs and expenses	16,852	14,850	19,564
Gain on sale of Hertz (Note 20)	–	–	1,095
Income/(Loss) before income taxes- Financial Services	1,224	1,966	4,953
TOTAL COMPANY			
Income/(Loss) before income taxes	(3,746)	(15,074)	1,054
Provision for/(Benefit from) income taxes (Note 19)	(1,294)	(2,655)	(855)
Income/(Loss) before minority interests	(2,452)	(12,419)	1,909
Minority interests in net income/(loss) of subsidiaries	312	210	280
Income/(Loss) before continuing operations	(2,764)	(12,629)	1,629
Income/(Loss) from discontinued operations (Note 20)	41	16	62
Income/(Loss) before cumulative effects of changes in accounting principles	(2,723)	(12,613)	1,691
Cumulative effects of changes in accounting principles (Note 28)	–	–	(251)
Net income/(loss)	$ (2,723)	$ (12,613)	$ 1,440
Average number of shares of Common and Class B Stock outstanding	1,979	1,879	1,846
AMOUNTS PER SHARE OF COMMON AND CLASS B STOCK (Note 21)			
Basic income/(loss)			
Income/(Loss) from continuing operations	$ (1.40)	$ (6.73)	$ 0.88
Income/(Loss) from discontinued operations	0.02	0.01	0.04
Cumulative effects of changes in accounting principles	–	–	(0.14)
Net income/(loss)	$ (1.38)	$ (6.72)	$ 0.78
Diluted income/(loss)	–	–	
Income/(Loss) from continuing operations	$ (1.40)	$ (6.73)	$ 0.86
Income/(Loss) from discontinued operations	0.02	0.01	0.03
Cumulative effects of changes in accounting principles	–	–	(0.12)
Net income/(loss)	$ (1.38)	$ (6.72)	$ 0.77
Cash dividends	$ –	$ 0.25	$ 0.40

Source: Ford Motor Company, 2007/Annual report, p. 55.

Consolidated balance sheet

Ford Motor Company and Subsidiaries
(in millions)

	December 31, 2007	December 31, 2006
ASSETS		
Cash and cash equivalents..	$ 35,283	$ 28,896
Marketable securities (Note 3)	5,248	21,472
Loaned securities (Note 3)	10,267	5,256
Finance receivables, net	109,053	106,863
Other receivables, net	8,210	7,067
Net investment in operating leases (Note 5)	33,255	29,787
Retained interest in sold receivables (Note 7)...................	653	990
Inventories (Note 8)...	10,121	10,017
Equity in net assets of affiliated companies (Note 9)......................	2,853	2,790
Net property (Note 11)...	36,239	36,055
Deferred income taxes...	3,500	4,922
Goodwill and other net intangible assets (Note 13)......................	2,069	3,611
Assets of discontinued/held-for-sale operations........................	7,537	8,215
Other assets	14,976	13,255
Total assets	$ 279,264	$ 279,196
LIABILITIES AND STOCKHOLDERS' EQUITY		
Payables	$ 20,832	$ 21,214
Accrued liabilities and deferred revenue (Note 15)........................	74,738	80,058
Debt (Note 16)...	168,530	171,832
Deferred income taxes...	3,034	2,744
Liabilities of discontinued/held-for-sale operations........................	5,081	5,654
Total liabilities...	272,215	281,502
Minority interests	1,421	1,159
Stockholders' equity		
Capital stock (Note 21)		
Common Stock, par value $0.01 per share (2,124 million shares issued and 6,000 million authorized)........................	21	18
Class B Stock, par value $0.01 per share (71 million shares issued and 530 million authorized)...............................	1	1
Capital in excess of par value of stock.............................	7,834	4,562
Accumulated other comprehensive income/(loss)........................	(558)	(7,846)
Treasury stock...	(185)	(183)
Retained earnings/(Accumulated deficit)...............................	(1,485)	(17)
Total stockholders' equity..	5,628	(3,465)
Total liabilities and stockholders' equity...............................	$ 279,264	$ 279,196

Source: Ford Motor Company, 2007/Annual report, p. 56.

A9.2   Ford market share, September 2008

Ford market share September 2008

Total vehicles per country (+/−2007)

Austria	7.5%	(+0.4%)
Belgium	8.0%	(+0.8%)
Switzerland	6.1%	(+1.9%)
Czeck Republic	10.5%	(+1.7%)
Germany	7.7%	(+0.8%)
Denmark	6.7%	(−2.4%)
Spain	8.2%	(1.4%)
France	5.3%	(+0.7%)
Finland	8.4%	(+0.2%)
Great Britain	14.9%	(−0.1%)
Greece	6.9%	(−0.7%)
Hungary	10.3%	(−1.6%)
Italy	7.7%	(+/−0.0%)
Ireland	16.3%	(+0.9%)
Norway	9.2%	(+1.5%)
Netherlands	10.2%	(+1.3%)
Portugal	7.3%	(+0.8%)
Poland	5.2%	(−1.8%)
Sweden	5.6%	(−0.8%)
Russia	4.2%	(−2.0%)
Turkey	16.0%	(−0.9%)
Total Europe	8.6%	(−0.7%)

Source: @Ford Europe, November 2008, p. 6.

Honda Motor Company Limited[*]

Some dream to escape the reality, some to change it forever.
Soichiro Honda, Founder of Honda Motor Co., Ltd.

Dreams inspire us to create innovative products that enhance mobility and benefit society. To meet the particular needs of customers in different regions around the world, we base our sales networks, research and development centres and manufacturing facilities in each region.
Honda Worldwide Philosophy[20]

Japan's renowned Honda Motor Company Limited is the world's largest manufacturer of motorcycles and one of the leading manufacturers of automobiles in the world. The company is recognized internationally for its expertise and leadership in developing and manufacturing a wide variety of products that incorporate Honda's highly efficient internal combustion engine technologies, ranging from small general-purpose engines to specialty sports cars. Approximately 19.3 million Honda products were sold worldwide during the fiscal year that ended 31 March 2008.

History

Soichiro Honda, the founder of Honda Motor Co., Ltd., was born in a poor family in Japan in 1906. He inherited his inborn manual dexterity and his curiosity about machines from his father, Gihei Honda. While doing his apprenticeship at Art Shokai, an automobile servicing company, the owner soon spotted the young man's star qualities. At the age of seventeen,

---

[*] This case was written by Ilona Szocs under the direction of Bodo B. Schlegelmilch and Björn Ambos, WU Vienna, Institute for Marketing and Management. It is intended to be used as the basis for class discussion rather than to illustrate the effective or ineffective handling of administrative situations. The case was made possible by the co-operation of Honda Motors.

Mr Honda became the accompanying engineer for the company's successful racing cars. In 1928, he opened a branch of Art Shokai in Hamamatsu, the only one of the owner's trainees who was granted this degree of independence. He was not just admired for his ability to repair machines, he was also given free reign for his talent as an inventor, later earning the title "the Edison of Hamamatsu."

In 1936, driven by a desire to move into manufacturing, Mr Honda set up the Tokai Seiki Heavy Industry and started to produce piston rings. The Second World War, however, took its toll on the new business, and it was not until 1946 when the Honda Technical Institute was established. Here, the motorizing of bicycles with war-surplus engines began and, later on, the production of engines.

Due to the success of the 2-stroke A-type 50cc engine, Honda Motor Co., Ltd. was formed in September 1948. Honda's innovative overhead valve design made its early 1950s Dream model a runaway success. As the market started to show signs of preference for 4-cycle engines, the company released the Honda 4-Stroke E-Type in 1951. It was the company's first highly successful motorcycle, selling 32,000 units per year by 1954 and paving the way for Honda's ongoing success. A few years later, Honda introduced the best-selling powered vehicle of all time, the 50cc Super Cub, which is still being produced today. Encouraged by the success, Honda expanded capacity and began exporting. American Honda Motor Company was formed in Los Angeles in 1959, accompanied by the slogan "You meet the nicest people on a Honda" in a campaign crafted to counter the stereotypical biker image.

In 1960, the company spun off the Honda Research and Development (R&D) Centre into an independent entity. During the 1960s, Honda added overseas factories and began producing lightweight trucks, sports cars, and minicars. The company began selling its tiny 600 model in the United States in 1970, but it was the Civic, introduced in 1973, that first scored with the US car market. Three years later, Honda introduced the Accord, which featured an innovative frame adaptable for many models. In 1982, Accord production started at the company's Ohio plant.

Former Honda engineer Nobuhiko Kawamoto was named president in 1990, a year before Soichiro Honda died. Kawamoto cut costs and continued to expand the company internationally. In 1997, Honda bought Peugeot's plant in Guangzhou, China, and boosted its US vehicle production by opening an all-terrain vehicle (ATV) plant in South Carolina in 1998. That year, Hiroyuki Yoshino, an engineer with US management experience, succeeded Kawamoto as CEO. In 1999, Honda and GM agreed to a deal in which Honda would supply low-emission V6 engines and automatic transmissions to GM, while Isuzu, a GM affiliate, would supply Honda with diesel engines. Later that year, Honda's R&D unit set up a solar-powered hydrogen production station in California as part of its efforts to develop renewable-energy fuel cell vehicles.

Years of research and experimenting with humanoid robotics technology brought the announcement of ASIMO in 2000, a highly advanced humanoid robot equipped with facial and gesture recognition. In 2005, Honda entered into a ten-year business alliance with Disneyland resort wherein the company would sponsor the theme park's anniversary festivities and exhibit ASIMO. Other recent activities include the introduction of the company's first pickup truck, the Honda Ridgeline, in 2006, and the first luxury motorcycle equipped with an airbag, the 2006 Gold Wing. In the same year, the group founded Honda Aircraft Company, a wholly owned subsidiary, which has developed Honda's first aircraft, the HA-420 Honda Jet.

Corporate profile

Headquartered in Tokyo, Japan, Honda employs a workforce of more than 170,000 and has a total of 397 subsidiaries and 104 affiliates in 28 countries (as of March 2008).[21] Its global network of subsidiaries and affiliates is working with strong compliance with the company's policy and principles. Honda operates under the basic principles of "Respect for the Individual" and "The Three Joys" – expressed as the joy of buying, the joy of selling and the joy of creating.[22] The company's mission statement stresses a global viewpoint and the commitment to supply products of the highest quality, yet at a reasonable price for worldwide customer satisfaction. In line with these principles, Honda emphasizes the individual aspect of each employee and the respect for the particular needs of customers in different regions around the world.

Japan's biggest automaker operates through four business divisions: the automobile business, motorcycle business, power products and other businesses and financial services. The automobile business division manufactures passenger cars, multi-wagons, minivans, sports utility vehicles, sports coupe and mini vehicles. Popular passenger car models include Legend, Accord, Civic and Acura. The motorcycle business produces a range of motorcycles, from the 50cc class to the 1800cc class cylinder displacement.[23] The line consists of scooters, sports motorcycles, commuter motorcycles, all-terrain vehicles and personal watercraft. The power products and other businesses segment manufactures commercial and residential-use machinery (for example, lawn mowers and snow blowers), portable generators and outboard motors. The company also makes engines for light business jets, fuel cells and humanoid robots. The financial services of Honda include retail lending, leasing to customers and other financial services, such as wholesale financing to dealers. Figure 9.3 shows the percentage of net sales by each of these four business divisions in fiscal year 2008.

The motorcycle business is one of Honda's strengths. Motorcycles are a basic means of transportation in many parts of the world, and demand is expected to grow in Asia and South America.[24]

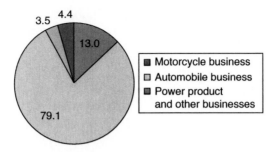

Figure 9.3 Percentage of net sales by business
Source: Based on Honda Annual Report 2008.

Since building its first manufacturing plant overseas, Honda has established independent local operations around the world for research, development, marketing and production.

Global organizational structure

Today, Honda has a complex organizational structure featuring both functional and divisional traits. It operates with a typical matrix structure (Appendix A9.1), which combines its regional headquarters activities with the business segment headquarters operations.

The group is headed by the Board of Directors, consisting of 21 directors (Appendix A9.2). The Board precedes the Executive Council, which is supported by the Business Ethics Committee. Corporate operations are split into six regional operations, namely, Japan, North America, Latin America, Europe/Middle and Near East/Africa, Asia/Oceania and China. A general manager from the Board of Directors or an operating officer is assigned to each regional headquarter and main division as well as to each R&D subsidiary. In addition, the Executive Council deals with important matters concerning management, and regional operating boards focus on matters concerning management of their respective regions. The main idea behind the six region strategy is that subsidiaries and dealers report directly to the regional headquarters located in Tokyo, Torrance, London, Sao Paulo, Bangkok and Beijing. The regional headquarters in turn report to Honda's main headquarters in Tokyo.

All functions are carried out on a base of strategic proposals coming directly from the regional headquarters. Regional headquarters develop a pan-regional strategy and each subsidiary is then responsible for its own local strategy, which has to be in line with the overall strategy of a particular region. The main responsibilities of the regional headquarters comprise product line development, pricing strategy, communication and PR functions and some back office functions (for example, marketing, logistics and administration). The subregional headquarters are mainly responsible for sales administration, marketing activities, information technology, service and warranty, accounting and human resources functions. The most important role of each regional office is quick and flexible reaction to different customers' needs as well as dealer network development.

Honda's head office is situated in Tokyo. Regional headquarters are located in Marysville, OH, (for North America), Sao Paulo, Brazil (for Latin America), Reading, United Kingdom (for Europe/Middle and Near East/Africa) and Bangkok, Thailand (for Asia/Oceania). In addition, the group holds subregional headquarters in many countries.

The headquarters in Japan plays a key role in global operations by working to develop advanced technologies and coordinate worldwide business efforts for optimal performance. As Honda continues to localize production around the world, its manufacturing bases in Japan are developing core engineering technologies to support operations overseas. The North American operations also play a vital role in Honda's global supply network. Honda operates 18 subsidiaries in this region, 15 of them located in the United States, two in Canada and one in Mexico. A 70 per cent profit has been gained by the American operation, which has a very strong influence over the Japanese office. Honda's European market share accounts for just 2 per cent, due to fierce competition and strong position of local car producers.

Manufacturing operations are situated in 40 separate factories (Appendix A9.3) around the world. Automobiles are mainly produced in Japan, the United States, Canada, Thailand and the United Kingdom; motorcycles are produced primarily in Japan, Brazil, India, Italy, the Philippines, Spain, Thailand and the United States (Appendix A9.4). Honda's sales activities cover all important car markets in Asia, Africa, Europe, North and South America and Oceania. Within the motorcycle area, the Kumamoto Factory is the most advanced operation of its kind in the world. Here, Honda focuses on high-efficiency and high-quality production systems to meet worldwide demand.

Approximately 96 per cent of Honda's overseas sales are made through its principal foreign sales subsidiaries, which distribute the company's products to local wholesalers and retail dealers.[25] Honda is enjoying brisk motorcycle sales, particularly in Asia where motorcycles are a popular mode of transportation. Honda has also completed the conversion of its entire motorcycle lineup to cleaner-burning four-stroke engines. On the automotive side, Honda gained market share in the United States through its entry in the light truck segment with the Ridgeline pickup. In Europe, Honda is capitalizing on the popularity of diesel models, and in China, the company is selling a lot of cars as the Honda brand grows in popularity.

One of Hondas goals is to find a balance between global integration and local responsiveness.[26] In 1994, the company developed a Five Region Strategy, comprising North America, Europe/Middle East/Africa, South

America, Asia/Oceania and Japan, in order to handle diverse demands in a more appropriate way. In 2003, Honda added one additional and rapidly increasing region: China.

Regarding revenues by geography, in the fiscal year 2008, Honda earned 50.8 per cent of its revenues from North America (predominantly the United States), 17 per cent from Japan, 12.5 per cent from Europe and 10.9 per cent from Asia. The other regions generated 8.7 per cent of total revenues.[27]

The group's R&D divisions operate independently as subsidiaries, allowing technicians to pursue their tasks with significant freedom. Product-related R&D is spearheaded by the Honda R&D Co., Ltd.; Honda R&D Americas, Inc., in the United States; and Honda R&D Europe (Deutschland) GmbH in Germany. R&D on production technologies centres on Honda Engineering Co., Ltd., in Japan and Honda Engineering North America, Inc. All of these entities work in close association with the company's other entities and businesses in their respective regions. Both Honda R&D Co., Ltd., and Honda Engineering Co., Ltd., are wholly owned by Honda Motor Company Ltd. and report directly to the main headquarters in Tokyo.

Honda invests heavily into its strong R&D capability to ensure further competitive advantages. These efforts lead to the development of innovative products, which allow the company to remain at the forefront of its respective businesses and differentiate its offerings in a highly competitive market. Honda has always been quick in responding to shifting market trends and in grasping opportunities. The company has spent a large amount of money for the development of hybrid vehicles, the demand for which is expected to increase. Another recent example is Honda's increased activity in R&D of alternative fuel vehicles. Total consolidated expenditures for the fiscal year 2008 amounted to ¥587.9 billion. Honda believes that it is important to strengthen the fundamentals of its product creation capabilities at home, in Japan. Unlike Toyota and other car producers, most of Honda's technology is developed by Honda itself, supplemented by some buy-in technology. Quality, innovation and technological improvement are key components of Honda's product development process. Honda has a two- to three-year cycle from development to production compared to a four-year average in the automotive industry. Although production is managed with tight control, Honda's organization for research is flat, which fosters innovation.

Although the company operates globally, it keeps its strong Japanese culture within internal affairs.[28] Top-level management of overseas operations is in general Japanese. Even though English is widely used as a language for day-to-day communication, Japanese is strongly preferred for managerial, business or product development activities when communicating with the main headquarters or other top managers from different regions. Therefore, Honda's way of doing business is unique in maintaining this homogeneity.

Honda in Europe

Honda started to export motorcycles to Europe in the 1950s. In 1963, it opened a motorcycle manufacturing plant in Belgium, the first such foreign-based facility for the company, followed in 1976 by a motorcycle plant in Italy. In Europe, Honda motorcycles are popular for their dynamic and environmental performance. Honda's strength in motorcycle sales was followed by the establishment of a power products factory in France in 1986, and the start of automotive manufacturing in the United Kingdom in 1992.

Since its establishment as Honda's European headquarter in 1989, Honda Motor Europe Ltd. has acted as a hub for the European facilities network, forming strong cooperative partnerships throughout Europe. Aiming to expand and strengthen its European operations, Honda delegated regional leadership to new subsidiaries established in Germany and France in 1994. Further, Honda R&D facilities were established in the United Kingdom, Germany and Italy and mandated to collaborate in the development of products tailored to the needs of local markets. To strengthen local production, Honda began automobile production in Turkey in 1997 and, in the fall of 2001, launched operations at a second factory in the United Kingdom. The UK facilities have become another vital link in Honda's global supply network, with Civic Type R exports to Japan beginning in the autumn of 2001 and CR-V exports to the United States beginning in the spring of 2002.

Honda aims to gain more strength in this intensely competitive market through developing models that are attuned to European tastes. It is promoting product development that meets regional needs by establishing a broad-based local network of company facilities and R&D offices.

In the past, for its operations in Europe, Honda used to have subsidiaries. Today, the company operates with branches instead, which control the dealers. The organization of regional headquarters started in 1994 and since that time, profitability has been improving. Honda is seeking reduction in the complexity of its operations in Europe through the three regional offices in Germany, France and Sweden, and one regional headquarters in the United Kingdom. Management is confident that the current matrix structure works well and gives a lot of autonomy in decision-making to the UK operation.

The European region headed by the regional headquarters, Honda Motor Europe Ltd. in London, is divided into two subregional headquarters: Honda Motor Europe North (HME North), located in Offenbach, Germany, and Honda Motor Europe South (HME South), located in Paris, France. HME North controls the branches in Germany, Austria, Belgium and the Netherlands while HME South controls the branches in France, Spain and Italy. Both HME North and HME South report to the regional headquarters in London while all the countries under these subregional headquarters report to their respective branch of HME. All the other countries that do not fall under these two umbrellas are covered from the UK head office and report directly to London. Honda established Honda Nordic, an executing arm of the European headquarters, headquartered in Malmö, Sweden, to manage operations in the Northern European countries of Sweden, Denmark, Finland, Norway, Estonia, Lithuania and Latvia. Furthermore, Honda Czech, Honda Poland, Honda Hungary and Honda Portugal are independent subsidiaries with typically a slim structure and a limited number of people, each covering various functions. They report directly to the regional headquarter in London. In CEE, Honda still works via subsidiaries and distributors, but is planning to merge them in the future into either HME North or South. Honda Motor Russia and Honda Turkey are separate subsidiaries, not covered by the HME North or South umbrella either. They are 100 per cent owned by Honda Motor Co., Ltd., and report to the regional headquarters in London. In addition, the African market is also part of the European regional headquarters. Sales volumes and margins in Africa and Europe are comparable. Similar marketing as in Europe can be applied to the Mediterranean African countries and South Africa as well. These are the territories where the biggest sales occur. Honda has established a depot in Nigeria, South Africa and Morocco in order to supply cars with parts in the African operation.

The reason for locating the regional headquarters in London is because Japanese companies traditionally prefer to put their head office in the United Kingdom because of the English language, which is more familiar to Japanese than, for example, French or Spanish. One other big reason for the choice has been Honda's existing factory in Swindon. The headquarters in Tokyo does not touch the day-to-day operations of the regional headquarters and subregional headquarters. However, it has a European section that supplies components to warehouses of the European offices. Honda's operations are in fact strongly controlled by each regional headquarters where the managing director is the top person in charge. This person controls about 90 per cent of the sales within the given region. The purpose is to respond quickly to the needs of the markets, which are very much diversified. This approach can lead, however, to many challenges and clashes of ideas on the administrative side. In addition, the rationale behind subregional headquarters is to be more efficient by combining back office functions such as advertising.

Research and product development

Regional headquarters include the function of R&D. Europe's R&D centres are based in the United Kingdom and Germany. Core R&D is done in Japan but adaptations to a major degree are done locally. Due to this fact, for example, the Accord for the European market differs from the one produced for the Japanese market and also from that for the American market. Different needs of the markets created dissimilar cars for each region, although the name of the car remained the same. For example, the style of the American Accord is more conservative. In Europe, where Honda's market share is much lower, the company needs to sell the car to a sportier segment in order to differentiate. As a result, the European Accord is more sporty and smaller than the American one. Unlike Toyota, Honda seeks to develop most of the technologies for its cars in-house. The company has a small number of buy-in technologies in cases where buying these from suppliers in Europe or the United States proves to be more economical or beneficial.

In the large majority of cases, the first original concept of the car is usually made by R&D in Japan. Engineers, managers and product directors in each regional headquarters are called to the Japanese R&D office to carry out discussions. At this point, the car does not have a name yet. Further discussions will follow with the regional model directors who eventually decide on the acceptance of the new model. The specification of the model to be sold in each territory takes place at the regional level. The R&D functions at the regional headquarters level are mainly concentrating on development and market adaptation rather than on basic research. With this approach, Honda is following a market adaptation strategy. Once the regional headquarters management decides which basic car concept to choose, a meeting with the marketing and sales department follows. After the price estimation is made in Japan, and based on the estimated sales volume, the final decision is made on whether it is worth starting production.

There is a strong belief in the Japanese business culture in the importance of involving top management in developing products. This is reflected also by the fact that the majority of ideas is coming from Japan. The President and CEO of Honda, Mr Fukui, believes in the importance of maintaining the development of main functions in Tokyo and thus to keep Japanese control. This way of thinking is related to the company's identity and is perceived as company culture. On the other hand, whenever it is appropriate, Honda seeks local knowledge, such as in case of pickup trucks for the American market, where the Japanese engineers do not have enough knowledge.

The European market

The biggest operation in Europe is in the United Kingdom from which about 50 per cent of Honda's European sales are gained. Compared to the United States, the needs and differences of the European market are greater. Europe is divided into north and south, which, according to Mr Aoki, Executive Vice President and Representative Director of Honda, is the Japanese way. The reason for this division was to maintain easier control and to meet the differences in northern and southern European needs. However, in the future, provided that the markets get closer and the differences in needs disappear or become weaker, Honda would reconsider restructuring its organizational structure in Europe. The key challenge is to find equilibrium, that is, to manage international uniformity and to meet local demands. Local carmakers such as BMW, Opel (GM), Renault, Volvo, Fiat or Audi were dominating this region long before Honda stepped in. As a result, many customers have a strong preference towards a brand. In addition, foreign companies like Toyota, Ford or Nissan made the market environment even more competitive. Sales in fiscal year 2008 in Europe were only about 25 per cent of those in the United States. According to Honda's senior management, the European car market is one of the most aggressive markets in the world to compete in. The fierce competition is caused by the model saturation and by a large number of car manufacturers. The four largest European car markets are Germany, the United Kingdom, Italy and France. One of the problems that Honda had to face in Europe resulted from the company's initial approach in treating the whole European region as if it were one unified market without any diversifications in demand. To redress this situation, Honda introduced, among other things, diesel engines in its most popular models, which are especially produced for the European region. Another dilemma for Honda comes with the different prices across Europe. The company is trying to adjust prices as much as possible in order to avoid grey imports. The European market, however, remains Honda's main challenge.

Nevertheless, the European market has a particular significance to Honda. It has been the most advanced and flexible market where Honda can gain a lot in terms of technology. Due to the fierce competition and top car manufacturers present in this region, Honda is able to benefit from the synergy effects and expand its global know-how.

Standardization in Europe

Honda does not need to change the specifications of the car according to each country because there is not much difference anymore in regulations across Europe. The only variation comes from the market and not from legal requirements. For example, Honda needs to have heated seats in Scandinavian countries or a hot light in France. Beyond these minor adaptations Honda does not add special features for every country. There is a stronger demand in northern Europe for luxury cars, while southern Europe demands more economical cars. These preferences can lead to different EXi models for each region, for example. Climatic differences and other factors, such as preferences for the car's body colour and the height of the human beings, must also be taken into consideration. For instance, in countries where it snows, a black interior is preferred. Heat capacities can differ as well. Moreover, the height of an average Nordic person is greater than the height of a person from southern Europe. Therefore, the volume of bigger cars sold in the Scandinavian countries is higher than the volume sold in the south. Local requirements also vary, and the key to success in each market is to listen to those requirements. As for marketing, each branch has a person in charge of advertising. Honda does not have a global agency, although the main logo and the main slogan are chosen by Tokyo. Local advertising, therefore, can vary in each operation. Benchmarking between different branches takes place on an irregular basis whenever there is a need for the exchange of ideas between territories.

Cultural issues

Honda's rationale behind having regional headquarters or subsidiaries is getting closer to the market, understand the market better and adapting the products more properly to the market. Although the company is said to be international, according to Aoki it is a "very Japanese company." He believes that a high degree of heterogeneity might lead to loss in identity. Although Mr Aoki claims that being homogeneous is fine to a certain extent, he says that the company's management is not always open to the demands of the local needs. Moreover, culturally based conflicts between the Japanese management and the local staff on the regional level are common. The obvious cultural differences start with very simple issues, like opening the door for women.

> The Japanese managers do not care how the door is going to be opened. So we just open the door and get out. No one in this country [Japan] follows that rule, because it's not in our culture. (Mr Aoki, Executive Vice President and Representative Director, Honda Motor Co., Ltd.)

As a result, European people often feel that Japanese managers do not have good manners. The cultural issues continue to rise during job interviews. In the Japanese culture, it is very important to ask certain questions, which would be considered inappropriate in many European countries because they are an intrusion into the person's private sphere. Such questions could be to ask "Do you have a flat?" or, especially to women, "Do you have a family?" Another challenge is created by the limited knowledge of English of the Japanese managers, which eventually leads to a communication problem. The conflicts thus filter down to the day-to-day operations in the regional headquarters. There are a lot of subtle differences between Japan and Europe in carrying out the business. Even the understanding of leadership works on different dimensions. When it comes to the concept of the responsibilities, Japanese managers listen to their staff's opinion, but in the end they take the responsibility and others are expected to follow. Another issue is the fact that top management positions are normally held by Japanese. This is in fact very practical because much of the communication with Japan has to be done in Japanese. However, local non-Japanese managers can feel de-motivated as far as their professional career and advancement are concerned.

One of Honda's strengths is its unity and conformity in terms of all Japanese management team sharing the same values, along with its strong corporate culture. Looking at Honda, the question arises whether the strength of a corporation lies in its diversity or in its similarity. Honda tries to share the same basic philosophy throughout all its global operations. This philosophy incorporates respect for the individual, value of peoples' time and the importance of being on the spot. Diversity in terms of different ideas is valued in Honda, and it is believed to create harmony. The common denominator, however, is that everybody wants to share the same corporate values, the same philosophy and the same basic principles. That is what makes Honda strong and unique. This message is conveyed to the associates internally or in their overseas departments and operations. The associates are versed in these ideas since joining the company. In Japan, there is more emphasis put on learning these principles, thus, the Japanese become ambassadors in getting these ideas across whenever they go outside Japan.

On the whole, being homogeneous seems to work very well for Honda. The question is, whether the time has come to handle the arising cultural problems more proactively and to open up for more heterogeneity amid today's globalized world.

European headquarters and subregional European headquarters relations

The European headquarters' role is to develop regional strategies. Based on those regional strategies, each subsidiary is responsible for developing its own local strategy in line with the total European strategy. The regions within Europe do not have much contact with each other because all activities are focused towards the European headquarters. Successes at one region sometimes can be copied by other regions, but managers do not see an urgent necessity to have frequent communication among themselves. The transfer of best practices is important, however, and if good ideas from one region should be followed in other regions, the managers do meet. Otherwise, managers at the same levels in different regions do not meet too often. All the information is centralized at the European headquarters where subsidiaries have to report. Contacts with other regions such as America or Asia and with the head office in Japan are almost nonexistent. Therefore, the transfer of knowledge in the company is missing, which eventually leads to weaknesses.

The subsidiaries are independent and generate their own expenses based on the budget approved by London. They are autonomous and flexible with regard to decisions in personal recruiting, discounts and so on; however, they have to stay within the business plan for the fiscal year. Sometimes subsidiaries have to receive approval from their respective regional office, which may be time-consuming and frustrating. On the other hand, regional balance has a high priority. If one country is overspending and another underspending, the balance can be kept.

Genba – The place where things are happening

Genba is the Japanese term for "the actual place where value is created," which Honda incorporated into its philosophy of doing business. Consequently, the headquarters in Japan will not interfere excessively with local operations' tasks, because it believes that the local staffs have the best knowledge on the local market situation. Therefore, the head office in Japan introduces the big guideline or goal to be achieved (for example, a target number in term of sales) and the local management is given a free hand in implementing this goal based on the regional specifics. However, for major decisions, local management has to get approval from the regional headquarters in London. The European headquarters in turn has to report to the headquarters in Japan about the total European operations. This report is of particular importance for global investors given that Honda is listed on the New York Stock Exchange.

According to Honda's senior management, combining functions on the regional level has its positive and negative sides. The President of Honda Czech, Mr Yokoyama said:

> If we have a regional headquarters in Warsaw, for example, it takes more time to report to the boss in Warsaw about what we want to do. And this boss, sitting in Warsaw, may not understand 100 per cent what is going on in Prague. ... I personally feel that regional headquarters is not the way for the future. (Mr Yokoyama, President, Honda Czech)

In the changing market conditions, each independent market in Europe needs to be addressed as quickly as possible. Thus, management has to make decisions quickly. Travelling to Frankfurt, Paris or Budapest, explaining the situation and asking for permission takes time as well as energy. On the other hand, Honda seeks to empower local people who have the best knowledge about the specific situation.

> Wherever we can enjoy economy of scale we will do it, but sometimes the taste is different. And for example dealer development – it is very difficult to understand what is going on daily or weekly basis if you are not in that country. And because business is lively and changing every day you have to act quickly. Speed is one of the most important things in the global business these days. And whatever happens, speed is a big handicap for a company and decision making. ... So whenever we can enjoy the economy of scale we share, but for important business decisions you have to be sitting in the office in Prague to make decisions about Prague. (Mr Yokoyama, President, Honda Czech)

Yokoyama further believes dealer development is one of the most important businesses in Honda's operations. In order to foster the dealership and to improve the quality of dealers, local Honda staff must communicate closely with the locals and speak their language. Some functions, such as inventories, are more advantageous to centralize. For instance, spare parts and components are done through the depot in Gent. This warehouse can supply almost all of the parts within 24 hours to any of the dealers. Thus, the countries can share the inventory. Similarly, some back office functions can be performed centrally instead of having duplicate functions in each country. One of the main reasons for centralized functions is cost saving. Functions at the subregional level include marketing strategy, packaging strategy and product lineup, commercial and public relations activities. As the Public Relations Manager for Corporate Investor Relations in London indicated: "Because we in the headquarters cannot know the details of the market needs, so that kind of request is coming from the regional operations" (Public Relations Manager for Corporate Investor Relations, Honda Motor Europe Limited).

Regional headquarters decide on the strategic overview, and subregional headquarters break it down depending on the market needs. Strategies or decisions that do not impact other countries outside the region are given to the top person within the subregion to decide. Wider reaching decisions, such as which models to bring into the whole region, are made on a pan-European basis. All major decisions are done by the Regional Executive Committee, which is comprised of the regional presidents of the subregions and the CEO. Each regional president has to be a member of the Executive Committee.

Honda's future in Europe

One of the challenges for Honda is how to organize itself in the future. Should it come up with more dynamic structures or will the current sub-regional approach hold well for the coming years? When the European headquarters was established, Honda did not foresee the creation of subregions. Subregions became a good idea over time. However, if in the future this idea does not hold, changes should be adopted. Another question is whether Honda will retain a global brand image on the one hand while it is stressing the "genba" philosophy on the other. What decisions should be delegated to each region and what should be done centrally are other unanswered questions.

Current Challenges and Future Prospects

Despite the fact that Honda is well diversified both geographically as well as in terms of the customer end markets that it serves, a weak economic outlook for its primary markets (Japan, the United States and the Eurozone) is already putting pressure on the revenues of the company. Japan's economy shrank more than 12 per cent during the final three months of 2008, which is a clear sign of how severely the global economic downturn has affected the world's second-largest economy. This poses a difficult situation for Japan, namely, an absolute disappearance of global demand for the country's products and a standstill in domestic demand. Japanese companies such as Honda, Toyota, NEC and Hitachi laid off thousands of employees during the first quarter of 2009 because of slowing consumer demand in the United States and Europe. Honda, after a substantial decline in sales, closed its UK plant in Swindon on 1 February 2009 for four months.[29] The company was also forced to cut jobs in Japan and reduced global production by 56,000 vehicles.[30]

Secondly, the worldwide automotive market is highly competitive, and Honda faces a strong rivalry from automotive manufacturers such as Toyota, Nissan, General Motors, Ford and Hyundai in various markets. In light of continuing globalization and consolidation, this competition is likely to intensify and eventually lead to lower vehicle sales.

Finally, Takanobu Ito, former Senior Managing Director, became the seventh President and CEO of Honda Motor Co., Ltd., in late June 2009. Undergoing this transition at a time of distress poses further challenges to Honda's global operations. Mr Ito stated: "This is a once-in-a-century crisis. I hope the market will begin to improve in the second half of this year or next year, but we can't act on that assumption."[31]

Appendix

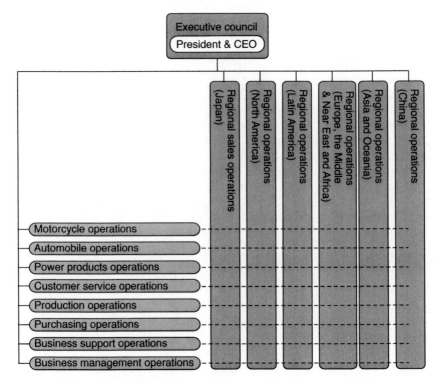

A9.3   Honda's organizational structure (as of 1 April 2006)

Source: http://world.honda.com/profile/organization/ (accessed 25 March 2009).

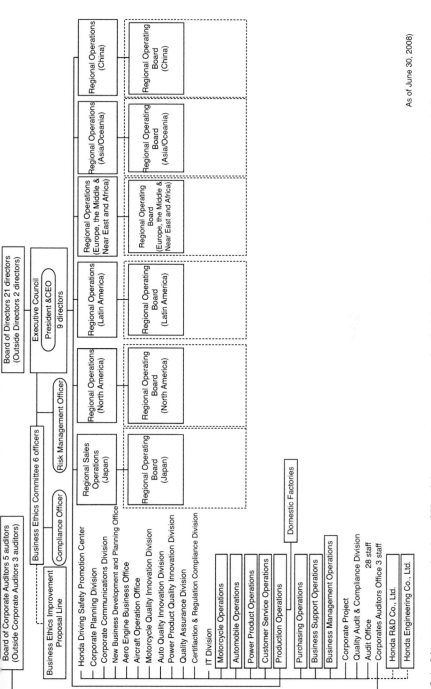

Board of Corporate Auditors 5 auditors
(Outside Corporate Auditors 3 auditors)

Board of Directors 21 directors
(Outside Directors 2 directors)

Business Ethics Committee 6 officers

Executive Council
President &CEO
9 directors

Business Ethics Improvement Proposal Line

Compliance Officer

Risk Management Officer

Honda Driving Safety Promotion Center
Corporate Planning Division
Corporate Communications Division
New Business Development and Planning Office
Aero Engine Business Office
Aircraft Operation Office
Motorcycle Quality Innovation Division
Auto Quality Innovation Division
Power Product Quality Innovation Division
Quality Assurance Division
Certifiaction & Regulation Compliance Division
IT Division
Motorcycle Operations
Automobile Operations
Power Product Operations
Customer Service Operations
Production Operations
Purchasing Operations
Business Support Operations
Business Management Operations
Corporate Project
Quality Audit & Compliance Division
Audit Office   28 staff
Corporates Auditors Office 3 staff
Honda R&D Co., Ltd.
Honda Engineering Co., Ltd.

Domestic Factories

Regional Sales Operations (Japan)
Regional Operating Board (Japan)

Regional Operations (North America)
Regional Operating Board (North America)

Regional Operations (Latin America)
Regional Operating Board (Latin America)

Regional Operations (Europe, the Middle & Near East and Africa)
Regional Operating Board (Europe, the Middle & Near East and Africa)

Regional Operations (Asia/Oceania)
Regional Operating Board (Asia/Oceania)

Regional Operations (China)
Regional Operating Board (China)

As of June 30, 2008)

A9.4 Management organization of Honda's corporate governance for decision making, execution, supervision and others

Source: Honda Motor Co., Ltd. Annual Report 2008.

231

A9.5 Principal subsidiaries (as of March 2008)

Region	Country of Incorporation	Company	Percentage ownership and voting interest	Main lines of business				Function
				Motor cycle business	Auto mobile business	Financial services business	Power product & other businesses	
Japan	Saitama	Honda R&D Co., Ltd.	100.0	*	***		**	Research & development
	Tochigi	Honda Engineering Co., Ltd.	100.0	*	***		**	Manufacturing and sales of equipment and development of production technology
	Saitama	Yachiyo Industry Co., Ltd.	50.5	*	***			Manufacturing
	Miyazaki	Honda Lock Mfg. Co., Ltd.	100.0	*	***		**	Manufacturing
	Shizuoka	Yutaka Giken Co., Ltd.	70.1	*	***		**	Manufacturing
	Nagano	Asama Giken Co., Ltd.	81.7	*	***		**	Manufacturing
	Saitama	Honda Foundry Co., Ltd.	82.1	*	***		**	Manufacturing
	Tokyo	Honda Motorcycle Japan Co., Ltd.	100.0	**				Sales
	Tokyo	Honda Finance Co., Ltd.	100.0			**		Finance
	Mie	Mobilityland Corporation	100.0				**	Others (Leisure)
	Tokyo	Honda Trading Corporation	100.0	*	***		**	Others (Trading)
	Mie	Honda Logistics Inc.	100.0	*	***		**	Others (Physical distribution)

Region	Country	Company	%					Sales
North America	U.S.A.	American Honda Motor Co., Inc.	100.0	*	***		**	Sales
		Honda North America, Inc.	100.0	*	*	*	*****	Coordination of Subsidiaries' operation
		Honda of America Mfg., Inc.	100.0	*	***			Manufacturing
		American Honda Finance Corporation	100.0			**		Finance
		Honda Manufacturing of Alabama, LLC	100.0		**			Manufacturing
		Honda of South Carolina Mfg., Inc.	100.0	**				Manufacturing
		Yachiyo of America Inc.	100.0		**			Holding company
		Honda Transmission Mfg. of America, Inc.	100.0		**			Manufacturing
		Honda Precision Parts of Georgia, LLC	100.0		**			Manufacturing
		Honda Power Equipment Mfg., Inc.	100.0				**	Manufacturing
		Honda R&D Americas, Inc.	100.0	*	***		**	Research & development
		Cardington Yutaka Technologies Inc.	100.0	*	***			Manufacturing
		Celina Aluminum Precision Technology Inc.	100.0		**			Manufacturing
		Honda Trading America Corporation	100.0	*	***		**	Others (Trading)
		Honda Engineering North America, Inc.	100.0	*	***		**	Manufacturing and sales of equipment and development of production technology

Continued

A9.5 Continued

			Percentage ownership and voting interest	Main lines of business					
Region	Country of Incorporation	Company		Motor cycle business	Auto mobile business	Financial services business	Power product & other businesses	Function
Canada		Honda Canada Inc.	100.0	*	***		**	Manufacturing and sales
		Honda Canada Finance Inc.	100.0			**		Finance
	Mexico	Honda de Mexico, S.A. de C.V.	100.0	*	***		**	Manufacturing and sales
Europe	Belgium	Honda Europe NV	100.0	*	***		**	Sales
	U.K.	Honda Motor Europe Limited	100.0	*	*	*	****	Coordination of subsidiaries' operation and sales
		Honda of the U.K. Manufacturning Ltd.	100.0		**			Manufacturing
		Honda Finance Europe plc	100.0			**		Finance
	France	Honda Motor Europe (South) S.A.	100.0	*	***			Sales
		Honda Europe Power Equipment, S.A.	100.0				**	Manufacturing and slaes
	Germany	Honda Bank GmbH	100.0			**		Finance
		Honda Motor Europe (North) GmbH	100.0	*	***		**	Sales
		Honda R&D Europe (Deutachland) GmbH	100.0	*	***		**	Research & development

234

Region	Country	Company	%				Business
	Italy	Honda Italia Industriale S.p.A.	100.0	**		**	Manufacturing and sales
	Spain	Montesa Honda S.A.	100.0	**			Manufacturing and sales
Asia	China	Honda Motor (China) Investment Co., Ltd.	100.0	*	***	**	Holding company and sales
		Jialing-Honda Motors Co., Ltd.	70.0			**	Manufacturing and sales
		Honda Automobile (China) Co., Ltd.	65.0		**		Manufacturing
		Honda Auto Parts Manufacturing Co., Ltd.	100.0		**		Manufacturing
	India	Honda Motorcycle and Scooter India Private Limited	100.0	**			Manufacturing and sales
		Honda Siel Cars India Limited	97.4		**		Manufacturing and sales
	Indonesia	P.T. Honda Precision Parts Manufacturing	100.0	*	***		Manufacturing
		P.T. Honda Prospect Motor	51.0		**		Manufacturing and sales
	Malaysia	Honda Malaysia SDN. BHD.	51.0		**		Manufacturing and sales
	Pakistan	Honda Atlas Cars (Pakistan) Limited	51.0		**		Manufacturing and sales

Continued

235

A9.5 Continued

Region	Country of Incorporation	Company	Percentage ownership and voting interest	Principal subsidiaries — Main lines of business				Function
				Motor cycle business	Auto mobile business	Financial services business	Power product & other businesses	
Philippines		Honda Philippines, Inc.	99.6	**				Manufacturing and sales
		Honda Cars Philippines, Inc.	74.2		**			Manufacturing and sales
Taiwan		Honda Taiwan Co., Ltd.	100.0		**			Sales
Thailand		Asian Honda Motor Co., Ltd.	100.0	*	*	*	****	Coordination of subsidiaries' operation and sales
		Honda Leasing (Thailand) Company Limited	100.0			**		Finance
		Honda Automobile (Thailand) Co., Ltd.	89.0		**			Manufacturing and sales
		Thai Honda Manufacturing Co., Ltd.	60.0	**			**	Manufacturing
		Honda Vietnam Co., Ltd.	70.0	*	***			Manufacturing and sales
Others	Argentina	Honda Motor de Argentina S.A.	100.0	*	***		**	Manufacturing and sales
	Brazil	Honda South America Ltda.	100.0	*	*	*	*****	Coordination of subsidiaries' operation and holding company

Country	Company				Business
	Honda Automoveis do Brasil Ltda.	100.0		**	Manufacturing and sales
	Moto Honda da Amazonia Ltda.	100.0	**	**	Manufacturing and sales
	Honda Componentes da Amazonia Ltda.	100.0	**		Manufacturing
Turkey	Honda Turkiye A. S.	100.0	*	***	Manufacturing and sales
Australia	Honda Australia Pty. Ltd.	100.0		**	Sales
New Zealand	Honda New Zealand Limited	100.0		**	Sales

Note: Percentage Ownership and Voting Interest include ownership through consolidated subsidiaries.
Source: Honda Motor Co., Ltd. Annual Report 2008.

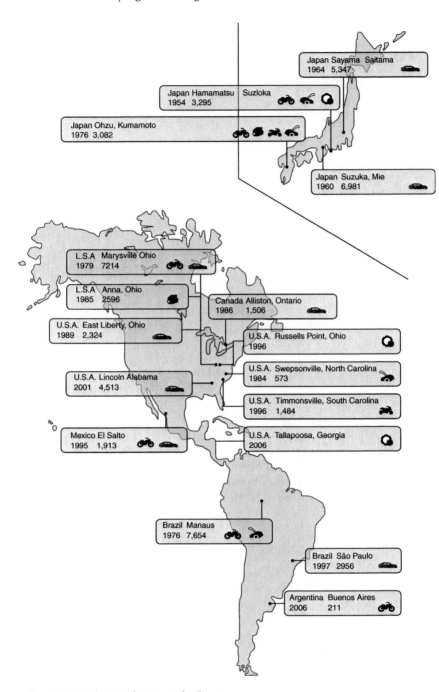

A9.6   Principal manufacturing facilities

Source: Honda Motor Co., Ltd. Annual Report 2008.

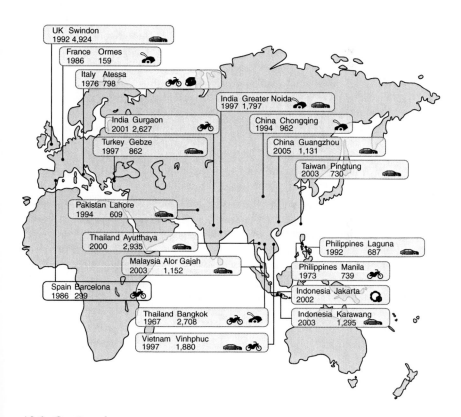

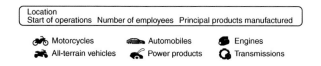

A9.6   Continued

10

Learning from the Sport Shoe Industry
Puma Prague*

Introduction

In late fall of 2005, Piotr Cichecki, general manager, was sitting together with the sales and retail director of Puma Prague discussing the marketing, sales and finance budget for the following year. The team was preparing the final budget proposal for 2006, which had to be sent to the regional headquarters. They were aware that pending changes to the corporate structure were soon to be implemented.

To date, all budgetary requirements were submitted directly to the regional headquarters (RHQ) in Salzburg, Austria, via direct vertical reporting lines. Presentations, discussions and final negotiations for the budget were undertaken by the regional director for Eastern Europe, Erwin Kaiser. The final decision for all budgetary decisions was made in corporate headquarters in Herzogenaurach, Germany. The subsidiaries such as Puma Prague received their budget allocation directly from the regional headquarters in Salzburg.

Over the last few years, Piotr Cichecki had developed a good and open relationship with his co-general managers in the other Eastern European countries. He had once asked the general manager for Warsaw to source some sport shoes for a key client because the deliveries from the suppliers were delayed. He could always contact Erwin Kaiser at RHQ when he had operational concerns. From time to time he would contact the Corporate Marketing Office at Herzogenaurach when there were marketing endorsement requests from the largest clients in Prague.

---

* This case was written by Gina Villanueva under the direction of Bodo B. Schlegelmilch and Björn Ambos, WU Vienna, Institute for International Marketing and Management. It is intended to be used as the basis for class discussion rather than to illustrate the effective or ineffective handling of administrative situations. The case was made possible by the co-operation of Puma.

Earlier in the year, there had been several news releases about a new organizational structure. The pending change in business structure perturbed Cichecki. In November, Cichecki was invited to participate in a global senior management meeting where the new business structure was to be presented.

Company history

Puma in the 1920s

Puma first originated from the entrepreneurial initiative of Rudolph Dassler. He began working at the age of 15 at the same shoe factory as his father where he learned the essential aspects of business and shoe production. Rudolf was young, assertive and motivated to learn his new trade. It was only after the First World War when he started to broaden his management awareness. He took a position at a porcelain factory and in a leather wholesale business in Nuremberg, Germany.

Rudolf Dassler went back to his hometown in Germany in the early 1920s to start a footwear manufacturing business with his brother, Adolf. In 1924, the Gebrüder Dassler Schuhfabrik was formally incorporated. Its main products were slippers and outdoor shoes. The brothers shared the responsibilities equally, with Rudolf handling the business and Adolf handling the production and technical operations. Within a few years, the brothers decided to phase out of the current product line due to difficulty in the markets. Instead the Dassler brothers decided to focus entirely on manufacturing sport footwear, specifically track shoes and football boots, which was an upcoming market at this time.

In 1925, the company received an order for about 10,000 pairs of athletic shoes from its first client: the sports club in Herzogenaurach. With its newfound image among sports persons and sporting good companies, the company grew despite the Great Depression in the late 1920s. A majority of the athletes in the 1928 Olympics wore Dassler shoes.

The split up

The company flourished in its chosen niche of sport footwear for the next few years. It started to sponsor star athletes in the midthirties to enhance its reputation. The track star Jesse Owens was wearing Dassler track shoes in the Berlin Olympics in 1936 when he won four gold medals in his events.

The Gebrüder Dassler Schuhfabrik continued to operate during the Second World War. In 1948, Rudolf and Adolf had a major falling out, which eventually led to the demise of the Dassler Company. The firm was split up into Adidas, which became Adolf's business, while Rudolf set up the Puma Schuhfabrik Rudolf Dassler. Workers in the Dassler Company were asked to choose which of the two new firms they would prefer to join. The brothers ceased all communications with one another. From that point, the two newly created companies would be competitors.

The Puma brand

The Puma brand would gradually gain recognition with the support of star athletes, especially runners and soccer players. In 1950, the Puma Atom shoe was worn by several German players at the first international soccer match post-Second World War. The Olympics event was another venue for the Puma brand. The success of the athletes wearing Puma shoes in the Helsinki Games catapulted the company into a new level. First, it opened the British market for the company. Second, Puma was awarded the rights as the "official shoe supplier" by the American Olympic Committee in 1952 and in 1956. The American women's 400-meter track team members were wearing Puma track shoes when they won the Olympic gold medal at the 1952 games. The soccer star Pele wore the Puma King shoes during these years.

Puma also developed its export business. By the late 1950s, Puma was a brand identified in 55 countries on five continents. Austria was chosen as the first licensed manufacturing location outside Germany. As the company continued to expand its presence overseas, the firm evolved from a sole proprietorship into a partnership called the Puma Sportschuhfabriken Rudolf Dassler Kommanditgesellschaft in 1959. The other co-owners in the company were Rudolf Dassler's wife and sons, Armin and Gerd. The export business covered 100 countries by 1962.

During the next decade the Puma brand was recognized for its innovative products. Puma developed the "vulcanization" process for soccer shoes in the early 1960s. This process "joined the soles to the uppers." All other sport shoe manufacturers were to adapt this new technology over the next few years. Around the same time, Puma also developed a "uniquely shaped sole for running shoes that supported the natural movement of foot when in motion." Puma was the first sport shoe manufacturer to use the Velcro brand strap.

Change in management and ownership

Armin Dassler took over the management of the company in 1974 when Rudolf Dassler died. He had managed the Austrian subsidiary in Salzburg since the early 1960s. The company continued to thrive under Armin's management and eventually went public in 1986. The company was then renamed Puma AG Rudolf Dassler Sport. Innovation was still an essential ingredient in the success of the business.

The S.P.A. technology was introduced by Puma in the mid-1970s. This process produced sport shoes with a higher heel that relieved tension on the Achilles tendon. The Puma Duo flex sole, developed by Armin Dassler in 1982, allowed the foot better mobility using special slots. The Trinomic sport shoe system, introduced in 1989, cushioned the runner's foot with hexagonal cells between sole and shoe. Other innovations included a window near the sole of children's shoes that allowed parents or sports guardians to determine if the sport shoe was still the perfect fit. The expensive Puma Disc System used a disc to tightened wires of athletic shoes instead of laces.

The Puma brand continued its momentum as star athletes wore Puma products. Many world-famous athletes from various sport disciplines carried the Puma logo on their sport shoes during the 1970s and 1980s: tennis stars Guillermo Villas, Martina Navratilova and Boris Becker; American football star Marcus Allen of the Oakland Raiders; baseball stars Jim Rice and Roger Clemens of the Boston Red Sox, as well as George Brett of the Kansas City Royals; and track stars Evelyn Ashford and Renaldo Nehemiah, to name a few.

Despite its success in brand awareness, profits slowly deteriorated in the late 1980s until it turned to losses by the early 1990s. Puma's athletic footwear still had high brand name recognition, but 50 per cent of sales originated from the lower-priced footwear sector by the mid-1980s. The product cycle of each type of model was short and required constant product innovation. This required investment in research and development costs as well as higher marketing costs for the new footwear. Margins drastically deteriorated by the late 1980s resulting in negative earnings for almost a decade.

By 1991, Puma International was founded. This served as the holding company for the profit centres in Australia, Austria, the Far East, France, Germany and Spain. Each division was independent of the other. In the same year, Proventus, a Swedish conglomerate, purchased Puma's outstanding common stock traded in Frankfurt and Munich while injecting DM50 million of fresh capital.

Similar to Adidas, Puma repositioned itself by focusing on the high-end, premium-priced footwear markets. Its main competitors became Nike and Reebok. This change in marketing strategy resulted in further financial losses as well as decreased sales. Market share position likewise decreased for Puma in the early 1990s. In addition, new product innovations such as the Puma disc further deteriorated Puma's already weak financial position.

In 1993, there was a need for a change in management. Jochen Zeitz became chief executive officer in late 1993. Under his leadership, Puma underwent a market-oriented "fitness program," which involved effective cost-cutting measures and organizational restructuring. This was phase one of the long-term company development. Zeitz aimed to streamline functions and create an entrepreneurial corporate culture. The purchasing and the product development departments were merged. A centralized distribution system was established.

The next step: Expansion after restructuring

By late 1996, Puma had re-established itself as a profiTable and successful market-driven company. New alliances and higher investment in international marketing and product development was the emphasis of the company in the mid- to late 1990s. Shareholders received dividends for the first time as the company achieved its highest sales in three years. Proventus reduced its holdings to 25 per cent via a stock offering at the Munich and Frankfurt Exchanges. In the same year, the Monarchy Regency movie and distribution firm purchased 12.5 per cent stake from Proventus. The other half of 12.5 per cent was purchased the following year. As the single largest shareholder, Monarchy was interested in building relationships in the sports world in order to diversify into new markets. Zeitz, on the other hand, believed that such an alliance would help Puma in its marketing efforts.

Puma started to concentrate on international business with emphasis on building the "sports lifestyle name" brand globally. An Italian subsidiary began operations in 1997. A new subsidiary was created in the United Kingdom in 1999. By this time, the United States became the most important market for Puma. The Japanese market was another important strategic market where license fees were still 10 per cent.

Puma continued to grow over the next few years by concentrating on its brand development. This was phase two of its corporate turnaround strategy.. It successfully landed long-term contracts as the official supplier for shoes and textiles for women's tennis teams in 1998. In the next year, Puma was one of four suppliers to the American National Football League. During the 2000 sports seasons, 13 National Football League football teams and 9 basketball teams wore Puma shoes. Serena Williams signed a five-year contract in 1998 for both promotional activities for Puma wear as well as movie and music engagements with Monarchy. The corporate strategy seemed to have worked as Puma's sales increased, especially in the United States. Now the company was well positioned for the future.

The Puma brand and culture in a momentum growth

By 2001, Puma continued to reposition its brand as "one of the most desirable sports life style brands in the world." Profits continued to grow. Brand recognition was further strengthened by direct investments in key markets such as Eastern Europe, Japan and South Asia. Strategic alliances were closed with several markets. Retail became a critical competent function for Puma. Expansion into in-store merchandising was given priority. The launch of store openings in high-density cities was another important step to extending the brand's visibility.

Compared to its competitors, Puma was still a small player in terms of the global sports merchandising market. In 2002, Puma launched phase three of its corporate growth strategy. Football and running were the key sports for Puma. Puma's management board knew that it had to be innovative and progressive for the future. They had to select a unique approach for the Puma brand and identify other types of sports that complemented the goal to be a desirable sports lifestyle brand. As a senior executive in Puma said, "Sports lifestyle is the challenge for a new market which realizes that consumers are demanding sporty products and styles that they can wear not only in the fitness studio or the pitch, but also in their free time." This was critical for the continued success of Puma as a company and the Puma brand.

In addition to the unique positioning of its brand, Puma aimed to promote its corporate culture. Management emphasized the values of "passion in the world of sporting endeavour; openness where teamwork flows seamlessly and empowerment; self-belief to make things happen; and an entrepreneurial spirit which demands a willingness to think outside the box."

By 2004, the Puma brand was identified as one of the most influential brands globally by a well-known market research firm. In June 2005, consolidated sales increased by 13.3 per cent, with global brand sales reaching €1.2 billion. Gross profit margin was above 53 per cent with net profit margins stabilizing at 12 per cent similar to the previous year.

In the fall of 2005, Puma had successfully positioned itself for the next phase of its corporate strategy. Phase four was referred to as the expansion, implying the expansion of product categories, the expansion of the non--Puma brand and a regional expansion. Management wondered if Puma AG's current corporate structure could sustain the demands required by this expansion strategy for the future.

Puma International and the Regional Hubs

Puma International has three virtual headquarters located in the United States (Boston), in Germany (Herzogenaurach) and in Hong Kong. Each virtual headquarters managed key functions such as Products, Brand, Product Supply and Growth in a matrix system. Each headquarters and each function is then subdivided into the three product categories of apparel, footwear and equipment (See Appendix A10.1).

The function Product refers to research and development and sourcing. The Brand function is for the marketing and strategic management of the brand. Product Supply function involves logistics, warehousing and supply services. The Growth function implies sales, after sales service and general distribution. Finance falls under the strategic planning subfunction.

According to Bauer, chief operating officer for Puma AG, regionalization is shaped by the similarities in the market conditions and cultural practices. Regionalization is possible when there are economies of scale, similarities in market conditions and practices, product harmony, price stability, complementary discount structures and an accounting system as a control mechanism. Regional hubs have central market competence in the region. A regional general manager ("RGM") must have a feel for how the regional market operates and how to lead the team. Regional marketing strategy and regional product management are important structures to have. The RGM must be able to identify the right product mix for markets within his area of responsibility. His leadership in managing each market as part of a whole region is critical to the success of the business. Therefore, human resources, finance, logistics and technology functions support the structure of the region. There are five core elements needed at the regional level: operating strategy, distribution systems, marketing strategy as applied in the national level, product strategy (which products can sell at the national level) and retail.

There is a regional hub in Hong Kong for Asia, one in Chile for Latin America, one in Boston for North America, one in Australia for the Pacific region, one in Germany for Europe and one in Austria for Eastern Europe, the Middle East and South Africa. The regional hubs are critical for being close to the market. Geographic groupings are the simplest given the time differences and the distance.

The overall goal is to create regional hubs in upcoming years. For example, France, Spain and Portugal could be a regional hub under one general manager. Another possible hub could be Eastern Europe with the Czech Republic, Poland, Bulgaria and Romania. There is also an Asian region with subhubs in Malaysia, Burma and Vietnam.

Regional headquarters in Salzburg, Austria

Puma AG owns 100 per cent of Puma Austria. Puma Austria is the 100 per cent owner of Puma Poland and Puma Prague in the Czech Republic. It is also part owner of the subsidiary in South Africa, India and the subhub in Dubai. As a regional headquarters, Puma Austria's main responsibility is the continued development of Eastern European business operations as well as the identification of opportunities in new, emerging markets. Puma Austria is also responsible for licensees and distributors in about 40 countries.

RHQ background and Erwin Kaiser

The main role of Puma Austria as a regional headquarters is to support the development of business operations in a geographic area. The regional headquarters was to expand the business operations in each country and identify opportunities to complete business deals. The regional headquarters showed distributors how Puma does business and imprinted the "Puma way": find a distributor and set up a business. All distributors in Eastern Europe fell under the auspices/responsibility of Puma Austria.

In the early 1990s, Erwin Kaiser undertook the task of developing the Eastern European countries. Austria was chosen as the regional basis due to the similarities in history and culture with the Eastern European countries. It was a time when Eastern Europe was coming out of the communist era and Cold War. The economic situation in these countries was still uncertain and unsTable for a multinational like Puma. It was difficult to do business given the ecopolitical situation. Kaiser decided to approach each market based on the customer demand and adjusted selected products to the local market conditions. One could describe the approach as "non-conformist" when compared to the corporate rules of Puma Holding AG. The goal was to first set up a marketing and sales operation in the local market for each country. In most cases, 70 to 80 per cent of the sales were based on the international collection. The remaining 20per cent are goods adopted for the local market preferences.

Under the leadership of Erwin Kaiser, Puma Austria successfully gained the know-how and the competence as the "specialist" to establish Puma as a new business in emerging and difficult areas. Unlike other regional headquarters heads, Kaiser felt he had the management freedom to carry out certain decisions. Puma Austria eventually served as the holding company for the Middle East and South Africa. There are discussions of setting up a Malaysian subsidiary that would eventually fall under the Hong Kong regional hub.

> As a manager from Warsaw explains, "The Austrian advantage is, however, that these guys are existing in these markets, since ages, since years. And my colleagues in Austria know much more about the market in Eastern Europe than my colleagues in Herzogenaurach. This is clear because they are responsible for this market for 15 years. Most of the guys in headquarters (Germany) have never been here before."

"Ideal" structure

The regional headquarters supported the Eastern European subsidiaries and start-up markets in all functions such as marketing, retail, logistics and finance. Each regional functional head is in touch with the functional heads in the subsidiaries such as Poland, the Czech Republic, Hungary, and so on. All major strategic decisions for the Eastern European subsidiaries are discussed with Puma Austria. All feedback regarding international problems and solutions is received by the Eastern European subsidiaries through Puma Austria. Each country general manager in Eastern Europe reports directly to Erwin Kaiser, the regional head.

Finance and budget

Finance and budgeting for Eastern Europe are centralized in Puma Austria. Each country reports its proposed budget to Puma Austria. The financial budget for the region is combined into one report for headquarters. Approval for each country budget is determined in regional headquarters. If a country general manager (GM) wants to make changes to the existing budget during an operating year, then there will be a consultation between the GM and Erwin Kaiser. If there were an issue regarding capital investment, then it would be essential to inform Erwin Kaiser.

Financial control stays at the level of the regional headquarters for the Eastern European subsidiaries. Costs and expenses are the responsibility of each country. The GM files the budget and is then in charge of expenditures. In order to manage the flow of financial information and general data, regional headquarters installed similar information and computer systems in all the Eastern European subsidiaries.

Sourcing and logistics

Puma Austria is responsible for the regional sourcing and logistics for Eastern Europe. There is a "custom-free" central warehouse in Austria that facilitates all purchases of the subsidiaries in the region.

Marketing

There is a global marketing competence in Boston and a European marketing centralized in Salzburg. In the event conflict and/or differences in opinions arise, then critical marketing issues will be referred back to Boston. Day-to-day administration for marketing operations is handled at the regional level. As Kaiser says, "We have become a company of meetings. There are unending meetings where each functional group meets with the regional specialists to discuss numerous issues."

Puma Prague

Current management and operations

Piotr Cichecki is the GM for the Czech Republic for Puma in Prague. He joined the company in October 2001 when the subsidiary was first established. Since then, Puma Prague has grown six times, achieving record sales. The operation initially started as a distributor with a policy of a quick turnaround of products and profit. As a subsidiary, direct investment in brand recognition for the local market became the primary goal. It was critical to establish the brand as a "sports lifestyle" in the Czech Republic. The Czech soccer national team carried Puma products, which facilitated the visibility of the brand. He says:

> Puma does not compete with Nike and Adidas directly. We do not want to be the biggest in the Czech Republic. We are concentrating more on fashion lifestyles. In the Czech Republic the Puma brand is very strong in the fashion lifestyle market. In sports Puma is number three here.

By mid-2005, the Puma brand was well established in the Czech market and was gradually developing in Slovakia.

Cichecki has overall responsibility for operations, which include finance, marketing, sales, logistics and human resources. Each function has a designated director in the Czech Republic who reports directly to him. Each director is also in touch with the regional head or European functional hub. He says:

> It is an interesting job. It is not like having just one particular focus. Actually it is the overall operation because we have to operate on both

sides. We do the wholesale here. Also, we do the overall retail here; retail operation and wholesale operation altogether.

In the fall of 2005, Puma Prague had 8 fully owned retail stores with a projected 60 stores planned for the next few years. The emphasis of Puma Prague was to expand in the retail section.

The retail store ownership initiative in Slovakia was expanded in January 2006. A legal entity had to be set up in Slovakia if a firm wanted to enter the retail market. A limited liability company was established in 2006, which is 100 per cent owned by Puma Prague. All existing distribution contracts expired by the end of December 2005.

Cichecki described his day-to-day management of Puma Prague as 60 per cent for operational issues and 40 per cent for strategic issues.

> Actually I am trying to make sure that we are in line with the budget ... that we sell to the right customers, right distribution channels, that we are in line with marketing and logistics is in function. And we put the right people and the people do what they are supposed to do ... It is difficult because you concentrate too much on the operational issues, for example legal issues, lawyers, new contracts for the retailers.

He communicated with Puma International (Herzogenaurach, Boston or Hong Kong) on a daily basis in terms of conference calls, video conference calls, and so on. In addition, there was a lot of administrative work via e-mail.

The employees hired since the beginning have all stayed with Puma Prague. Cichecki made sure that each new person "fit" with the rest of the team. To date, the attrition rate has been zero.

Marketing and promotion

Puma AG allows for cultural differences in marketing its products. As such, Cichecki felt that Puma Prague had a high level of autonomy and flexibility in developing its marketing strategy for the local Czech markets. The national marketing strategy had to coincide with the framework of the global strategy of Puma AG. Puma Austria as regional headquarters recognized the ability of Puma Prague in executing its marketing strategy and did not demand for things to be done in any particular way. Sometimes Cichecki felt that Puma Prague was quite independent of Puma Austria. "They would say, 'This is your budget, your responsibility. Do it your way'!"

Even if a global campaign or materials were used, Puma Prague included its own local content with each campaign. Most campaigns were differentiated locally based on the activities such as the events or athlete sponsored. Depending on the budget, Puma Prague would sometimes have to contact the marketing group at regional headquarters in Austria regarding certain high-resolution pictures and PR materials. Kaiser and his team held the database of all information. "We would need to go through the pipeline even if the discussion was in HQ Herzogenaurach" (Erwin Kaiser, Regional Managing Director, Puma Austria).

Product development

Puma Prague normally participated in sending feedback on the product samples and styles directly to the global hub for product development in Boston. Localized preferences were also reported so that changes in colour, style or feature could be added to the global collection. Then all orders from the Eastern European countries for the upcoming global collection were sent to the regional headquarters at Puma Austria.

There was a grouping of product orders for standard products in the collection for the region. Each pair of sport shoes had a specific style that was for a specific market/country. Cichecki and his team aimed to make the best product choice for the Czech market. Sometimes Puma Prague ordered the trendier products directly via the French or Italian subsidiaries because regional headquarters had no access to these trendier products. Take the example of the Ferrari collection. It was launched in Italy, but Cichecki was interested in having this collection for the Czech Republic, so he contacted the GM in Italy directly. Regional headquarters and corporate headquarters knew that there was in-buying among the subsidiaries directly.

Sourcing/warehousing

Puma Austria as regional headquarters was a support organization in terms of sourcing. All the Eastern European affiliates and subsidiaries ordered all goods directly from Puma Austria. It consolidated the orders of Puma Czech Republic, Poland, Austria, Russia and others. This centralized sourcing via Puma Austria facilitated each country's efforts to reach the minimum order quantities required by the supplier. Puma Prague had its own warehouse, which served as a central depot for both the Czech Republic and Slovakia.

Interaction with regional headquarters Puma Austria

In Cichecki´s opinion, Puma RHQ Austria was a "good service organization with competences." Its main function was as support for marketing, sourcing and related activities as well as human resources. It was now viewed as a consulting service.

Puma Austria was an essential ingredient in setting up the business operations in the Czech Republic and other Eastern European countries. They contacted Kaiser as the regional headquarters head on a daily basis. Cichecki describes the reporting lines.

Cichecki reported directly to regional headquarters in Austria. However, Puma AG had an open communication channel. Sales and marketing issues were handled directly with the hub in Germany; while finance and sourcing were still important functions carried by Puma Austria. If he had marketing issues to settle, Cichecki "discussed everything with the marketing department in headquarters." If there were outstanding issues in finance, then he would contact the finance person in Salzburg regional headquarters.

In the current scenario, Cichecki was not even sure if he had an official boss. If he needed something specific, then he had to discuss it with some guys in Germany, in Austria and in Boston. "It is not like having one person. You just report and communicate with Austria. Actually, it is a multi-cultural link. Our finance director communicates directly with Puma Germany in many issues."

In some cases, Cichecki needed to negotiate with three or four persons located in different cities. He wanted to open a concept store in the Czech Republic. First, he had to discuss this with Puma International Retail located in Germany. The second step was to discuss the budget investment with the Finance Director in Puma headquarters, who was also located in Germany. The third person he contacted was Erwin Kaiser in the regional headquarters, Puma Austria in Salzburg. But Kaiser was not interested with this new project because this was "not his business." Finally, Cichecki needed to speak to the marketing persons located in Boston regarding his ideas for a localized Czech Republic version of the Puma concept store. In other words, Cichecki need to persuade international marketing Boston, international finance and international retail to get the green light to go ahead with the project. If the international retail director said no but Cichecki wanted to undertake the project, then the strategic planning director asked, "Who decides?" No one knew the answer.

> The process can be very slow. In Austria they will call to Germany. That would be very complicated. Everyone knows his competences. If I need something from Boston, I will call Boston or to Germany... For example, for international spot marketing the guy sits in Herzogenaurach. Nobody had a clue about it in Austria. So we discussed it... That's what I like about this structure.
>
> On the one hand, it is very complicated. On the other hand, it gives you flexibility to negotiate with them and to persuade the people. If you had one boss, it is sometimes easier to make a decision. On the other hand, you have no chance if he says no. It depends on the negotiation skills and on the argument.

Cichecki felt that Puma Prague did not need a regional headquarters in Austria anymore given the growth of business in the Czech Republic. He felt that the role of Puma Austria as RHQ for Eastern European countries would lessen. "Honestly, I think we will lose the interdependency we have now." Its role, however, in the development of other operations in other countries such as those in the Middle East area was critical. India and Dubai are currently still part of the Austrian coverage.

Relations with other subsidiaries

By 2005, Puma Prague had outperformed Poland and Hungary in terms of sales per capital and profit margin returns. Cichecki, however, felt that comparisons were not that critical as each market was different. *"It is not about competition. It is about cooperation."* There was some kind of cooperation, exchange of ideas and information flow of success stories through international meetings.

There were sport shoe replicas from the Czech national soccer team that sold successful. The GM of Poland then contacted Cichecki to inquire how Puma Prague had launched this sales campaign. Similarly, Cichecki had contacted the Hungarian GM to learn how the Blue Star jeans label was launched in Hungary. In another scenario, Cichecki called the GM in Warsaw to purchase 3,000 pairs of sport shoes from its existing stock. The supplier was late in delivery to Prague, and Cichecki had promised the stock to a top client. Puma Prague received the shoes in 48 hours.

Cichecki also tried to maintain an open and cordial relationship with the larger subsidiaries such as Italy, France and Norway. Day-to-day operational cooperation normally existed between the smaller subsidiaries and the larger ones. The open communication was important, such as when requesting direct orders for trendier products.

The Puma culture was essential in the development of the subsidiaries´ cooperative and communicative environment. There were international meetings where ideas were presented, concepts discussed and projects planned. There were 12 regional meetings per year (once a month) and about 4 international meetings, which also included the distributors. In addition, there were GM meetings, marketing meetings, international retail meetings and so on. Communication was the key.

Upcoming changes

Piotr Cichecki knew that Puma AG's long-term strategy was to consolidate the established subsidiaries in Eastern and Western Europe. Currently, all the Eastern European operations report directly to the Puma Austria RHQ. The larger subsidiaries were very independent and reported directly to the RHQ in Germany or to the "hub competence."

There was to be one general manager for all of Europe. Cichecki would report directly to the GM for Europe. The European regional headquarters will be located in Herzogenaurach in Germany together with Puma AG headquarters. A total of 28 countries would fall under this division. This would include all EU countries plus Switzerland. There would also be GMs for North America, South America, Africa, Asia and Australia.

Now there was going to be one direct boss for Cichecki. No one could say formally what the changes would be. Cichecki felt that:

> There is uncertainty about what's going to happen now in this chain. Of course, you created some good communication links to regional hubs. And now all those links will be cut off to establish really new communication links. And actually these are things which create attention.

There was, however, the issue of competences. Certain subsidiaries and regions are better in finance or sales or product design. Then there is marketing, which is centralized in Boston headquarters and Hong Kong headquarters. Setting budgets would be a battle if Europe were taken as one region. There would no longer be a regional headquarters to protect the smaller, less-established subsidiaries.

With the pending changes looming, Cichecki was not sure how to address the next phase in the corporate growth strategy for Puma Prague. Should he continue to rely on Puma Austria for financing and accounting data? Was it important to inform regional headquarters about the selection of product styles for the national collection? Where and how would Puma Prague source its products for the next year? How would Puma Prague now handle its key account clients who also have a presence in other European countries? Rumour had it that additional virtual layers would be inserted in the already complex multicultural matrix structure.

> That's still a question mark. I think that will be kind of hybrid. It will not change from day one. To be honest I don't know the exact structure because now this is sure what's going to happen. But we will have a discussion about it when it is official. But for the period of half a year Austria will be our sourcing base for us. It will not change as we have placed the orders for the next season. Now we are making orders for the autumn/winter 2006... It will take some time to change the complete structure. Puma International or whatever it will be.

A10.1 Appendix

Puma's corporate structure is a virtual matrix. The vertical axis represents the virtual headquarters ("VHQ") whereby each VHQ is a functional competence centre. The horizontal axis represents the regional headquarters such as Puma Austria.

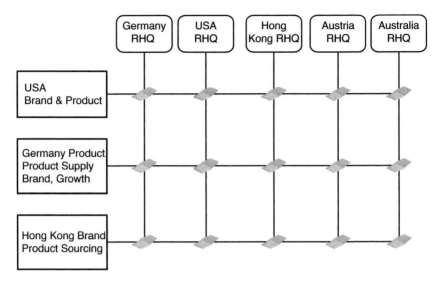

A10.1   Virtual matrix corporate structure as of July 2005

A10.2   Puma AG's corporate values

Puma's corporate values as quoted from the corporate web site:

Our Values

PUMA plans to evolve the organization through the fostering of unique company values, all compatible with the personality of the brand. These can be best summarized in four words: Passion, Openness, Self-belief and Entrepreneurship.

Passion.   PUMA is not a business that manufactures and sells soap powder or ballpoint pens or instant coffee. It is a business rooted in the passionate world of sporting endeavour. The history of the brand resonates with the echoes of great athletes and legendary performances, celebrated in stadiums across the globe. PUMA makes products designed to facilitate the individual achievements that evoke the most passionate responses.

Openness.   Today's marketplace is one of the fastest changing and dynamic on the planet. To respond quickly and effectively in this environment demands a culture of openness, where opinions can be shared without fear of blame and where old wisdom can be questioned without the fear of antagonism. In this culture, respect and understanding flourish naturally, teamwork flows seamlessly, barriers dissolve and a much over-used word, empowerment, takes on real meaning.

Self-belief. Global businesses face new challenges every day. It is the quality of the people in these businesses and their belief in their own abilities that enable these challenges to be overcome. Puma's recognition of this is reflected in its determination that everyone in the company understands and embraces the company values, as well as benefits from the experience and integrity of their colleagues. Only with self-belief will individuals have the confidence to make things happen, take the tough decisions and realize their ambitions for themselves and, ultimately, for the business.

Entrepreneurship. Few businesses succeed without great ideas. PUMA has been built on them and needs them to flow relentlessly hour by hour, day by day. This demands a willingness to think outside the box, to zig where others zag and to seek inspiration beyond the more obvious boundaries of our business universe. Such creativity has inspired the PUMA brand strategy. It will also be needed to make it a reality.

A10.3 Selected financial information for Puma AG

Business phase	Momentum			Investment				Restructuring (1995)		
Consolidated sales	1,530.3	1,274.0	909.8	598.1	462.4	372.7	202.5	279.7	250.5	211.5
Gross profit	794.0	620.0	396.9	250.6	176.4	141.7	108.2	102.3	94.0	79.0
Gross profit margin (%)	51.9	48.7	43.6	41.9	38.2	38.0	35.8	36.6	37.5	37.4
Consolidated profit	258.7	179.3	84.9	39.7	17.6	9.5	4.0	34.6	42.8	24.6
Net profit margin (%)	16.9	14.1	9.3	6.6	3.8	2.6	1.3	12.4	17.1	11.7
Total assets	942.3	700.1	525.8	395.4	311.5	266.6	222.9	176.6	147.7	106.5

Source: http://about.puma.com.

Inside the Nike Matrix[*]

> To bring inspiration and innovation to every athlete in the world, if you have a body, you are an athlete.
>
> Nike's mission statement

Introduction

"We are on the offense, always" is boldly printed on the front page of Nike's Annual Report 2008.[1] According to Phil Knight, Nike's founder, "Business is war without bullets." And indeed, Nike is very much a growth company with an ever-expanding portfolio and a tremendous brand value. And it's been doing well. Hence, Mark Parker, CEO and president of Nike, proudly commented on the company's 2008 performance: "I'm very pleased with how we have enhanced the position, performance, and potential of all the brands and categories in the NIKE, Inc. family."[2]

Growth, however, creates structural challenges. This is all the more true for global players such as Nike Inc. that need to juggle trade-offs of local responsiveness and global integration on a daily basis. Hence, this case takes a look behind the scenes and focuses on how Nike manages and structures its worldwide operations. In particular, aspects of regional management and the splitting of functions and responsibilities between global headquarters and regional headquarters in Europe are highlighted.

Key facts and figures

Headquartered in Beaverton, Oregon, Nike Inc. is the largest seller of athletic footwear and athletic apparel in the world and is traded on the New

---

[*] This case was written by Barbara Brenner under the direction of Bodo B. Schlegelmilch and Björn Ambos, WU Vienna, Institute for International Marketing and Management. It is intended to be used as the basis for class discussion rather than to illustrate the effective or ineffective handling of administrative situations. The case was made possible by co-operation of Nike.

York Stock Exchange.[3] For the fiscal year ending 31 May 2008, Nike reported record revenues of USD18.6 billion, a USD2.3 billion increase over the previous year's earnings, or a 14 per cent increase with growth in every region and every business unit (see Appendix 1).[4] Gross margins improved by more than a percentage point to a record high of 45 per cent, and earnings per share grew by 28 per cent.

Nike operates on six continents, employs more than 30,000 people worldwide and has a workforce of more than 800,000 workers in contract factories.[5] The leading designer, marketer and distributor of athletic footwear, apparel, equipment and accessories is represented by 14 Niketowns, more than 200 Nike Factory Stores, 12 Nike Women stores and more than 100 sales and administrative offices around the world. Nike products are distributed under the Nike brand and Nike Inc. affiliate brands such as Bragano, Bauer Nike Hockey, Cole Haan, g Series, Hurley, Converse, Chuck Taylor, All Star, One Star, Jack Purcell, Starter, Team Starter, Asphalt, Shaq and Dunkman.[6]

In 2008, the footwear segment generated revenues of USD9,732 million, apparel sales amounted to USD5,234 million and equipment sales reached USD1,069 million in all three major regions. Total pre-tax income increased by 14 per cent to USD2,509 million in fiscal 2008.

The Nike brand includes footwear, apparel and equipment in six core categories: running; basketball; football (soccer); women's fitness, golf, and tennis; men's training; and sport culture.[7] Nike products are sold through Nike-owned stores and independent distributors in more than 160 countries.[8] Footwear and apparel production is outsourced to independent manufacturers outside the United States, while equipment is produced both in and outside the United States.[9] Nike works with 137 contract factories in the Americas, 104 in Europe, the Middle East and Africa (EMEA), 252 in North Asia, and 238 in South Asia.[10]

History snapshot

Bill Bowerman and Phil Knight founded the company Blue Ribbon Sports in 1964. Both contributed USD500 to the partnership and managed to sell 300 pairs of Tiger running shoes within three weeks. In 1972, they introduced a novel brand of athletic footwear called Nike, named after the Greek goddess of victory. In 1980, the company went public, and within a year, Nike became the predominant brand of the company. In 1986, corporate revenues surpassed USD1 billion for the first time. With the Swoosh trademark logo and its slogan "Just do it," Nike crafted a unique brand image in the 1980s.[11] Nike underwent a period of substantial expansion in the 1990 starting with the acquisition of Cole Haan, an American luxury brand, followed by other major strategic acquisitions such as the ice hockey equipment brand Bauer (1994) and Converse (2003). [12]

Key regions

A geographical breakdown of Nike's revenues shows that the majority of revenues are made outside the US market. In fiscal 2008, non-US sales (including non-US sales of Cole Haan, Converse, Exeter Brands Group, Hurley, Nike Bauer Hockey, Umbro, and Nike Golf) accounted for 57 per cent of total revenues, compared to 53 per cent in fiscal year 2007.

In 2008, with USD6,378 million accounting for 40 per cent of Nike's total sales, the United States was Nike's single most important market. USD5,620.4 million or 35 per cent of its global revenues were achieved in the EMEA region. The Asia-Pacific region recorded sales of USD2,881.7 million or 18 per cent of Nike's global sales (Nike Annual Report 2008). Finally, with USD1,154.1 million, the Americas region made the smallest share. Thus, together with other smaller markets, Nike's global sales were approximately USD18 billion in fiscal year 2008, up by 14 per cent compared to the previous year (see Figure 10.1).

Nike sells athletic footwear and apparel in more than 160 countries worldwide via Nike-owned retail stores, independent distributors and licensees (see Table 10.1). The Nike brand accounts for more than 90 per cent of Nike's total revenues.[13] In 2006, USD13 billion out of USD14.9 billion were generated by the Nike brand (Nike 2006a: 27). Nike's most significant worldwide customer is the retail chain Foot Locker, which accounted for around 10 per cent of Nike's global brand sales in fiscal year 2006.

United States

All roads at Nike lead to Beaverton, Oregon, where Nike's world headquarters is located. Distribution facilities and customer service centres are based in Memphis, Tennessee, and Wilsonville, Oregon. All over the United States, Nike's US-based subsidiaries include Cole Haan Holdings Inc. in Maine,

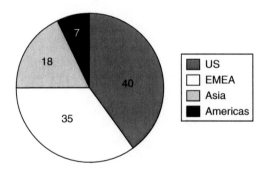

Figure 10.1   Breakdown of revenues per region (per cent), 2008
Source: Nike Annual Report 2008.

Table 10.1   US retail stores in 2008

US retail stores	Number
Nike Factory Stores	121
Nike Stores (incl. Nike Women Stores)	14
Niketowns	12
Nike Employee-Only Stores	3
Cole Haan Stores (Factory Stores etc.)	102
Converse Stores (Factory Stores etc.)	35
Hurley Stores	9
Total	296

Source: Nike Annual Report 2008, p. 4.

Table 10.2   Non-US retail stores

Non-US retail stores	Number
Nike Factory Stores	141
Nike Stores and Employee-Only Stores	46
Niketowns	3
Nike Employee-Only Stores	12
Cole Haan Stores (Factory Stores etc.)	57
Hurley Stores	1
Total	260

Source: Nike Annual Report 2008, p. 4.

Bauer Nike Hockey Inc. in New Hampshire, Hurley International LLC in California, Nike IHM Inc. in Oregon, Converse Inc. in Massachusetts and Exeter Brands Group LLC in New York.[14]

In addition to Nike's principal properties, the company leases other properties outside the United States, including 22 production offices, 93 sales offices and showrooms, 76 administrative offices and 418 retail stores and factory outlet stores.[15] Moreover, the company runs some 296 retail stores in international markets (see Table 10.2).

Nike's US home base represents the company's most important single market (see Appendix 2). However, with only 4 per cent growth from 2007 to 2008, this region was outperformed by other regions with distinctively higher growth rates, such as the EMEA region (19 per cent growth) or Asia-Pacific (26 per cent growth). Nevertheless, with USD6,378 million representing 40 per cent of Nike's total sales, the United States remained Nike's single most important market.[16] With a 20 per cent market share in the athletic shoe market, Nike is currently the dominant leader in this segment in the United States.[17] Nike's major competitors in the US footwear market include Adidas Reebok, Brown Shoe, the Jones Apparel Group, Timberland and Wolverine World Wide. Footwear revenues increased by 6 per cent in 2008, compared to 2007 up to USD4,326.8 million, apparel revenues grew by 2 per cent to USD1,745.1 million and equipment revenues fell by 5 per cent to USD306.1 million.[18]

EMEA

Nike first started selling its products in Europe in 1978 and established its first European headquarters two years later.[19] Prior to setting up its European headquarters for the EMEA region in the Netherlands in 1999, Nike coordinated its European activities from the United Kingdom and Germany (Nike 2006a: 17). Mainly financial, tax and other economic incentives paired with excellent language skills and the favourable central location found in Hilversum[20] induced Nike to relocate its regional headquarters from Frankfurt to the Netherlands.[21] Figure 10.2 provides an overview of the 27 countries within the EMEA region.

The following countries are included in the EMEA region: Austria, Belgium, Bulgaria, Croatia, Czech Republic, Denmark, Finland, France, Germany, Greece, Hungary, Ireland, Israel, Italy, Lebanon, the Netherlands, Norway, Poland, Portugal, the Russian Federation, Slovakia, Slovenia, South Africa, Spain, Sweden, Switzerland, Turkey and the United Kingdom. As a result of restructuring processes, Israel, which is in the Middle East, is also part of the EMEA region. Similarly, Africa has also reported to the regional headquarters in Hilversum since 2000.[22]

Although EMEA represents Nike's largest region in terms of territory, it is only Nike's second largest region in terms of revenues.[23] In fiscal year 2008, EMEA accounted for 35 per cent of Nike's global sales or USD5,620.4 million, which is an increase of 19 per cent compared to the previous year. Overall growth in the region was driven by the emerging markets, including Russia, Turkey and South Africa. Nike and Adidas-Reebok are the leading companies in the athletic footwear sector in the European footwear market. In 2008, some 55 per cent of Nike's European sales were in the footwear segment, with running being the most dominant category, followed by soccer. The category running shoes accounts for 30 per cent of total sales of athletic footwear in Europe. In the running segment, Nike faces strong competition from Asics and New Balance while Adidas-Reebok and Umbro are major rivals in the soccer segment.[24]

Asia-Pacific

The Asia-Pacific region is Nike's number one region in terms of manufacturing and represents Nike's third largest region in terms of revenues.[25] Currently, the Asia-Pacific region comprises Australia, China, Hong Kong, India, Indonesia, Japan, Korea, New Zealand, Singapore, Malaysia, Philippines, Thailand, Sri Lanka, Taiwan and Vietnam.

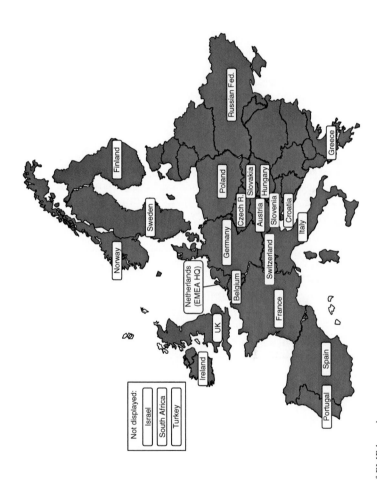

Not displayed:
Israel
South Africa
Turkey

Figure 10.2 Map of EMEA region
Source: Nike.com.

The Americas

Canada, Mexico and South America make up the Americas region. Nike has subsidiaries in five countries within the region: Argentina, Brazil, Chile, Mexico and Canada.[26] The Americas region is Nike's smallest region in terms of sales.

Inside the Nike matrix

Nike Inc. comprises 44 wholly owned subsidiaries, of which seven are US-based (see Figure 10.3). All subsidiaries, except for Nike IHM Inc., Triax Insurance Inc. and Nike (Suzhou) Sports Company Ltd., deal with the design, marketing, distribution and sale of athletic and leisure footwear, apparel, accessories and equipment.[27] The US-based Nike IHM Inc. manufactures plastics and Air-Sole shoe-cushioning components, the Hawaii-based corporation Triax Insurance Inc. is an insurance company, and the Chinese-based Nike (Suzhou) Sports Company Ltd. manufactures footwear and Air-Sole shoe-cushioning components. Nike's US subsidiaries comprise Nike Golf, Cole Haan Holdings Inc., Bauer Nike Hockey Inc., Hurley International LC, Converse Inc. and Exeter Brands Group LLC.[28]

Nike has a five-year strategy to ensure global growth and sustain or build market leadership of the Nike brand and affiliated brands for the period 2006 to 2011. Top-line revenue is planned to grow from USD15 billion to USD 23 billion by 2011.[29] Ongoing product innovation, brand leadership and retail experience as well as further regional expansion will be part of the strategy. Geographically speaking, Nike expects further growth in its US home turf, the United Kingdom, Japan and China but also in Russia, India and Brazil.

Nike is organized by a matrix structure, which entails multiple responsibilities and reporting lines for each unit, which might be problematic.[30] However, Nike's performance figures seem to tell a different story. Nike

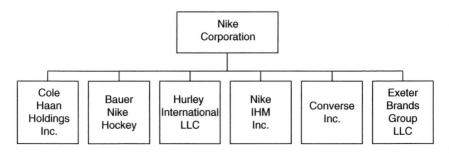

Figure 10.3 Subsidiaries of Nike Inc.
Source: Nike.com.

executives point to the importance of leadership in a matrix structure:

> The other sort of interesting thing is, there is always a lot of discussion on organizational structure within Nike and when you first enter this company, you just wonder how it can actually work, this matrix structure. Seems like there is no clear line accountability, it must be very hard to get a decision made here...that's kind of your initial reaction when you are coming from the outside and you hear people describe how it works. But then after you are here for a while you notice that...here leaders are able to get decisions made very quickly and are able to get people aligned behind decisions and actually get a lot of support when you move things through. And the organization moves quite fast and is quite innovative and so while it looks like it should be slow and bureaucratic and not moving, it is not. (Mr Alebeek, Vice President for Operations, Nike Head Office)

However, Nike decided to introduce an additional layer of hierarchy by establishing a regional headquarters for EMEA where the matrix structure is also replicated at a regional level. In the following section, the functions and responsibilities of the management on different hierarchical levels are introduced (see Figure 10.4). We start on top by scrutinizing the functions of the global headquarters.

Global headquarters

The global headquarters is not only on the top of the hierarchical decision-making pyramid of the group, but it is also in charge of three of Nike's four major markets and manages regional operations in the United States, the Americas and Asia Pacific.[31] Instead of having individual regional headquarters (RHQs) in these regions, the infrastructure that runs these markets is

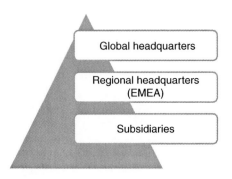

Figure 10.4 Nike hierarchy

located at the global headquarters[32] The EMEA region, on the other hand, is managed by the European RHQ. Structure is of utmost importance to Nike's global headquarters:

> Structure prioritizes where you spend your time and because [you are] getting completely inundated with information if you don't have a sort of structure. And so the fact that you need a Nordic walking shoe to be successful in Norway is irrelevant to our business. [...] I am using this just as an example, but we don't [want our] people here to give the same level of attention to a Nordic walking shoe from Norway as they would give to a basketball shoe that could be used in many markets across the globe. So I think that's part of what you do with the structure, you filter out some of the information that maybe frontline information, [...] We need to be prioritized [...] and to create a structure in a right way, then the right information flows very quickly. (Mr Alebeek, Vice President for Operations, Nike Head Office)

Structure needs to be supported by a strong organizational culture and corporate identity. The headquarters needs to create a common identity where everybody feels and identifies with a company culture that embraces closeness to the end consumers' needs. If that common understanding is present, streamlined and centralized structures are not a barrier to stay in touch with the local consumer end, but essentially enable the company to pick up important trends.

> I think part of how you make sure you stay very close to the consumer is not through a structure but that's part of a cultural thing where everybody feels that it's their job to really understand what happens at the consumer end and I think that the structure does not necessarily include that or facilitate that from happening, that's more. That is something that's driven by the culture where everybody in the end knows that our job is to identify and solve consumer needs and translate them into product needs, [...] a general, cultural mindset that everybody has in this company to be innovation and consumer focused all the time. (Mr Alebeek, Vice President for Operations, Nike Head Office)

On average it takes Nike 18 months to design and manufacture a product.[33] Research, product development and design are largely the responsibility of the global headquarters in Oregon. Given the sheer numbers of product developments – 30,000 to 40,000 per year – Nike needs to constantly scout for new trends on the markets. Although apparel is designed on a regional level, footwear design remains the responsibility of the global headquarters. Although some footwear designers are located at Hilversum, R&D facilities are largely centralized at one place.

Producing consumer goods, Nike needs to react quickly to ever-changing consumer preferences and to adjust its product mix accordingly. Therefore, product features and colours are changed and updated on an ongoing basis. Doing so allows Nike to stay innovative while at the same time achieving a certain continuity that is sought after by consumers.

Nike uses information technology systems, such as SAP, across the supply chain to ensure an efficient inventory management and timely shipping to customers. Most product sourcing is managed globally and organized by product type (footwear, apparel, equipment).

> Most of the sourcing of products is managed globally. Again the reason for that is that we are trying to rationalize globally how we set up our resource base as most of our products are made in Asia. It wouldn't be efficient for everyone in the regions to work with the same factories, almost compete with each other for volume commonality structures. We basically plan, forecast the demand regionally, place purchase orders regionally and then manage purchase orders with the factories globally. (Peter Ruppe, Vice President for Global Equipment, Nike Head Office)

Planning and forecasting of the demand and placing of orders are affected on a regional level, while purchase orders with the factories are managed globally. Because most of Nike's products are manufactured in Asia and sold worldwide, effective operations are seminal. In 2006, contract suppliers located in China, Vietnam, Indonesia and Thailand manufactured some 30 per cent of total Nike brand footwear.[34] Nike's brand apparel is mostly produced by contract manufacturers located in some 40 countries including Bangladesh, China, Honduras, India, Indonesia, Malaysia, Mexico, Pakistan, Sri Lanka, Taiwan, Thailand, Turkey and Vietnam. Manufacturing is rather scattered. For example, Nike's largest footwear factory has a share of around 6 per cent of total footwear production in 2006. Also, raw materials are largely obtained locally.[35]

Outsourcing production to such a large degree requires sophisticated logistics: 21 distribution centres in Europe, Asia, Australia, Africa and Canada are needed to get the goods from the factories to the customers.[36] Efficient operations are therefore the key to Nike's success.

Counterfeiting is a big issue for Nike, because its greatest competitive edge is essentially its brand. However, it is quite common in the sports goods industry that competing companies share the same production halls. Consequently, Nike also shares some facilities with its major business rivals such as Adidas. In order to prevent unique knowledge from disappearing, Nike tries to establish trusted and long-standing relations with manufacturers, and Nike buildings are subject to tight security measures. Moreover, Nike makes sure that R&D facilities are kept separate from competitors. As one manager said:

We have a separate development centre, separate stuff for that and things staying there. So we try everything we can to create as much competitive separation as possible. [...] At the same time we build a great loyalty, we have factory groups that have been working with us for thirty years. You know they are not owned by Nike but they have grown to become very wealthy managers and owners by being our partners and trusting us.

Marketing campaigns are created at the global headquarters and later adapted to local needs. Typically, local athletes are hired for local marketing campaigns. However, global campaigns integrate testimonials from athletes who are often famous soccer players like Ronaldo.

We were very US centric, some argue that we are still are. We are a US brand up in the North West of Oregon, high passion about very specific sports and early in our development those sports were uniquely American in their heritage....We didn't care about soccer until the early 1980s. (Peter Ruppe, Vice President for Global Equipment, Nike Head Office)

Regional headquarters

Nike's European regional headquarters is located in the Netherlands and is responsible for 27 countries in the EMEA region. The latter is further divided into three countries and four sub-regions. Although larger country markets such as Italy and France do report individually to the headquarters, smaller country markets are grouped into subregions (see Figure 10.5). AGSS is consti- tuted by Austria, Germany, Switzerland and Slovenia. The CEMEA (Central

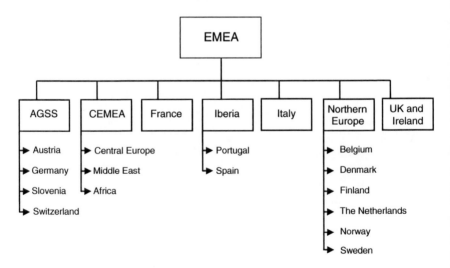

Figure 10.5   EMEA region

Europe, the Middle East and Africa) region – split into CEMEA North and CEMEA South – encompasses Bulgaria, Croatia, the Czech Republic, Greece, Hungary, Israel, Lebanon, Poland, Russia, Slovakia, South Africa and Turkey. The Iberia subregion includes Portugal and Spain. Northern Europe comprises Belgium, Denmark, Finland, Norway, the Netherlands and Sweden.

The main reason for introducing an additional layer of hierarchy on a regional level is to reduce complexity and enhance transparency throughout the group. In the words of a senior manager:

> Part of what happened when I was in Europe was that the GM at that time that came in said, how do we reduce the number of direct reports that I have. And he basically created at that time seven geographic direct reports, consisting of the big five countries, which were UK, France, Germany, Italy, Spain (Iberia), and then he created Northern Europe, which was the Benelux and the Nordic countries together and then Central Europe, Middle East he put under one. Later that was modified a little bit, Austria and Switzerland was put to Germany so that became a sub-region. And the thing what you are really trying to do is to manage the number of direct reports you have.

In some Eastern European countries, Nike still cooperates with distributors that will successively be taken over in the future to get more control over the brand management. Consequently, subsidiaries will be set up in these markets in order to pursue a differentiation strategy that ensures consistent brand positioning.

> Over time we started to bring distributors in-house or buying them out or terms eclipsed we started to build a structure on a country level. So we never had stressed having the idea of having a regional structure from a very early stage and literally up to this point we have really never gone back to fundamental questions.
>
> Where we have been structured I would say in the last five years, has been very much looking at the intersection between geographies, so countries' roles up into product structures, regions and product-based business units focused on creation of product for [...] geographies and that's aligned by footwear, apparel or is within equipment. And that's been the main way that we have structured. [...] on the product based side is a lot of the discipline around [...] operations, sourcing, supply chain, setting up the ability to deliver product into market. [...] At the geography level, certainly there is a need to then take the backing work and make sure that we are delivering for customers, the wholesale business we deal with. Most of our business goes through retailers that are not Nike owned. So we are transacting at that level. So you know regionally there is a heavy discipline towards managing the account base and

how we interact with those accounts, making sure we make delivery for them, so a lot of supply chain activity based upon doing that. And then in addition to that, the marketing aspects how we are going to communicate what our offering is or how we going to build the brand through the communication that we have. And then in addition, there is feedback that comes back to the product creation process to make sure that from a regional basis that we are understanding the markets and delivering what is being required. So that's very fundamentally the way it's structured. Underneath that is an operations unit [...] and somewhat in better than somewhat be coupled the product in region structure that we have. (Peter Ruppe, Vice President for Global Equipment, Nike Headquarters).

The reasons for building subregions are manifold: First, synergies can be derived by grouping countries: AGSS was created to streamline operations (for example, marketing, logistics and finance) across the group.

Second, reducing the number of reporting lines facilitates coordination and speeds up decision-making. Grouping single markets into regions helps to filter and funnel local demands. The more countries are integrated into a subregion, the lower is the total number of direct reports to the European regional headquarters.[37]

Third, subregional structures provide support for individual markets. Smaller, less important markets are given a voice within the group of countries:

Part of the idea here is that when you do the sub-grouping you are trying to allow a group to have a better voice but at the same time a lot of the goals are at the other side of it. (Peter Ruppe, Vice President for Global Equipment, Nike Headquarters).

A subregion manager reports these local requirements to the European regional headquarters. By doing so, issues raised by a seemingly unimportant market can be amplified by regional structures and are granted more attention within the MNC than without regional structures. Hence, the regional headquarters not only bundles information flows and enables synergies, but also needs to manage surfacing tensions, which come with aggregation. The more aggregated single subsidiaries are into groups, the more they crave attention. Nike's grouping criteria are manifold:

So it is a matter of effectively trying to cluster, and say this makes sense. Generally for Central and Eastern Europe, and this EMEA region, generally there is a relatively fast growing region for us, so the mindset has been a lot different than in some of the other parts of the geography. Only the bigger five countries outside of Germany are independently run. It's really just that Europe, that Central European AGSS, it's the only one that is otherwise a sub cluster within that region and we felt, hey, we can get better leverage where we can do that. (Hubertus Hoyt, General Manager for AGSS, Nike Regional Headquarters)

Countries are clustered according to consumers' similarities. For example, French or British consumers are different from consumers in Austria, Germany, Switzerland and Slovenia, which are countries that have been aggregated in the AGSS subregion. Similarly, regions are based on the similarity of retail structures across countries.[38]

Geographic location per se is also a reason for clustering. Although there are surely differences among geographically proximate countries (for example, Nordic countries), there are also similarities. Undoubtedly, trade-offs need to be made when grouping countries. Other reasons for building subregions are market size and market development stage of single-country markets.

Nike's underlying structural logic, the matrix, is replicated at the regional level (see Figure 10.6). Managerial responsibility is broken down by business unit (apparel, equipment and footwear) and function (human resources, operations, finance, marketing and sales, including retail).

In short, Nike's European regional headquarters has a strong integrative role within the region. It seeks to coordinate country and regional strategies and pools resources to increase the efficiency of regional operations. Also, Nike realizes synergies by strongly cooperating horizontally across business units.

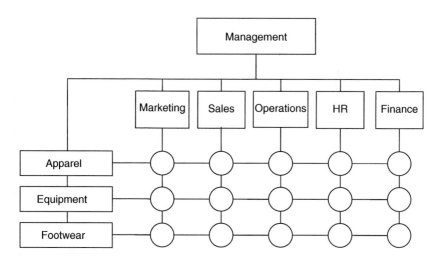

Figure 10.6 Regional matrix structure

The main driver for establishing a regional headquarters was the necessity to aggregate market knowledge at the regional level. Moreover, the regional headquarters enables Nike to achieve leverage effects in financial and management operations as well as in supply chain management. A regional headquarters executive explains:

> So we value, we are bringing in the idea that there is a value aggregating knowledge about a market up to a regional structure and then feeding it in and aggregate it as opposed to having everything come unfiltered from thirty or forty different gather points out of Europe into the head office. (Peter Ruppe, Vice President for Global Equipment, Nike Head Office)

New product development for Nike products, in particular for shoes, is largely done at the global "product engine" in three global R&D centres. Hence, the accountability for products is at the headquarters where the main decisions are made. At the same time, the regional headquarters needs to make sure that they scout around for local stimuli, pick up important local trends and quickly feed those back to the global headquarters. Essentially, R&D and design issues are handled centrally at the global headquarters in Oregon. Therefore, effective communication is called for rather flat hierarchies and collaboration. A senior manager explains:

> We try to be as flat as we can. The ideal behaviour at the end of the day is that Japan is a unique market, Tokyo is an epicentre for trends, we got a group of people in Beaverton, Oregon, responsible for trend and creating product is really fresh and brand based. It would be better to listen to Tokyo, right? That's what we ultimately try to accomplish. If we make the world's best football boots, right, well the world's best football players on a normal basis aggregate in Europe every year. So if we sit in Kansas and say, we are going to engineer the best football boots and listen to the University of Kansas football team. No! We are going to be in Western Europe. So they way what we actually do is all in partnership.

Thus, global Nike collections are often a joint effort: Global and regional designers go into the field to carry out consumer research and consumer analyses because of varying consumer preferences within Europe. Fashion-oriented Italian consumers, for example, are found to prefer product features different from more performance-oriented German consumers. The soccer line, for instance, was jointly designed by the designer teams of the headquarters and the regional headquarters. They went to local clubs (for example, Arsenal) to work out products and make product adjustments with players.

In Europe, global products are adjusted to regional demands. Also, regional apparel, equipment and shoe collections are especially developed for Europe. All European products originate from the regional product engine. Some 700 new models per season are coming out in Europe. Countries do not develop any products, but their input is incorporated into the European shoe collection. The countries are in charge of filtering consumer insights in regard to products and sports categories and reporting local product requirements to the regional headquarters, which are afterwards forwarded to the global product engine. Each country has employees who are responsible for individual product categories.[39] They meet regularly to discuss specific product features, for example, functionality of a running shoes, colours, price points and so on. Based on these briefings, new collections are created. This way Nike ensures that all regional and local product requirements are covered. However, not the entire product range is available in all country markets. Nike also develops products with regional customers (such as Hervis Sports and Intersport) individually in order to supply them with exclusive models.[40]

Strategic marketing, including investment decisions and product concepts, for EMEA is done by the regional headquarters. As one senior regional headquarters manager explains:

> At the regional level, what we mainly try to do is look at how you disseminate your marketing messages and how you communicate [...] you have to make sure that you are on track in terms of the imaging and storytelling. So marketing becomes a key function there.

Five big marketing campaigns per annum are drafted either regionally or globally. In order to adjust for cultural differences, some campaigns are tailored to the European market. For instance, given the popularity of soccer in Europe, Nike sponsors some of the best soccer teams (for example, FC Barcelona) and players (for example, Ronaldinho).[41] Also, celebrity endorsements vary by region based on local popularity differences.

Although Nike produces many regional campaigns not all are necessarily implemented on a country level. Also, uniformity has its limits; hence, generic advertising campaigns are developed for the region as a whole and are adapted locally. Basically, countries do have an advertising budget assigned for local activities, but need to seek approval by the regional headquarters to ensure that their activities are in line with Nike's corporate identity.

Foot Locker is Nike's major pan-European key account, representing some 10 per cent of Nike's global net sales in 2006.[42] In order to effectively manage key accounts, Nike has joint teams consisting of members from the single countries and the regional headquarters.

Pricing strategies are also centrally decided on at the regional headquarters. Consequently, there is a uniform discount system for all European sales. All sales agreements deviating from that rule need to be approved by the regional headquarters.

Operations, that is, supply chain management, which comprises all activities from manufacturing to delivery, are another important function of the regional headquarters. Although the supply chain is managed by product type (footwear, apparel and equipment), the logistics and customer delivery sides of the supply chain are organized by the regional headquarters within the region. Customers are supplied directly by factories and distribution centres.

In an effort to gain more control over their distributors, Nike took over most distributors during the 1980s and the 1990s. Ongoing optimization processes lead to the formation of a single European distribution centre in Laakdal, Belgium.

Subsidiaries

Nike's subsidiaries enjoy some autonomy within clearly set boundaries. Projects exceeding the limits set by the regional headquarters or global headquarters do need the approval of the region. Basically, operational country-level decisions can be made by the subsidiaries themselves. Although subsidiaries largely implement plans, there is some room for local initiatives and adaptation as well.

Appendices

A10.4 Selected financial data

	Financial History				
	2008	2007	2006	2005	2004
	(In millions, except per share data and financial ratios)[a]				
Year Ended May 31,					
Revenues ($)	18,627.0	16,325.9	14,954.9	13,739.7	12,253.1
Gross margin	8,387.4	7,160.5	6,587.0	6,115.4	5,251.7
Gross margin (%)	45.0	43.9	44.0	44.5	42.9
Net income	1,883.4	1,491.5	1,392.0	1,211.6	945.6
Basic earnings per common share	3.80	2.96	2.69	2.31	1.80
Diluted earnings per common share	3.74	2.93	2.64	2.24	1.75
Weighted average common shares outstanding	495.6	503.8	518.0	525.2	526.4
Diluted weighted average common shares outstanding.	504.1	509.9	527.6	540.6	539.4
Cash dividends declared per common share.	0.875	0.71	0.59	0.475	0.37
Cash flow from operations	1,936.3	1,878.7	1,667.9	1,570.7	1,518.5
Price range of common stock					
High	70.60	57.12	45.77	46.22	39.28
Low	51.50	37.76	38.27	34.31	24.80
At May 31,					
Cash and equivalents ($)	2,133.9	1,856.7	954.2	1,388.1	828.0
Short-term investments	642.2	990.3	1,348.8	436.6	400.8
Inventories	2,438.4	2,121.9	2,076.7	1,811.1	1,650.2
Working capital	5,517.8	5,492.5	4,733.6	4,339.7	3,498.1
Total assets	12,442.7	10,688.3	9,869.9	8,793.6	7,908.7
Long-term debt	441.1	409.9	410.7	687.3	682.4
Redeemable Preferred Stock	0.3	0.3	0.3	0.3	0.3
Shareholders' equity	7,825.3	7,025.4	6,285.2	5,644.2	4,781.7
Year-end stock price	68.37	56.75	40.16	41.10	35.58
Market capitalization	33,576.5	28,472.3	20,564.5	21,462.3	18,724.2
Financial Ratios					
Return on equity (%)	25.4	22.4	23.3	23.2	21.6
Return on assets (%)	16.3	14.5	14.9	14.5	12.8
Inventory turns	4.5	4.4	4.3	4.4	4.4
Current ratio at May 31	2.7	3.1	2.8	3.2	2.7
Price/Earnings ratio at May 31	18.3	19.4	15.2	18.3	20.3

Note: [a] All share and per share information has been restated to reflect the two-for-one stock split effected in the form of a 100% common stock dividend distributed on April 2, 2007.
Source: Annual Report 2008.

A10.5 Breakdown of revenues per region, 2007–2008

	Fiscal 2008	Fiscal 2007	FY08 vs FY07 % Change (In millions)	Fiscal 2006	FY07 vs FY06 % Change
US region					
Footwear	$ 4,326.8	$ 4,067.2	6%	$ 3,832.2	6
Apparel	1,745.1	1,716.1	2%	1,591.6	8
Equipment	306.1	323.8	(5)%	298.7	8
Total US	6,378.0	6,107.1	4%	5,722.5	7
EMEA region					
Footwear	3,112.6	2,608.0	19%	2,454.3	6
Apparel	2,083.5	1,757.2	19%	1,559.0	13
Equipment	424.3	358.1	18%	313.3	14
Total EMEA	5,620.4	4,723.3	19%	4,326.6	9
Asia Pacific region					
Footwear	1,499.5	1,159.2	29%	1,044.1	11
Apparel	1,140.0	909.3	25%	815.6	11
Equipment	242.2	214.9	13%	194.1	11
Total Asia Pacific	2,881.7	2,283.4	26%	2,053.8	11
Americas region					
Footwear	792.7	679.6	17%	635.3	7
Apparel	265.4	193.9	37%	201.8	(4)
Equipment	96.0	79.0	22%	67.8	17
Total Americas	1,154.1	952.5	21%	904.9	5
	16,034.2	14,066.3	14%	13,007.8	8
Other	2,592.8	2,259.6	15%	1,947.1	16
Total revenues	$ 18,627.0	$ 16,325.9	14%	$ 14,954.9	9

Source: Annual Report 2008.

11
Conclusion

Dynamic competence relays

We started this book with a positive statement on globalization. In concluding the book, we want to reiterate this positive tone. More importantly though, we would like to reemphasize that casting the debate in the polar extremes misses the multifaceted complexity that exists in reality. There is an important regional dimension between globalization and localization that is too often neglected. There are too many fine-grained stages of integration versus responsiveness that are missed in the debate. Contrasting only standardization versus adaptation is far too bold to capture the fine-grained intricacies of the international marketing process. And in a similar vein, centralization versus decentralization inevitably fails to reflect the subtleties in strategy development and implementation.

As our data and case examples consistently show, the world is not flat in a Friedman sense. In fact, it is doubtful that even *within* regions, such as Europe, we will lose this "spiky landscape" in the near future. In the data presented in Chapter 2, where we analysed the extent to which common ground exists between Spain and Slovakia or Italy and Ireland, we observed that Europe remains a rather diverse continent. Although many European countries are faced with the same challenges and the unifying force of the European Union is pushing countries closer together, many differences still prevail. These differences are deeply rooted in the individual countries' cultures and traditions and are not likely to disappear rapidly in the near future.

Nevertheless, the European consumer market does show signs of consolidation, and we observed a path towards increased European homogeneity. Yet this homogeneity is a regional homogeneity and not an interregional homogeneity; the importance of a regional focus will not disappear. Even though the European Union has excellent commercial ties with its international trading partners, for European countries, the European market will remain far more important than trade with the rest of the world. However, using the importance of intraregional trade to announce an end of globalization is equally exaggerated, unless we apply a very narrow definition of what globalization actually is. Again, the debate should not be cast in extremes but to allow for a middle ground.

To achieve global advantages, firms need to know how to win regionally. To this end, for much of the book, we looked at the strategies and structures for winning this regional game in one of the key regions of the globe, namely, Europe. More specifically, we undertook a more detailed look at the integration responsiveness dilemma experienced by many multinational firms and outlined the common organizational responses to manage this dilemma. Based on this debate, we developed the argument that the quest for superior performance may be determined at the regional level. This suggests that firms venturing beyond the home region may gain by tilting the global matrix towards a more regional approach that is consistent with regional strategy.

Recognizing the need for superior regional performance is one thing, achieving superior regional performance is another! To develop a stellar regional strategy, multinationals need to resolve a number of pertinent questions. It starts with the rather mundane-sounding question: what is a region? Evidently, companies answer this differently. Some split Europe into European Union and non-European Union, others divide into Western Europe and CEE, while some even create entities called EMEA, into which they merge all of Europe.

Having settled on their particular definition of a region, multinationals need to decide how to manage it. Should companies manage the region with a regional headquarters or without? Would it make more sense to have a regional desk at corporate headquarters outside Europe? If the company opts for regional headquarters within Europe, where should it be located? And what about subregions? Which companies need them and which do not?

Although the answers to these questions are largely isocratic to the companies involved, we also demonstrated that managers need to follow some general rules in order to make these important decisions. Our data show that, in addition to market similarities, managerial considerations constitute the main drivers for the grouping of individual markets. In fact, the structure multinational firms adopt to manage the region tends to reflect the maturity and diversity of the business. More mature organizations usually adopt a more fine-grained subregional or mixed market approach within Europe; smaller organizations go for a single regional headquarters structure.

Our analysis also reveals that maturing organizations often reconsider their original decision for the location of the regional headquarters. Soft factors as well as internal resource and power considerations have a greater impact on this decision than economic factors like tax benefits. Thus, given the prevalence of internal and managerial factors, multinational firms are well advised to take a closer look at their organization's resources and capabilities when making decisions about regional headquarters and regional management.

Leaving questions of location and structure behind us, we then focused on the complex task of managing a regional headquarters. Being squeezed between global and local interests, regional headquarters often serve as the main pressure point in the organization. To mitigate this pressure, we argue for clear roles, responsibilities and reporting lines. Moreover, successful regional headquarters are usually equipped with wide-ranging degrees of autonomy and have an important say in corporate strategy development.

If managed well, regional headquarters fulfil both an entrepreneurial charter and an administrative charter. From the data we analysed, it seems that the entrepreneurial charter *gains* momentum over time. Furthermore, it is here where subsidiary managers perceive the regional headquarters to add most value to their operations. Consequently, we argue that it is wrong to view regional headquarters merely as administrative centres that lose in importance as the organization matures.

Part II of our book analyses the challenges faced by US and Japanese multinationals operating in Europe. Specifically, we focused on the automobile, sport shoe and apparel and pharmaceutical industries, where we took a detailed look at the European strategies and structures of three US and three Japanese multinationals. For the United States, we discussed Ford, Nike and Pfizer and showed that they use rather different approaches in establishing and managing their European operations.

The autonomous style of Ford resulted in a fragmented regional headquarters structure whereas Nike and Pfizer both have a centralized base in terms of key business functions or geographic groupings. We also observed that all analysed US multinationals are rather hierarchical but make frequent use of informal teams that support and strengthen the information sharing and communication within the headquarters, regional headquarters and the local country operations.

In comparison, the three Japanese companies we investigated – Honda Motors, Asics and Astellas – appear to face stronger challenges in managing their European operations. Problems, conflicts and misunderstandings between the headquarters in Japan and the regional headquarters in Europe often appear to arise due to misperception of the Japanese style of management and culture. As a consequence, Honda, Asics and Astellas still prefer to maintain tight control over their regional headquarters and subsidiaries in Europe.

In the third part of the book, we aimed to highlight the best practices in each of the three industries we analysed. To this end, in each of our three industries, we took a closer look at two of the leading companies we identified. For the pharmaceutical industry, we developed case studies for Astellas and Boehringer, for the automotive industry we focused on Ford and Honda, and for the sport shoe and apparel industry we showed what can be learned from Puma and Nike. The case studies give concrete examples on how firms actually manage their regional operations. All cases can also serve as the basis for classroom discussion.

Taken collectively, our data demonstrate that multinationals can, and do, develop region-specific advantages. The organizational architecture selected to serve the region is a crucial element in delivering these advantages. Different types and mandates of regional headquarters have emerged and are largely driven by the type of industry, the national culture and corporate heritage of the multinational, as well as the distribution of recourses and power within the multinational. Although regional headquarters fulfil an administrative function, their entrepreneurial role is arguably more important. The entrepreneurial role of regional headquarters adds most value to the multinational and assumes increasing importance as the organization matures. Passing on best practices, encouraging subsidiaries to adopt new business models and developing innovative products and processes turns well-managed regional headquarters into what we like to call "dynamic competence relays" that accomplish a pivotal role in the fabric and strategy of global multinationals.

Notes

1 Introduction

1. Levitt, Theodore (1983, May–June) "The Globalization of Markets," *Harvard Business Review*, 61, pp. 92–102; Yip, George (2002) *Total Global Strategy II,* Upper Saddle River, NJ, Prentice Hall.
2. Bartlett, Christopher A. and Ghoshal, Sumantra (1998) *Managing Across Borders: The Transnational Solution,* Cambridge, MA, Harvard Business School Press.
3. Buzzell, Robert D. (1968) "Can You Standardise Multinational Marketing?" *Harvard Business Review,* 46 (6), pp. 101–14.
4. Picot, Arnold, Reichwald, Ralf and Wigand, Rolf, T. (1996) *Die grenzenlose Unternehmung,* Wiesbaden, Gabler Verlag, pp. 351–411; Brooke, Michael Z. (1984) *Centralization and Autonomy – A Study of Organizational Behavior.* London: Holt, Rinehart and Winston.
5. Levitt, Theodore (1983, May–June) "The Globalization of Markets," *Harvard Business Review,* 61, pp. 92–102.
6. Ghemawat, Pankaj (2003) "Semiglobalization and International Business Strategy," *Journal of International Business Studies,* 34(2), pp. 138–42; Ghemawat, Pankaj (2005) "Regional Strategies for Global Leadership," *Harvard Business Review,* 83(12) pp. 98–109; Ghemawat, Pankaj and Ghadar, Fariborz (2006) "Global Integration ≠ Global Concentration," *Industrial and Corporate Change,* 15(4), pp. 595–623; Ghemawat, Pankaj (2007) *Redefining Global Strategy: Crossing Borders in a World Where Differences Still Matter,* Cambridge, MA, Harvard Business School Press.
7. Rugman, Alan M. and Verbeke, Alain (1992) "A Note on the Transnational Solution and the Transaction Cost Theory of Multinational Strategic Management," *Journal of International Business Studies,* 23(4), pp. 761–71; Rugman, Alan M. and Verbeke, Alain (2004) "A Perspective on Regional and Global Strategies of Multinational Enterprises," *Journal of International Business Studies,* 35(1), pp. 3–18; Rugman, Alan M. (2005) *The Regional Multinationals – MNEs and "Global" Strategic Management,* Cambridge, Cambridge University Press; Rugman, Alan M. (2007) *Regional Aspects of Multinationality and Performance,* Research in Global Strategic Management, Vol. 13, Oxford, Elsevier.
8. Osegowitsch, Thomas and Sammartino, Andé (2008) "Reassessing (Home-) Regionalisation," *Journal of International Business Studies,* 39(2), pp. 184–96; and the reply by Rugman, Alan M. and Verbeke, Alain (2008) "The Theory and Practice of Regional Strategy: A Response to Osegowitsch and Sammartino," *Journal of International Business Studies,* 39(2), pp. 326–32.
9. Gupta, Anil K. and Govindarajan, Vijay (2004) *Global Strategy and Organization,* New York, John Wiley & Sons, Inc.
10. Rugman, Alan M. and Verbeke, Alain (2008) "The Theory and Practice of Regional Strategy: A Response to Osegowitsch and Sammartino," *Journal of International Business Studies,* 39(2), p. 330.
11. Usunier, Jean-Claude and Sissmann, Pierre (1986, Spring) "L'intercultural au service du marketing," *Harvard-L'Expansion,* (40), pp. 80–92.

12. Douglas, Susan and Wind, Yoram (1987) "The Myth of Globalization," *Columbia Journal of World Business*, 22(4), pp. 19–29.
13. Nachum, Lilach and Zaheer, Srilata (2005) "The Persistence of Distance? The Impact of Technology on MNE Motivations for Foreign Investment," *Strategic Management Journal*, 26(8), pp. 747–67.
14. Szulanski, Gabriel (1996) "Exploring Internal Stickiness: Impediments to the Transfer of Best Practice within the Firm," *Strategic Management Journal*, 17, Special Winter Issue, pp. 27–43; Von Hippel, Eric (1994) " 'Sticky Information' and the Locus of Problem Solving: Implications for Innovation," *Organizational Science*, 5(1), pp. 98–118.
15. Zaheer, Srilata (1995) "Overcoming the Liability of Foreignness," *Academy of Management Journal*, 38(2), pp. 341–63; Zaheer, S. and Mosakowski, Elaine (1997) "The Dynamics of the Liability of Foreignness: A Global Study of Survival in Financial Services," *Strategic Management Journal*, 18 (6), pp. 439–64.
16. Krawchenko, Anton (2007) "OMV/MOL: Protectionist Threat Raised," Energy Business Review, August 3, http://www.energy-business-review.com/article_feature.asp?guid=FB89FD60-B3B3–4D45-AEAB-56106716EC53 (accessed 23 March 2008).
17. http://www.abcmoney.co.uk/news/14200787706.htm (accessed 23 March 2008).
18. Perlmutter, Howard (1969, January–February) "The Torturous Evolution of the Multinational Corporation," *Columbia Journal of World Business*, pp. 9–18.
19. Wind, Yoram, Douglas, Susan P. and Perlmutter, Howard V. (1973, April) "Guidelines for Developing International Marketing Strategies," *Journal of Marketing*, 37, pp. 14–23.
20. Malhotra, Naresh K., Agarwal, James and Baalbaki, Imad (1998) "Heterogeneity of Regional Trading Blocks and Global Marketing Strategies: A Multicultural Perspective," *International Marketing Review*, 15(6), pp. 476–506.
21. Bartlett, Christopher A. (2003) "P&G Japan: The SK-II Globalization Project," Harvard Business School (9–3003-003).
22. Ibid., p. 12.
23. For the entire research project, we developed many more case studies. However, for this book we selected only six.

2   The European Market

1. European Commission (2008d) *European Economic Statistics*, Luxembourg, © copyright European Communities, p. 87.
2. European Commission (2008b) *Europe in Figures – Eurostat Yearbook 2008*, Luxembourg, © copyright European Communities, p. 355.
3. European Commission (2008a) *European Union International Trade in Services – Analytical Aspects*, Luxembourg, © copyright European Communities, p. 9.
4. European Commission (2008d) *European Economic Statistics*, Luxembourg, © copyright European Communities, p. 87.
5. European Commission (2008c) *Panorama of European Union Trade – Date 1999–2006*, Luxembourg, © copyright European Communities, p. 5.
6. Ibid., p. 22.
7. Ibid., p. 17.
8. Ibid., pp. 28–31.
9. Ibid., pp. 36–40.
10. Ibid., p. 40.

11. Ibid., pp. 44–46.
12. Ibid., pp. 46–47.
13. European Commission (2008a) *European Union International Trade in Services – Analytical Aspects*, Luxembourg, Office for Official Publications of the European Communities, p. 9.
14. Ibid., pp. 9–11.
15. Ibid., p. 13.
16. European Commission (2008b) *Europe in Figures – Eurostat Yearbook 2008*, Luxembourg, Office for Official Publications of the European Communities, p. 358.
17. European Commission (2008a) *European Union International Trade in Services – Analytical Aspects*, Luxembourg, Office for Official Publications of the European Communities, p. 13.
18. Ibid.
19. UNCTAD (2007) *World Investment Report 2007: Transnational Corporations, Extractive Industries and Development*, New York and Geneva: United Nations Publication; European Commission (2008a) *European Union International Trade in Services – Analytical Aspects*, Luxembourg, Office for Official Publications of the European Communities, p. 100.
20. European Commission (2008a) *European Union International Trade in Services – Analytical Aspects*, Luxembourg, Office for Official Publications of the European Communities. p. 101.
21. UNCTAD (2007) *World Investment Report 2007: Transnational Corporations, Extractive Industries and Development*, New York and Geneva: United Nations Publication, p. 70.
22. Ibid., pp. 68–69.
23. Ibid.
24. European Commission (2008e) *European Foreign Direct Investment Yearbook 2008 – Data 2001–06*, Luxembourg, Office for Official Publications of the European Communities, p. 12.
25. Chebel D'Appollonia, Ariane (2002) "European Nationalism and European Union." In: Anthony Pagden, ed., *The Idea of Europe: From Antiquity to the European Union*, Cambridge, Cambridge University Press, pp. 171–91.
26. Fontaine, Pascal (2006) *Europe in 12 Lessons*, Luxembourg, Office for Official Publications of the European Communities, p. 5.
27. Ibid., p. 29.
28. Smith, Stuart (2007) "The Not-So-United States of Europe," *Marketing Week*, 30(14), p. 21.
29. Fontaine, Pascal (2006) *Europe in 12 Lessons*, Luxembourg, Office for Official Publications of the European Communities, p. 6.
30. Ibid.
31. Ibid.
32. Ibid.
33. Ibid., p. 32.
34. Rogers, John H. (2007) "Monetary Union, Price Level Convergence, and Inflation: How Close is Europe to the USA?" *Journal of Monetary Economics*, 54 (2007), p. 787.
35. Aistricht, Matti, Saghafi, Massoud M. and Sciglimpaglia, Don (2006, Spring) "Expectations Unfulfilled?" *European Business Forum*, p. 32.
36. Fontaine, Pascal (2006) *Europe in 12 Lessons*, Luxembourg, Office for Official Publications of the European Communities, p. 30.

37. Ganesh, Jaishankar (1998) "Converging Trends Within the European Union: Insights from an Analysis of Diffusion Patterns," *Journal of International Marketing*, p. 32.
38. Fontaine, Pascal (2006) *Europe in 12 Lessons*, Luxembourg, Office for Official Publications of the European Communities, p. 30.
39. Aistricht, Matti, Saghafi, Massoud M. and Sciglimpaglia, Don (2006, Spring) "Expectations Unfulfilled?" *European Business Forum*, p. 32.
40. European Commission (2007a) *Consumers in Europe – Facts and Figures on Services of General Interest*, Luxembourg, Office for Official Publications of the European Communities, p. 31.
41. Rehman, Scheherazade S. (1998) "The Euro as a Global Trade Currency," *The International Trade Journal*, 12(1), p. 52.
42. Nadler, Paul S. (2003) "The Euro and You," *Secured Lender*, 59(5), p. 36.
43. Ibid., p. 34.
44. "Will the Dollar Play Second Fiddle?" *Financial Executive*, March/April 1999, 15(2), p. 10.
45. Fontaine, Pascal (2006) *Europe in 12 Lessons*, Luxembourg, Office for Official Publications of the European Communities, p. 34.
46. Morphy, Erika (2001) "To Coin a Phase," *Global Business*, 17(4), p. 30.
47. Rich, Georg (2004, Fall) "The Euro After Five Years," *The Brown Journal of World Affairs*, 9(1), p. 242.
48. Ahlber, Johan, Garemo, Nicklas and Naucler, Tomas (1999) "The Euro: How to Keep Your Prices Up and Your Competitors Down," *The McKinsey Quarterly*, 2, p. 113.
49. Rich, Georg (2004, Fall) "The Euro After Five Years," *The Brown Journal of World Affairs*, 9(1), p. 249.
50. European Commission (2008b) *Europe in Figures – Eurostat Yearbook 2008*, Luxembourg, Office for Official Publications of the European Communities, p. 162.
51. Council of Europe, "Bologna for Pedestrians," http://www.coe.int/t/dg4/highereducation/EHEA2010/BolognaPedestrians_en.asp (accessed 6 October 2008).
52. European Commission (2007c) "The Bologna Process – Towards the European Higher Education," http://ec.europa.eu/education/policies/educ/bologna/bologna_en.html (accessed 6 October 2008).
53. "The Bologna Declaration of 19 June 1999 – Joint Declaration of the European Ministers of Education," http://www.bologna-bergen2005.no/Docs/00Main_doc/990719BOLOGNA _DECLARATION.PDF (accessed 5 October 2008).
54. Eurostat Database 2008, Luxembourg, Office for the Official Publications of the European Communities.
55. European Commission (2008i) *i2010 – Strategy for an Innovative and Inclusive European Information Society*, Luxembourg, Office for Official Publications of the European Communities, pp. 1–2.
56. European Commission (2008b) *Europe in Figures – Eurostat Yearbook 2008*, Luxembourg, Office for Official Publications of the European Communities, p. 482.
57. Bialas-Motyl, Anna (2008) "Regional Road and Rail Transport Networks – Density Highest Not Only in Capital Regions," *Eurostat – Statistics in Focus*, 28, p. 2.
58. Ibid., p. 1.

59. European Commission (2005) *Trans-European Transport Network: TEN-T Priority Axes and Projects 2005*, Luxembourg, Office for Official Publications of the European Communities, p. 6.
60. Ibid.
61. Colm, Kelly (2008) "Ireland," *International Tax Review*, 2008 World Tax Supplement, Vol. 18, pp. 241–5.
62. Cuddeford, Horag Jones (2004) "CEE in the EU: When East Meets West," *Brand Strategy*, September 2004, p. 24.
63. European Commission (2008b) *Europe in Figures – Eurostat Yearbook 2008*, Luxembourg, Office for Official Publications of the European Communities, p. 25.
64. Lanzieri, Giampaolo (2008) "Population in Europe 2007: First Results," *Eurostat Statistics in Figures*, 81, p. 1.
65. Euromonitor International (2008) *Eastern Europeans Returning Home*, London, p. 4.
66. Miles, David (1997, November) "Economic Implications of European Demographic Change," *Economic Outlook*, 22(1), p. 18.
67. Gianniakouris, Konstantinos (2008) "Ageing Characterises the Demographic Perspectives of the European Societies," *Eurostat Statistics in Figures*, 72, p. 2.
68. Cervellati, Matteo and Sunde, Uwe (2005, December) "Human Capital Formation, Life Expectancy and the Process of Development," *The American Economic Revue*, 95(5), p. 1653.
69. European Commission (2008h) Eurostat News Release – Population Projections 2008–60, 119/2008 – 26 August 2008, p. 1.
70. Laff, Michael (2008) "Number Crunch," *T+D*, American Society for Training and Development, Alexandria, May 2008, 62(5), p. 14.
71. European Commission (2008b) *Europe in Figures – Eurostat Yearbook 2008*, Luxembourg, Office for Official Publications of the European Communities, p. 39.
72. United Nations (2007) *World Population Prospects – The 2006 Revision*, New York, Department of Economic and Social Affairs, p. 55.
73. Rich, Georg (2004, Fall) "The Euro after Five Years," *The Brown Journal of World Affairs*, 9(1), p. 243.
74. Benoit, Bertrand (2007, December 15) "High Benefits for German Jobless," *Financial Times London (UK)*, p. 7.
75. Rich, Georg (2004, Fall) "The Euro after Five Years," *The Brown Journal of World Affairs*, 9(1), p. 243.
76. Euromonitor International Database (2008), London.
77. Ibid.
78. Knudsen, Trond Riiber, Randel, Andreas and Rugholm, Jørgen. (2005) "The Vanishing Middle Market," *The McKinsey Quarterly*, 4, pp. 6–8.

3 Managing the Integration Responsiveness Dilemma

1. Bartlett, Christopher A. and Ghoshal, Sumantra (1998) *Managing Across Borders: The Transnational Solution*, Cambridge, MA, Harvard Business School Press.
2. See, for example, the collective body of work by Rugman and colleagues. For example: Rugman, Alan M. and Verbeke, Alain (1992) "A Note on the Transnational Solution and the Transaction Cost Theory of Multinational Strategic Management," *Journal of International Business Studies*, 23(4), pp. 761–71; Rugman, Alan M. and Verbeke, Alain (2004) "A Perspective on Regional and

Global Strategies of Multinational Enterprises," *Journal of International Business Studies*, 35(1), pp. 3–18; Rugman, Alan M. (2005) *The Regional Multinationals – MNEs and "Global" Strategic Management*, Cambridge, Cambridge University Press; Rugman, Alan M. (2007) *Regional Aspects of Multinationality and Performance*, Research in Global Strategic Management, Vol. 13, Oxford, Elsevier. See also the recent book by Pankaj Ghemawat. Ghemawat, Pankaj (2007) *Redefining Global Strategy: Crossing Borders in a World Where Differences Still Matter*, Cambridge, MA, Harvard Business School Press.

3. See Ambos, Björn and Schlegelmilch, Bodo (2005, Spring) "In Search for Global Advantage," *European Business Forum*, 21, pp. 23–4.
4. Grant, Robert (2008) *Contemporary Strategy Analysis*, Malden, MA, Blackwell.
5. Interview with one Asics Senior Manager in Kobe, Japan.
6. Ferdows, K., Lewis, M., and Machuca, J. (2004, November) "Rapid-Fire Fullfillment," *Harvard Business Review*, pp. 104–10.
7. Bartlett, Christopher A. and Ghoshal, Sumantra (1998) *Managing Across Borders: The Transnational Solution*, Cambridge, MA, Harvard Business School Press.
8. Stopford, J. M. and Wells, L.T. 1(972) *Managing the Multinational Enterprise*, New York, Basic Books.
9. Bartlett, Christopher A. and Ghoshal, Sumantra (1998) *Managing Across Borders: The Transnational Solution*, Cambridge, MA, Harvard Business School Press.
10. John B. Cullen and K. Praveen Parboteeah (2008) *Multinational Management: A Strategic Approach*, 4th edition, Mason City, IA, Thomson.
11. Bartlett, Christopher A. and Ghoshal, Sumantra (1998) *Managing Across Borders: The Transnational Solution*, Cambridge, MA, Harvard Business School Press.
12. Wolf, Joachim (1997) "From 'Starworks' to Networks and Heterarchies? Theoretical Rationale and Empirical Evidence of HRM Organization in Large Multinational Corporations," *Management International Review*, 37, pp. 145–169.
13. Ambos, Björn and Reitsperger, Wolf (2004) "Offshore Centers of Excellence: Social Control and Success," *Management International Review*, 44, pp. 51–65.
14. Whittington, Richard and Mayer, Michael (2000) *The European Corporation: Strategy, Structure and Social Science*, Oxford, Oxford University Press.
15. Rugman, Alan M. (2005) *The Regional Multinationals – MNEs and "Global" Strategic Management*, Cambridge, Cambridge University Press.
16. Osegowitsch, Thomas and Sammartino, Andé (2008) "Reassessing (Home-) Regionalisation," *Journal of International Business Studies*, 39(2), pp. 184–96.
17. Rugman, Alan and Verbeke, A. (1992) "A Note on the Transactional Solution and the Transaction Cost Theory of Multinational Strategic Management," *Journal of International Business Studies*, 23(4), pp. 761–71.
18. Rugman, Alan M. (2005) *The Regional Multinationals – MNEs and "Global" Strategic Management*, Cambridge, Cambridge University Press.
19. Ghemawat, Pankaj (2007) *Redefining Global Strategy: Crossing Borders in a World Where Differences Still Matter*, Cambridge, MA, Harvard Business School Press.
20. Ibid.
21. Much of the international trade theory focused on the fact that countries can gain by focusing on producing goods and services in which they possess a relative comparative advantage and trade international with other nations. Similar, recent conceptualizations of the MNC have stressed its superior ability to recombine knowledge across markets and thus create superior value for the firm.
22. In reality the argument we are trying to map here is much more complex. Yet research commonly agrees that to absorb incoming knowledge, firms need to possess a certain level of absorptive capacity (related knowledge) to make sense

of the incoming information. Thus, if the knowledge bases differ too much, knowledge transfer is less likely to be successful. Multinational firms have been heralded to gain key advantages by exactly achieving these transfers on an interregional basis. However, the evidence so far suggests that this endeavour is rather difficult for multinational firms to achieve.

23. Campbell, A. and Goold, M. and Alexander, M. (1995, March–April) "Corporate Strategy: The Quest for Parenting Advantage," *Harvard Business Review*, pp. 120–32.
24. Lehrer, M. and Asakawa, K. (1999) "Unbundling European Operations: Regional Management and Corporate Flexibility in American and Japanese MNCs," *Journal of World Business*, 34, pp. 267–86.
25. Lehrer, M. and Asakawa, K. (1999) "Unbundling Europeon Operations: Regional Management and Corporate Flexibility in American and Japanese MNC's." *Journal of World Business*, 34, pp. 267–86, copyright, with permission from Elsevier.
26. See Birkinshaw, J., Bouquet, C. and Ambos, Tina (2007) "Managing Executive Attention in the Global Company," *Sloan Management Review*, 48(49), pp. 39–45.

4 Developing Regional Structures

1. The concept of the triad was first initiated by Kenichi Ohmae in 1985, but has assumed centre stage in the work by Rugman and colleagues. See Ohmae, K. (1985) *Triad Power: The Coming Shape of Global Competition*, New York, The Free Press.
2. Press release by Norsat International Inc. in response to opening its regional headquarters in Lausanne, Switzerland, early 2009.
3. See, for example, Håkanson, Lars and Ambos, Björn (2008, July 1–3) "The Antecedents of Psychic Distance," presented at the Academy of International Business, Milan, Italy.
4. See Ghemawat, Pankaj (2001, September) "Distance Still Matters: The Hard Reality of Global Expansion," *Harvard Business Review*, 79(8), pp. 137–47.
5. See Birkinshaw, Julian, Bouquet, Cyril, and Ambos, Tina (2007) "Managing Executive Attention in the Global Company," *Sloan Management Review*, 48(49), pp. 39–45.
6. In this *Harvard Business Review* article "Regional Strategies for Global Leadership," Ghemawat in fact argues that, by centering scholarly investigation on regional headquarters rather than regional strategies, previous research has come closer to studying the wallet than its content. And while Ghemawat has a strong point to make, one should not ignore that even those firms that he considers home-base centred do possess a "centre" within that region that is managing the business activity. Thus, in reality, we will see only a few firms that do not have a structure to support their regional business activities.
7. See Ghemawat, Pankaj (2005) "Regional Strategies for Global Leadership," *Harvard Business Review*, 83(12), pp. 98–109.
8. See Schütte, H. (1996) *Regional Headquarters of Multinational Corporations*. Ph.D. dissertation, Universität St. Gallen, St. Gallen, Switzerland.
9. Andersson, Ulf and Forsgren, Mats (1996) "Subsidiary Embeddedness and Control in the Multinational Corporation," *International Business Review*, 14(5), pp. 473–86; Andersson, Ulf, Forsgren, Mats, and Holm, Ulf (2002) "The Strategic Impact of External Networks: Subsidiary Performance and Competence Development in the Multinational Corporation," *Strategic Management Journal*, 23(11), pp. 979–96.

10. We used Nvivo statistical software and content analysis to establish the linkages and associations among the constructs.
11. We used IMD data from the World Competitiveness Index and location information on regional headquarters in six countries to compute a correlation between location choice and competitiveness score.
12. The fact that the general manager's name Kaiser is the German term for *emperor* adds some humour to the story.
13. The lead country in this sense is usually defined as the market with the largest sales for the corporation or the largest operation.

5   Managing Regional Headquarters

1. See Chini, T., Ambos, B. and Wehle, K. (2005) "The Headquarters-Subsidiary Trench: Tracing Perception Gaps within the Multinational Corporation," *European Management Journal*, 23(2), pp. 145–53.
2. Asakawa, K. (2001) "Organizational Tension in International R&D Management – The Case of Japanese Firms," *Research Policy* 30, pp. 735–57; Chini, T., Ambos, B. and Wehle, K. (2005) "The Headquarters-Subsidiary Trench: Tracing Perception Gaps within the Multinational Corporation," *European Management Journal*, 23(2), pp. 145–53.
3. Though it has to be said, these differences are not always statistically significant.
4. As in the previous chapter, we used content analysis of the interview data to compute the graph and to determine relationships among the constructs displayed.
5. The distinction between entrepreneurial and integrative functions of headquarters goes back to Chandler (1962, 1991) and has been applied in many studies including, Bikinshaw, Julian, Braunerhjelm, Pontus, Holm, Ulf, and Terjesen, Siri (2006) "Why Do Some Multinational Corporations Relocate Their Headquarters Overseas?" *Strategic Management Journal*, 27, pp. 681–700; Lasserre, P. (1996) "Regional Headquarters: The Spearhead for Asia Pacific Markets," *Long Range Planning*, 29, pp. 30–7 and many others. For Chandler's original work, see Chandler, Alfred (1991) "The Functions of the HQ in the Multibusiness Firm," *Strategic Management Journal*, 12, pp. 31–50. Chandler, Alfred (1962) *Strategy and Structure: Chapters in the History of American Industrial Enterprise*, Cambridge, MA, MIT Press.
6. Asakawa, K. and Lehrer, M. (2003) "Managing Local Knowledge Assets Globally: The Role of Regional Innovation Relays," *Journal of World Business*, 38, pp. 31–42.
7. See Yeung, H., Poon, J. and Perry, M. (2001) "Towards a Regional Strategy: The Role of Regional Headquarters of Foreign Firms in Singapore," *Urban Studies*, 38(1), pp. 157–83.
8. Enright, Michael (2005a) "Regional Management Centers in the Asia Pacific," *Management International Review*, Special Issue, pp. 59–82; Enright, Michael (2005b) "The Roles of Regional Management Centers," *Management International Review*, Special Issue, pp. 83–102.

6   US Companies in Europe: Going East

1. Ford Annual Report 2006, p. F.
2. A complete definition of each brand is presented in the case study on Ford in Chapter 9.

3. A further write-up on Nike and its brands is presented in the case study on Nike in Chapter 10.
4. Nike press release, November 2007.
5. Nike Annual Report 2008.
6. A further description of the EMEA countries and subregions can be found in the case study "Inside the Nike Matrix" in Chapter 10.
7. The matrix structure is located in the case study "Inside the Nike Matrix" in Chapter 10.
8. Interview with Mr Peter Ruppe, headquarters.

7 Japanese Companies in Europe: Going West

1. Honda's corporate philosophy is based on the Japanese belief of harmony with nature. As such, the individual is an important part of the cycle of nature. These corporate philosophies are presented in the Honda case study in Chapter 9.
2. As quoted from a corporate report of Honda Inc.
3. An organization structure of Honda Motor Europe Ltd. is presented in the Honda case study in Chapter 9.
4. Asics Annual Report 2006a:2, p. 69.
5. These countries were not subsidiaries as of the time of the research interview and are, therefore, not shown in Figure 7.3 above.
6. This is as described during the interview of a senior manager in 2006.
7. This refers to Lassere's typology.
8. Astellas Company Profile 2006.
9. Strawberryfrog is a global advertising agency appointed to develop a global marketing strategy for Asics.
10. The latter refers to the historical meaning of the Asics acronym (Paul and Shark 2007).

8 Learning from the Pharmaceutical Industry

1. Economist Intelligence Unit (2004) "Japan Healthcare: Price Cuts Force Pharma Merger," pp. 19–20 http://web.ebscohost.com/ehost/pdf?vid=14& hid=8&sid=2277353c-68d2–4973-89b9–2b0eef11f004%40sessionmgr11 (accessed 15 March 2009).
2. Hill, Ray (2004) "The Japanese Pharmaceutical Industry – On the Road to Change," IMS Health MIDAS, Sept. 2004; pp. 16–21.
3. Economist Intelligence Unit (2004) "Japan Healthcare: Price Cuts Force Pharma Merger," pp. 19–20 http://web.ebscohost.com/ehost/pdf?vid=14& hid=8&sid=2277353c-68d2–4973-89b9–2b0eef11f004%40sessionmgr11 (accessed 15 March 2009).
4. Economist Intelligence Unit (2004) "Japan Healthcare: Merge or Else"; pp. 13–15, see also, Hill, Ray (2004) "The Japanese Pharmaceutical Industry – On the Road to Change," IMS Health MIDAS, Sept. 2004; Economist Intelligence Unit (2004) "Japan Healthcare: Price Cuts Force Pharma Merger," pp. 19–20 http:// web.ebscohost.com/ehost/pdf?vid=14&hid=8&sid=2277353c-68d2–4973-89b9– 2b0eef11f004%40sessionmgr11 (accessed 15 March 2009).
5. Pharmaceutical Executive (2008) "Corporate Profile: Astellas."
6. Datamonitor (2008) Astellas Pharma Inc.

288   *Notes*

7. IMS Health (2006) "Top 10 Pharmaceutical Markets Worldwide, 2005," *http://www.imshealth.com/vgn/images/portal/cit_40000873/21/46/79016672PharmaTrends16CORR1.pdf* (accessed 4 October 2006); see also, OECD (2005) "Health at a Glance. OECD Indicators 2005," *http://www.sourceoecd.org/socialissues/9264012621* (accessed 2 July 2006); OECD (2006) "OECD Health Data 2006," June 2006, *http://www.oecd.org/health/healthdata* (accessed 3 July 2006).
8. Markovic, J. (2002) "The European Pharmaceutical Industry – Opportunities and Challenges," *Business Briefing: Global Healthcare Issues*, 20(3), pp. 22–27.
9. Avison, B. (2003) "Pharma Market Authorization Strategies," Business Insights, http://www.bi-interactive.com/index.aspx?Lang=en&MainPage=renderContent&StoryID=100395&ReportID=29&Highlight=pharma%20market%20authorization%20strategies%20#top (accessed 15 March 2009).
10. Datamonitor (2006) "The European Pharmaceutical Industry.
11. Turner, N. (2004, July) "Pricing Climate Heats Up in US and Europe," *Pharmaceutical Executive*, 24(7), pp. 64–74.
12. Datamonitor (2006) The European Pharmaceutical Industry.
13. Moses, Z. (2002) "The Pharmaceutical Industry Paradox: A Strategic Analysis of the Countertrends of Consolidation and Fragmentation," Business Insights, http://www.bi-interactive.com/index.aspx?StoryID=82169&ReportID=68&Lang=en&MainPage=renderDownload (accessed 15 March 2009).
14. Datamonitor (2006) The European Pharmaceutical Industry. Koberstein, W., Petersen, C. and Sellers, L. J. (2000) "The Mergers. Miracles, Madness, or Mayhem?" *Pharmaceutical Executive*, 20(3), pp. 48–61.
15. Pajwani, P. (2004) "Has the Consolidation Wave Gone Too Far? Should the Industry Consider Deconsolidating Next?" *International Journal of Medical Marketing*, 4(3), pp. 224–227.
16. Pfizer (2006a) "Pfizer 2005 Annual Review," *http://www.pfizer.com/pfizer/annualreport/2005/annual/review2005.pdf* (accessed 22 June 2006). Pfizer (2006b) "Pfizer 2005 Financial Report," *http://www.pfizer.com/pfizer/annualreport/2005/financial/financial2005.pdf* (accessed 22 June 2006).
17. GSK (2006a) "GSK Annual Review 2005," *http://www.gsk.com/investors/reps05/annual-review-2005.pdf* (accessed 22 June 2006). GSK (2006b) "GSK Annual Report 2005," *http://www.gsk.com/investors/reps05/annual-report-2005.pdf* (accessed 22 June 2006).
18. Sanofi-aventis (2005) "sanofi-aventis 2004 Annual Report," *http://en.sanofi-aventis.com/Images/050418_ar2004_en_tcm24-2539.pdf* (accessed 1 September 2006). Sanofi-aventis (2006) "sanofi-aventis 2005 Business Report," *http://en.sanofi-aventis.com/Images/060418_ar2005_en_tcm24-13000.pdf* (accessed 22 June 2006).
19. Pajwani, P. (2004) "Has the Consolidation Wave Gone Too Far? Should the Industry Consider Deconsolidating Next?" *International Journal of Medical Marketing*, 4(3), pp. 224–227.
20. Moses, Z. (2002) "The Pharmaceutical Industry Paradox: A Strategic Analysis of the Countertrends of Consolidation and Fragmentation," Business Insights, http://www.bi-interactive.com/index.aspx?StoryID=82169&ReportID=68&Lang=en&MainPage=renderDownload (accessed 15 March 2009).
21. http://www.pmlive.com/pm_europe.cfm?showArticle=1&ArticleID=5208&print=1 (accessed 15 April 2006).
22. EFPIA (2006) "The Pharmaceutical Industry in Figures. 2006 edition," European Federation of Pharmaceutical Industries and Associations.

23. Pharmaceutical Executive (2005): "Drugs Too Expensive: People Support Importation and Price Controls to Bring Prices Down," p. 36, www.pharmexec. com (accessed 17 March 2009).
24. http://www.pmlive.com/pm_europe.cfm.
25. Cambridge Pharma Consultancy (2004) "Pricing and Reimbursement Review 2003," Cambridge Pharma Consultancy, IMS Health Management Consulting, *http://www.imshealth.com/vgn/images/portal/cit_40000873/53/34/ 49596330PRReview2003_FINAL.pdf* (accessed 23 August 2006); see also, Cambridge Pharma Consultancy (2005) "Pricing and Reimbursement Review 2004," Cambridge Pharma Consultancy, IMS Health Management Consulting. *http://www.imshealth.com/vgn/images/portal/cit_40000873/49/16/74409641PRR EVIEW2004_FINAL.pdf* (accessed 14 August 2006); Danzon, Patricia M. and Ketcham, Jonathan D. (2003) "Reference Pricing of Pharmaceuticals for Medicare: Evidence from Germany, the Netherlands and New Zealand,".= NBER Working Paper 10007, *http://www.nber.org/papers/10007* (accessed 22 August 2006).
26. Cambridge Pharma Consultancy (2004) "Pricing and Reimbursement Review 2003," Cambridge Pharma Consultancy, IMS Health Management Consulting, *http://www.imshealth.com/vgn/images/portal/cit_40000873/53/34/49596330PRRevi ew2003_FINAL.pdf* (accessed 23 August 2006). Cambridge Pharma Consultancy (2005) "Pricing and Reimbursement Review 2004," Cambridge Pharma Consultancy, IMS Health Management Consulting, *http://www.imshealth.com/ vgn/images/portal/cit_40000873/49/16/74409641PRREVIEW2004_FINAL.pdf* (accessed 14 August 2006); Danzon, Patricia M. and Ketcham, Jonathan D. (2003) "Reference Pricing of Pharmaceuticals for Medicare: Evidence from Germany, the Netherlands and New Zealand," NBER Working Paper 10007, *http://www.nber. org/papers/10007* (accessed 22 August 2006).
27. Bennett, P., Parker, T. and Manning, A. (2003) "Generics Battle Heats Up," *Pharmaceutical Executive* 23(4), p. 52.
28. EFPIA (2006) "The Pharmaceutical Industry in Figures. 2006 Edition," European Federation of Pharmaceutical Industries and Associations.
29. "Value through Innovation" was chosen as the group's corporate vision by shareholders and management in 1993.
30. Reference pricing is a procedure with which governments try to cut costs. External referencing looks up prices for certain drugs in other countries and uses the lowest price. Also "internal referencing" is used in which products with similar therapeutic effect are grouped together and for every group a relatively lower all-in price is determined. The reimbursement system is then aligned so that the patients must pay for the drug themselves if the drug price is higher than the reference price.
31. The centrality of an organizational unit in a network of multiple units refers to the extent to which all major transactions in the network go via this unit. A very central unit is then considered to have substantial power and influence on the whole network. Further readings: Ghoshal, S. and Bartlett, C. A. (1990). "The Multinational Corporation as an Interorganizational Network," Academy of Management. The Academy of Management Review 15(4), pp. 603–625.

9   Learning from the Automotive Industry

1. Datamonitor, Ford Motor Company, November 2008, p. 4.
2. Datamonitor, Ford Motor Company, November 2008, p. 18.

3. National Public Radio, 3 March 2009, http://www.npr.org/templates/story/ story. php?storyId=5168769 (accessed 5 March 2009).
4. Datamonitor, Ford Motor Company, November 2008, p. 18.
5. Datamonitor, Ford Motor Company, November 2008, p. 21; @Ford North America, January 2009, p. 3.
6. Just-auto, competitor analysis, Ford: 2009 company profile edition 1: Competitor analysis. Just – Auto. Bromsgrove: February 2009, p. 11.
7. ACEA, European Automobile Manufacturers' Association, www.acea.be (accessed 7 January 2009).
8. http://www.at.ford.com/news/publication/pages/FordNorthAmerica (accessed July 21).
9. @Ford Europe, November 2008, p. 7.
10. *"Ford* of *Europe* CEO sees rough ride until 2010," Automotive News, 83(6338), 15 December 2008, p. 18.
11. Ford Motor Company, 2007 Annual Report, p. 10.
12. Frink, Lyle (2008) "Hyundai to double engine output in Europe," Automotive News Europe, 13(20), 29 September, p. 22.
13. CSM Worldwide, www.csmauto.com (accessed 5 March 2009).
14. ACEA, European Automobile Manufacturers' Association (2008) *EU Economic Report February 2008.*
15. ACEA, European Automobile Manufacturers' Association, Regulations and Standards, www.acea.be (accessed 20 March 2009).
16. Datamonitor, Ford Motor Company, November 2008, p. 24.
17. ACEA, European Automobile Manufacturers' Association, CO_2 Emissions, www. acea.be (accessed 20 March 2009).
18. Ford Motor Company, 2007 Annual Report, p. 2.
19. Datamonitor, Ford Motor Company, November 2008, p. 4.
20. http://world.honda.com/profile/philosophy/ (accessed 16 March 2009).
21. Honda Worldwide, URL: http://world.honda.com (accessed 16 March 2009).
22. Honda Motor Co., Ltd., Annual Report 2008, title page.
23. MarketLine (Datamonitor): Honda Motor Co., Ltd., Company Profile, December 2008, p. 5.
24. Honda Motor Co., Ltd., Annual Report 2008, p. 12.
25. Honda Worldwide, URL: http://world.honda.com (accessed 16 March 2009).
26. Kovacikova, Tkac (2007) *Regional Strategies and Structures within the Automotive Industry,* Master's Thesis, WU Vienna, p. 85.
27. MarketLine (Datamonitor): Honda Motor Co., Ltd., Company Profile, December 2008, p. 22.
28. Kovacikova, Tkac (2007) *Regional Strategies and Structures within the Automotive Industry,* Master's Thesis, WU Vienna, p. 84.
29. BBC News, "Honda's Four-Months Break Begins," URL: http://news.bbc.co.uk (accessed 25 February 2009).
30. Honda Cuts Jobs and Production," URL : http://money.cnn.com/2009/01/16/ autos/ honda_cuts.reut/index.htm (accessed 22 March 2009).
31. *Financial Times* online, "Honda Names Ito as New Chief Executive," URL: http:// www.ft.com/ (accessed 23 February 2009).

10   Learning from the Sport Shoe Industry

1. Nike Annual Report 2008.
2. http://www.nike.com.

3. http://www.nike.com/nikebiz/ (accessed 12 February 2009).
4. 2008, Nike Annual Report, p. 4.
5. http://www.nikebiz.com/company_overview/ (accessed 1 February 2009).
6. http://www.nike.com/nikebiz/ (accessed 8 February 2009).
7. http://www.nike.com/nikebiz/news/ (accessed 3 February 2009).
8. Nike (2008) "Company Overview – The Facts," http://www.nikebiz.com (accessed 11 February 2009).
9. Lorenz, K. and Hennrich, A. (2007) *Regional Headquarters of MNCs in the Sports Industry,* Unpublished Master's Thesis, WU-Wien.
10. http://www.nike.com/nikebiz/ (accessed 13 February 2009).
11. http://www.nikebiz.com/company_overview/ (accessed 13 February 2009).
12. http://www.nike.com/nikebiz/ (accessed 10 February 2009).
13. Lorenz, K. and Hennrich, A. (2007) *Regional Headquarters of MNCs in the Sports Industry,* Unpublished Master's Thesis, WU-Wien.
14. http://www.nike.com/nikebiz/ (accessed 2 February 2009).
15. Lorenz, K. and Hennrich, A. (2007) *Regional Headquarters of MNCs in the Sports Industry,* Unpublished Master's Thesis, WU-Wien.
16. Nike Annual Report 2008, p. 4.
17. http://www.hoovers.com/nike/ (accessed 8 February 2009).
18. Nike Annual Report 2008.
19. http://www.nike.com/nikebiz/ (accessed 7 February 2009).
20. http://www.nfia.com/ (accessed 31 January 2009).
21. http://www.nike.com/nikebiz/ (accessed 27 January 2009).
22. http://www.nike.com/nikebiz/ (accessed 2 February 2009).
23. http://www.nike.com/nikebiz/ (accessed 8 February 2009).
24. Lorenz, K. and Hennrich, A. (2007) *Regional Headquarters of MNCs in the Sports Industry,* Unpublished Master's Thesis, WU-Wien.
25. http://www.nike.com/nikebiz/ (accessed 12 February 2009).
26. http://www.nike.com/nikebiz/ (accessed 14 February 2009).
27. Lorenz, K. and Hennrich, A. (2007) *Regional Headquarters of MNCs in the Sports Industry,* Unpublished Master's Thesis, WU-Wien.
28. Ibid.
29. http://www.nike.com/nikebiz/news/ (accessed 12 February 2009).
30. Joyce, William F. (1986) "Matrix Organization: A Social Experiment," *Academy of Management Journal*, 29(3), pp. 536–31.
31. http://www.nike.com/nikebiz/ (accessed 13 February 2009).
32. http://www.nike.com/nikebiz/ (accessed 13 February 2009).
33. Lee, Louise (2000, February 21) "Can Nike Still Do It? CEO Phil Knight Is Struggling to Rebuild the Shoemaker from Top to Bottom," *Business Week*.
34. Lorenz, K. and Hennrich, A. (2007) *Regional Headquarters of MNCs in the Sports Industry,* Unpublished Master's Thesis, WU-Wien.
35. Nike Annual Report 2006.
36. Nike Annual Report 2007.
37. Lorenz, K. and Hennrich, A. (2007) *Regional Headquarters of MNCs in the Sports Industry,* Unpublished Master's Thesis, WU-Wien.
38. Senior Manager, Nike Switzerland.
39. Ibid.
40. Ibid.
41. http://www.nike.com/nikebiz/news/ (accessed 12 February 2009).
42. Nike Annual Report 2006.

Index